PEACE ECOLOGY

PEACE ECOLOGY

RANDALL AMSTER

Paradigm Publishers
Boulder • London

Copyright © 2015 Paradigm Publishers

Published in the United States by Paradigm Publishers, 5589 Arapahoe Avenue, Boulder, CO 80303 USA.

Paradigm Publishers is the trade name of Birkenkamp & Company, LLC, Dean Birkenkamp, President and Publisher.

Library of Congress Cataloging-in-Publication Data

Amster, Randall.
  Peace ecology / Randall Amster.
     pages cm
  Includes bibliographical references and index.
  ISBN 978-1-61205-297-7 (paperback : alk. paper)
  ISBN 978-1-61205-656-2 (consumer ebook)
  1. Human ecology. 2. Environmental ethics. 3. Peace-building. I. Title.
  GF41.A455 2014
  304.2—dc23

                                                                    2013049384

Printed and bound in the United States of America on acid-free paper that meets the standards of the American National Standard for Permanence of Paper for Printed Library Materials.

Designed and Typeset by Straight Creek Bookmakers.

19 18 17 16 15   1 2 3 4 5

For my mother, who always supported my ideas, and my father, who always challenged me to support them.

✳

Contents

✳

ACKNOWLEDGMENTS

This book was written in a time of great turmoil, both personally and politically. After nearly two decades of living in the desert, my family and I embarked on a cross-country move to a vastly different climate, environmentally and culturally speaking. During the course of writing this book, I changed jobs, went from a farm to the city, homeschooled a child, and endured various ailments and growing pains. Yet all of these personal vicissitudes pale in comparison to those in evidence on the global stage. With each passing day, domestic and international politics grow cruder and more Machiavellian. Economic crises that are largely fomented by elite interests are used to further retrench the minimal safety net clung to by underpaid working people—and those are the fortunate ones, when compared to the plight of *de facto* slaves and those casually dispossessed by war and corporate colonization. All the while, the planet's life-giving capacities are impinged by a ruthless machine of human consumption, hell-bent on drilling, digging, blasting, and fracking its way to a continued state of ostensible plenty that flouts the laws of nature at every turn. The rapacious destabilization of climate systems is merely one way this manifests, and the specter of inevitability begins to set in as irreversible thresholds are crossed.

In many ways, writing a book on peace ecology during such an era has represented a therapeutic release from the relentlessness of the world's machinations, presenting a clean slate from which to nudge reality down a gentler, saner fork in the road. At the same time, a sense of cognitive dissonance would often threaten to set in, as the remoteness of peace in our time and ecological balance in the world remain evident, and as the prospect of living a truly peaceful and environmentally sustainable life in this era continually recedes toward the vanishing point. Such are the interior dilemmas an author is wont to indulge, providing grist for the mill and, perhaps more importantly, serving as a reminder of how high the stakes are and why it matters to keep trying to right the ship while there is still time—even through the relatively remote act of writing a book. I have no illusions that any single work will be instrumental in turning things around, but I do know that we all have the power to raise our voices—and doing so, indeed, just might.

This book was produced from a place of connection and compassion, for the world and its living creations, even as the process of writing can be isolating and solipsistic. None grasp this duality more than those who live with the author, and so my first debt of gratitude goes to my family—my partner, Leenie, and my sons, Arlo and Zeno, who are always my inspiration for writing at all. A circle of supportive friends and colleagues is necessary for a project like this, providing guidance and reassurance in ways as to which most remain unaware. Myriad scholars and activists offered daily inspiration across the years and through the airwaves, reflected if at all in the bibliography but again largely unaware of their influence. More tangibly, authors are only as good as their editors, and Jennifer Knerr at Paradigm Publishers was a consistently thoughtful sounding board throughout this process. The anonymous reviewers likewise provided cogent feedback that greatly improved the manuscript. Any errors or misconceptions are of course my responsibility, but that is of minor consequence compared to the risk of not venturing out.

Specific support was provided by many people, often in the form of locating references and honing ideas. I am certain to omit some, but the list includes Geoff Boyce (University of Arizona), Dan Millis (Sierra Club), Jay Walljasper (On the Commons), Tom Fleischner (Natural History Institute), Luis Fernandez (Northern Arizona University), the incredible students in my classes over the years, and the Interlibrary Loan coordinator at Prescott College. Others generously provided quotes and/or living examples of the themes covered here, including Pancho Ramos Stierle (Casa de Paz), Nipun Mehta (ServiceSpace), Tree (Free Farm), Stephanie Knox Cubbon and Hannah

Renglich (PeaceMeal), and Annie Symens-Bucher (Canticle Farm). Still others bestowed their blessing on this work through their generous endorsements, for which I am grateful: John Clark, Chellis Glendinning, Betsy Hartmann, Dennis Lum, and Kent Shifferd. I greatly admire all of you and am pleased beyond mere words to have your support.

Finally, I want to acknowledge venues where earlier versions of the concepts covered here were incubated and developed. Portions of the Introduction are published here with the permission of Cambridge Scholars Publishing. Various online media outlets provided a forum for the cultivation of core ideas, including *Truthout*, *Common Dreams*, *Huffington Post*, *Counterpunch*, *New Clear Vision*, and the *Journal of Sustainability Education*. Prior to and during the course of this project I gave numerous public presentations and conducted workshops on themes directly related to the nexus of peace and ecology, at conferences held by the Peace and Justice Studies Association, the National Peace Academy, the Wisconsin Institute for Peace and Conflict Studies, and the Ahimsa Center at Cal Poly Pomona; additional similar events were held at venues including Barry University, Wilfrid Laurier University, Georgetown University, University of Baltimore, University of Manitoba, Prescott College, Fort Lewis College, Naropa University, and the Prescott Unitarian Universalist Fellowship. I am grateful for the dialogue and feedback I have received in all of these outlets over the years, and I look forward to more such positive exchanges as this work makes its way into the hands of readers who, ultimately, will be the real unsung heroes of the story as the ideas presented here will, I hope, yield concrete actions.

Introduction
From the War Economy to Peace Ecology

The desert is a stark, solitary, and seemingly lifeless landscape—unless one knows where to look. Living in the southwestern United States for nearly two decades has taught me to appreciate the subtle ways that life ekes out an existence in harsh environs. Desert living tends to cultivate a resilient capacity to make do with the available resources at hand, and to be able to sustain oneself during lean times that include extended drought and intermittent vegetation. Perhaps the most profound lesson from the desert is the deeply rooted sense of life's inherent interconnectedness and the overarching mutual interdependence that allows each species to sustain itself. In the desert, nothing can survive in isolation; the food chain involves a complex ebb and flow between animal and plant populations, and in the case of the latter the roots literally run deep in search of scarce water supplies. Life is hardened in the desert, conditioned by extremes of hot and cold, drought and flood, abundance and scarcity—in many ways coming to represent the conditions of life everywhere on a finite planet with a rapidly destabilizing environment. This book represents an effort to reconcile the localized lessons I have gleaned during an era rife with rampant global change.

As human cultures grow and evolve, so too does our understanding of the ways in which the various facets of our lives are interconnected. From the impetus of globalization and new networks of technology and communication, to the challenges of resource depletion and planetary climate change, there is a nascent yet pervasive understanding that we are all part of a whole system. The potential for this emerging sensibility to promote greater unity and empathy is palpable, even as conceptual and pragmatic difficulties with a "one world" model are likewise prevalent. Still, the notion of a holistic framework—equally the province of ecology and peace—is appealing to many, and in some instances it has begun to take on an air of inevitability. Navigating this brave new world has become a cutting-edge crucible for all disciplines of human thought, particularly as we seek to imagine and create "safe harbors" in an increasingly uncertain present. This introductory chapter highlights these challenges and opportunities, focusing in particular on how we can move from a militaristic mindset to the promise of peace ecology.

The War Problem

War is a dominant motif in our social and political interactions. It is waged in response to almost every perceived threat, constituting the baseline method of resolving conflicts or solving societal issues. This is the case despite a lack of evidence suggesting that war actually works, at least in terms of addressing root causes and underlying issues. The so-called war on terror waged principally by the United States in the new millennium is a case in point, as it now constitutes the longest continuous war in the nation's history and seems to keep adding new fronts (and creating new enemies) in the process. Even with the best of intentions (rhetorically, if not in actual practice) as with the "war on poverty" or the "war on crime," the war motif only tends to exacerbate the problem and generally leaves us no closer to a tangible solution. War, in short, occupies the playing field but rarely, if ever, wins the game.

Another critical feature of war is that it exists simultaneously on a number of mutually reinforcing levels. When the United States invaded Afghanistan, it was billed as a war on Al Qaeda and those who would harbor them, including the Taliban (who were actually then-recent US allies). It was also asserted, in something of a side note, that the effort was intended to liberate Afghan women from oppression and mistreatment. Less well known, although not entirely absent from the dialogue for more careful readers of the news, were issues of resource control including oil and gas transport from the Caspian Basin and the presence (established by the Soviets decades earlier) of potentially trillions of dollars in rare-earth minerals essential to the workings of the digital age (Risen 2010). In waging the war in Afghanistan, which at times has spilled over into neighboring Pakistan akin to how the Vietnam War spilled into Cambodia, myriad episodes of "collateral damage" have ensued in which civilians (including women and children) have been either mistakenly killed or killed ancillary to attacking other targets.

Yet another unspoken casualty of this war has been the environment and landscape itself. Unexploded munitions (including massive numbers of landmines), toxic substances, the devastation of continual bombing, the resource drain and wastes created by foreign troops, and the loss of habitats and arable lands are all outcomes of the war in Afghanistan (cf. Sanders 2009, 125–142)—and of many of the wars waged all over the world. The recognition of the environment itself as a casualty of war is a relatively recent phenomenon, although in practice war has been environmentally unfriendly throughout recorded history. This is apparent to such an extent that there is even a book for young readers called *War and the Environment*, observing that "no part of the environment is safe from the crippling effects of warfare" and concluding in stark terms that as long as war exists "we cannot hope to save our environment from the effects of the fighting" (Sirimarco 1993, 12, 27). There is also the obvious toll that war takes on economic systems, consuming vast financial resources in order to be waged, as well as the enormous health-related costs associated with caring for the growing number of victims and veterans who have been physically and psychologically impacted by war. Thus, when we seek to understand and evaluate war and its impacts on modern society, we need to consider the multiple levels on which it is waged, as David Suzuki has movingly discerned:

> War is a social, economic and ecological disaster. It is totally unsustainable and must be opposed by all who are concerned about meeting the real needs of all people and future generations. The effect of war is most immediate for those who are killed or maimed or made homeless, but the social and ecological consequences reverberate for generations. Among the children who survive, we still don't know the full extent

of the psychic damage they have suffered or the degree to which their problems are transmitted to successive generations. War is the ultimate atrocity that dehumanizes victor and vanquished alike; divorcing children from parents, separating families, smashing communities, it deprives its victims of their basic need for love and security in the company of their fellow beings. (1999, 169)

In 1935, Major General Smedley Butler famously wrote that "war is a racket," referring to the ways in which war tends to serve the interests of the wealthy by exploiting the poor as soldiers, controlling resources for private enterprise, and running up huge costs (and oftentimes lucrative contracts) in waging it. Butler likened his years of military service to working as "a racketeer, a gangster for capitalism"—and in the process produced one of the most trenchant critiques of modern war. Much of Butler's analysis remains applicable today, perhaps even more so in many ways, as war has become a permanent feature of the economic and political landscape. Indeed, one of the defining features of warfare in the twenty-first century is that issues of economics and resources are increasingly being touted openly as factors of "national security" and thus as legitimate bases for war. Wars today can be waged without any clear exit strategy, and it increasingly appears to be the case that the United States in particular (though not exclusively) is prepared to engage in multigenerational warfare on a planet with dwindling natural resources, a rising population, and the expansion of potential threats from other actors on the global stage. In this light, we begin to understand how war against one another and war against the earth correlate.

All of this suggests that anyone concerned with social and environmental justice ought to expressly tackle the "war issue" as a leading factor in their analysis. And yet, perhaps because it is so pervasive, war tends to be less robustly confronted in many treatments of sociopolitical and ecological issues. When we read works on race or gender, the prison system, economic inequality, food and water justice, climate change, and the like, they are oftentimes silent on the central role that war (and a war mentality) plays in the confluence of factors defining the issue. In the United States, however, where military expenditures comprise about half of all federal spending annually, it is clear that war is connected to every other issue even by virtue of economics alone. In relation to environmental issues in particular, war is deeply entangled, from the growing resource basis of conflict to the production of massive carbon emissions driving climate change. Indeed, by many accounts, humankind has been waging a long "war on the environment" that is by now pushing to the brink the planet's capacity to continue supporting human life—seemingly yielding an unfortunate vicious cycle that is driving more conflict and greater environmental degradation in the process.

Somewhat surprisingly, then, we have seen in recent years an increasing tendency on the part of various environmental actors to embrace the rhetorical logic of war. A January 18, 2013, segment on "carbon and cash" that aired on the environmentally themed radio program "Living on Earth," for example, opened with this remark: "When it comes to fighting climate disruption, trees are some of the most effective front line soldiers." Environmental advocates and organizations have been resorting more frequently to the explicit language of war in highlighting the need for urgent action, and some have even begun embracing tools of combat in pursuit of their ostensible pro-environment agendas. An opinion article in the *Boston Globe* (Kayyem 2012), for instance, specifically asserted that "we're in a war against climate change," touting recent developments in post-disaster scenarios such as Hurricane Sandy in which "environmental activists found an unexpected ally: the military." In an influential edited volume on peace and conservation issues, Saleem Ali (2007, 339) concluded by advocating for "a transformation of the military's role to one of a ranger force ... accomplishing conservation tasks." Others have issued calls for us to "harvest" and "repurpose" military technologies and capacities as a move toward building a sustainable economy (Kramer and Pemberton 2013). And in December of 2012, the World Wildlife Fund announced (in an article that included a header image of camouflaged "guards" in a remote natural setting) that it had received a large grant to develop new technologies aimed at "detection and deterrence" of poachers, including the use of "remote aerial survey systems" potentially akin to what are more commonly known as "drones."

The military and political establishment itself has likewise begun to draw environmental concerns together with security issues. A 2009 editorial in the *New York Times* cited as "accepted wisdom" among the national security establishment the following sentiment: "Proponents of climate change legislation have now settled on a new strategy: warning that global warming poses a serious threat to national security. Climate-induced crises like drought, starvation, disease and mass migration, they argue, could unleash regional conflicts and draw in America's armed forces, either to help keep the peace or to defend allies or supply routes." In a scathing critique of this increasing resort to militaristic language and tools around environmental issues, a report in *Truthout* (Mychalejko 2013) characterized this as a potential form of "green imperialism" in which advocates for stronger measures to address climate change and promote sustainability could unwittingly serve the more narrow interests of nationalism and the maintenance of US hegemony in terms of resource control and unilateral action. The article asserts that viewing environmental issues "through a national security framework divides the world between us and them, while reinforcing the dangerous notion of American exceptionalism," and concludes that this is a "dangerous road" that reflects a tendency toward domination and exploitation while ignoring "peaceful democratic measures" for engaging environmental challenges that can be effective in both short- and long-term contexts.

Despite this opening analysis, this is not primarily a book about war. Rather, it is about the ways in which the sorts of problems both created and confronted by war can also become steps toward peace. It is about how the same set of global conflicts over resources, population, and climate that are increasingly at the root of war might also be among the most potent drivers of peaceful relations. It is about how nearly every crisis in the modern era is also a profound opportunity, not merely to find short-term solutions to pressing problems, but more so to establish deeper ways of being in the world that address the foundational issues driving the problems in the first place. It is about how the very same strategies that are often touted as helping people adapt to the pervasive environmental issues in our midst (e.g., localism, alternative energy, lessening one's "footprint") can also be powerful methods for averting the occurrence of the crises in the first place. This book, in short, is about *peace ecology*, emphasizing the positive ways in which we can move beyond the ravages of the war economy.

Terms of Engagement

In order to undertake such an ambitious agenda, we need to define our terms with more precision. We will consider the broad and often misunderstood concept of *peace* in both its negative (i.e., prevention of war and violence) and positive (i.e., creating conditions favorable to peaceful societies) senses. Peace is more than just the absence of war; it is also the promotion of societies in which violent conflict, both internally and externally, is not a dominant feature and is minimized as much as possible. This does not mean that peace entails the absence of conflict altogether, but more so necessitates the minimization of violent conflict coupled with well-developed processes for addressing and resolving conflicts in healthier ways that do not merely lead to more of it (as is often the case in "winners and losers" systems such as those widely in practice today). In order to manifest such a world, it is necessary to address basic structural conditions in society, in the overarching belief that the root causes of violent conflict are connected to issues such as education, health, opportunity, and participation in governance.

Additionally, we will also look at peace from a number of distinct yet related levels of application. *Peacemaking* is the name for the practices and processes brought to bear in the event of a conflict, usually applied during the conflict in order to help resolve or remediate the dispute. *Peacekeeping* is the set of initiatives undertaken after a conflict has occurred, and focuses on efforts to help keep the peace and prevent the renewal of hostilities or additional conflicts from arising. *Peacebuilding* can take place before, during, and after a conflict, emphasizing the formation of the structural conditions necessary to create a peaceful society such as those noted above. Sometimes these terms are used interchangeably and with significant overlap, with the salient point being that there are well-developed practices available to prevent conflicts from running rampant and resulting in the devastation of warfare. Moreover, the making, keeping, and building senses of peace all possess environmental components that apply in concrete situations from species and habitat protection to human health and safety concerns (see Mische and Harris 2008). In this sense, we come to understand peace—despite its frequent mischaracterization as being amorphous or idealistic—as having a substantial empirical grounding, one that emphasizes both its pragmatic methods and its visionary attributes equally.

Like peace, the concept of *ecology* is also susceptible to an expansive definition. As a scientific field in its own right, ecology considers the full dimensions of the relationship between living organisms and their environment, as well as the ways in which those organisms relate to one another. Beyond this exploration of biotic and abiotic interconnections (including concepts of biodiversity, evolution, adaptation, and mutual feedback loops), ecology more colloquially has come to be understood as any holistic analysis of the interactions among components of a complex system. Thus, for example, *urban ecology* looks at factors including city planning, demographics, architecture, housing, transportation, open spaces, water and air quality, and animal life within a given geographical location. The concept of *human ecology* explores the evolution of human life on earth, including the trajectory of societies and technologies as well as the impacts of human existence on the evolution of other species and the balance of the physical environment. Ecology is often used interchangeably with concepts like *environmentalism, sustainability,* and *resilience,* especially when highlighting integrative processes and the complex patterns of interconnection that exist within human societies and natural ecosystems alike.

Peace ecology is more than merely a conceptual synthesis of peace and ecology. In essence, it contemplates the ways in which the same environmental processes that often drive conflict—e.g., resource depletion, anthropogenic climate change, food and water shortages—can also become profound opportunities for peaceful engagement. When confronted with a crisis, as with hurricanes and earthquakes, recent research indicates that people are actually more likely to cooperate than they are to compete, and that instances of violence in such situations are the exception rather than the norm (e.g., Solnit 2009). Aside from the context of an acute disaster, when people in a community work together to produce food or conserve shared resources, they can simultaneously build bonds of trust and mutual respect that serve to both forestall conflicts and help resolve them nonviolently when they arise. People around the world who strive to manage scarce essential resources (as with sensitive watersheds) often find that their mutual reliance on the resource transcends even profound cultural and political differences—and in some cases even warring parties have found ways to work together positively on such issues. Informed by schools of thought including *social ecology* (connecting sociopolitical hierarchies with environmental problems) and *deep ecology* (emphasizing humankind's disturbance of the natural world as the cause of social issues), peace ecology is concerned equally with the human-human and human-environment interfaces as they impact the search for peace at all levels.

Despite increasing attention paid to these issues in both policy-oriented and activist-minded circles, relatively little has been written in terms of in-depth analysis as to how and why environmental issues can become triggers for peace rather than war. Having said that, a significant body of literature has emerged in recent years around areas such as *environmental peacemaking* and *environmental security* that broaches these subjects, and likewise a spate of relevant writing on *food/water justice* and *climate justice* has appeared. From an activist perspective, organizations such as Greenpeace have long linked the lessons of nonviolent action with the need to redress the planet's most pressing environmental issues. These efforts will serve to inform the analysis here, helping to frame the issues and also suggesting avenues where more attention is needed. For instance, what is it about environmental issues in particular that suggests the utility of a peacemaking perspective? We might surmise that as a larger-than-human set of relationships and factors, "the environment" is capable of transcending our differences and, in our mutual reliance upon it for survival, tends to foster a sense of common humanity. We can suppose further that the earth, with its regenerative and self-regulating planetary attributes in evidence, possesses an inherent capacity to function as a healing medium that can serve to mediate human conflicts and provide a shared mode of exchange among relative equals. We may even ascribe to this some spiritual or metaphysical significance as a working explanation.

Thus, while the concept of peace ecology as a viable alternative to the war economy has been suggested by the extant literature, a more precise understanding of how and why it works has yet to be undertaken. Doing so is a primary purpose of this text, with the caveat that the nascent "answers" presented here are complex, subtle, and open to further inquiry. The intention of this work is to bring together for the first time in one place the range of issues contemplated by peace ecology, to understand their genesis and highlight the ways in which crises and opportunities around them are interlinked, and in the end to foster an integrative perspective on contemporary social and ecological challenges through the lens of *peace* as a multi-leveled pursuit that touches upon frames from the personal and communal to the national and global. It is a substantial task, to be sure, but is an essential and urgent one in a rapidly changing world where escalating disasters (both "natural" and "man-made") are a central feature of the landscape.

This book engages these issues by emphasizing specific aspects of the problem in the context of an integrative framework that views the myriad challenges before us as inherently interlinked—and moreover as profound opportunities for pursuing a different path based on peace rather than war, and on environmental sustainability rather than degradation. The chapters presented here focus individually on unique topics, yet are also intended to work together as a synthesis of the potential represented by the emerging field of peace ecology. Following this introduction, Chapter One begins by looking at concepts of scarcity and abundance, inquiring as to some of the civilizational underpinnings of the critical issues we are facing today, and looking at the prospect of establishing a "structural peace" that challenges prevailing dogma about humankind's propensity toward competitive, conflictual, and violent tendencies when it comes to living with one another and on the earth. Taking something of an historical trajectory, Chapter Two considers the potential role of the commons in promoting peace and sustainability, and the ways in which the loss of the commons (both literally and figuratively) has hastened the advent of crises including perpetual warfare, climate destabilization, and environmental degradation.

As possible antidotes to these challenges, in Chapter Three we explore the burgeoning movements centered on the production and distribution of food, sometimes under rubrics such as *food justice* or *food sovereignty*, and how community-oriented and bioregional food systems can serve to promote the values of peacemaking (by transforming resource conflicts) and peacebuilding (by mitigating their occurrence in the first place). Similarly, we will consider the manner in which the essential resources of human life (e.g., food, water, energy) are increasingly commodified though forces of privatization and commercialization, as well as how efforts to reclaim the material bases of life can simultaneously serve the interests of peace and sustainability. Extending this analysis, Chapter Four looks at various manifestations of an emerging "free economy" perspective that is working to contend with dominant patterns of profit-seeking and commodification in favor of a reinvigorated spirit of the commons that builds community while helping to promote structural peace through processes including empathy, compassion, and solidarity. Together, these opening chapters articulate a perspective that seeks to move us from being reactive to becoming proactive in our collective engagement with the substantial challenges before us, in the belief that our window of time in which to act is short.

Picking up these themes, Chapter Five considers in greater detail how contemporary crises, including both acute disasters and longer-term challenges such as climate change, present potentially grave consequences and imperil the continuance of human habitation on the planet. At the same time, such short- and long-term crises represent unique opportunities to demonstrate and implement another narrative, one premised on a spirit of mutual aid and resiliency that can serve as strategies for deeper transformation of seemingly intractable challenges; indeed, as almost every contemporary disaster indicates, peacebuilding is a prevalent norm. As Chapter Six details, a potent indication of these processes can be found in the cases describing how resource conflicts can be transformed into opportunities for collaboration instead, serving to help prevent and resolve conflicts while promoting environmental sustainability at the same time. While such practices often happen at the local and/ or regional levels, there are also many inspiring examples to be found across national borders (including the particular case of the militarized US-Mexico border), as discussed in Chapter Seven, demonstrating the potential for peace ecology to function as a basis for converting an era of perpetual warfare into one of possible peace.

Ultimately, the twin challenges of endemic warfare and escalating degradation are thoroughly interconnected, both as functions of "hardware" (e.g., resources, habitats, climate) and "software" (e.g., ideologies, mythologies, narratives). While the crises of the modern era are obviously grounded in tangible, material matters, they are also the products of deeply held belief systems and ways of looking at the world around us (and our collective place in it) that are so ingrained as to be largely invisible, as detailed in Chapter Eight. It is becoming apparent that solving our inherently complex and potentially cataclysmic human problems cannot be accomplished merely in piecemeal fashion, but rather entails a holistic approach that strives to integrate various initiatives into a larger project that works toward the overall stabilization of human-human and human-environment relationships at all levels of engagement—in essence comprising a union of peacemaking, peacekeeping, and peacebuilding efforts from the personal to the planetary. In this sense, as the Conclusion to this volume asserts, we come to understand peace ecology as equal parts pragmatic and utopian, as both a set of concrete practices and a vision for altering our collective trajectory away from the precipice and toward greater balance.

Frameworks for Inquiry and Matters of Scale

The foregoing constitutes a wide ambit for any single written work to encompass. The intention here is to raise these issues in a meaningful way and to bring together various emergent "best practices" that have been accruing in recent years around the core concepts envisioned by peace ecology. The text seeks to raise as many questions as it answers, striving at the least to set forth the working terms and concepts for continued analysis and discussion of the crucial issues of our time. Indeed, it often appears that the range of crises before us possesses a "kitchen sink" feel: resource depletion, privatization of essentials, endemic poverty, a widening wealth/power gap, mass migrations of people due to war and environmental degradation, loss of arable lands, toxification of water and air, climate destabilization, failure of political institutions, media consolidation, lack of education toward viable alternatives, and more. Even more confounding is the looming sense that these issues are all somehow interrelated, mutually reinforcing, and thus increasingly impossible to disentangle for purposes of direct engagement on any of them.

Such a realization, once critically commenced, can be overwhelming and potentially disempowering. Where exactly is one to start in terms of engaging these myriad crises? I am often asked this question, and usually respond "anywhere" even as it is apparent that not all actions are created equal. If the "solution" to climate change, for example, is posited as either "changing the global economic system" or "changing one's light bulbs" (with few points demarcated in between), then it is small wonder that little progress has thus far been made. Matters of scale abound, from the intensely personal (e.g., dietary practices, consumer choices, spiritual beliefs) to the eminently global (e.g., geopolitics, wars between nations, planetwide environmental problems). Conceptually, it is often difficult to associate particular issues with specific scales. For instance, food is increasingly a globally produced commodity that still comes down to individual tastes and patterns of consumption; imperialism and war, conversely, appear as global issues and yet are waged and largely funded by individuals. Moreover, while food and war may appear as distinct issues, they are becoming more and more intertwined as resource conflicts devolve upon essential items and as access to life's basics is increasingly militarized.

The basic framework advanced here is that we ought to embrace this complexity and the interconnected nature of the issues before us as a pathway toward critical engagement and effective action. The discrete variables and familiar scales of prior epochs have become tenuous in a fully wired world defined by global networks that are accessed primarily through personal delivery devices; similarly, the notion that there is any longer a viable space outside of capitalism is waning as its associated technologies of surveillance and conveyance expand. Today, the relevant actors on the world stage include multinational corporations and international nongovernmental organizations (NGOs), nation-states and politicians, regional associations, and community-based organizations—as well as individuals uploading their profiles and making consumer choices. While media hegemons and military contractors ostensibly exert greater influence on our collective course of action, it is also the case that small-scale efforts possess a capacity to impact the whole today in ways that were not practicable a generation ago. Whether local initiatives in themselves will be sufficient to stem the tide of pandemic conflict and degradation is not clear, but it is hard to imagine change occurring at wider scales without them. Indeed, we might say metaphorically that the path to peace and sustainability lies in individuals and communities laying a foundation of cobblestones across which politicians and executives will be encouraged to walk. The inverse image of a road constructed for us by elite interests has by now shown itself to be a dead end.

These observations are not offered lightly, nor should we consider their efficacy in dichotomous terms. Global institutions, like local ones, are still composed of actual individuals performing a multitude of tasks. There is no simple prescription for resolving the crises before us, no definitive policy injunction or rhetorical invocation sufficient by itself to turn the tide. Just as contemporary crises present themselves as a panoply of interlinked issues, it will take a confluence of actors working at every level of engagement to nudge us along a different axis in our sociopolitical and environmental practices alike (cf. Philpott and Powers, eds. 2010). While there may be a longing for structural change and revolutionary possibilities, we cannot in the meantime ignore the reality of more mundane demands placed on our lives and the virtues of less dramatic evolutionary transformation. As such, the overarching aim of this text is not about offering a specific set of recommendations; rather, the intention is to encourage a perspective that helps us move from perpetually reacting to escalating crises and destructive conflicts toward proactively constructing societies in which conflicts and crises are less prevalent and are more widely understood as potential opportunities—opportunities for transforming our practices and increasing bonds of solidarity and empathy among human communities and between humankind as a whole and the balance of the earth's systems. Such an ambitious goal is rendered plausible by reference to concrete cases and aspirational suggestions alike, weaving together the transdisciplinary strands of inquiry comprising the burgeoning rubric of peace ecology.

Toward an Ecology of Peace

The field of peace studies as both a body of knowledge and a set of action-oriented principles is uniquely situated to directly embrace these issues and challenges and to serve as a bridge between the social sciences and the environmental sciences. Thoroughly interdisciplinary by its very nature—including in its framework strands of history, political science, psychology, sociology, criminology, religion, and philosophy, among others—the field of peace studies already is prone to holistic thinking about social problems and potential solutions. Moreover, as an academic field with a values-based perspective woven into its moniker, there is a deeper sense of being comfortable engaging ethical issues in a manner that is neither premised on achieving an unattainable objectivity nor consumed by academic tendencies to bifurcate theory and action. Simply put, peace studies represents a natural arena for ecological thinking, in the strong sense of striving to understand complex interrelationships and mutual interdependencies.

Notwithstanding this inclination, peace studies on the whole has yet to fully embrace environmentalism among its many transdisciplinary explorations. This is not entirely the case, of course, and there are many fine examples in the literature and history of the field expressing connectivity with environmental matters, including Johan Galtung's consideration of primitive war and the implications of "rank-disequilibrium," Elise Boulding's writings on utopian communities and their relationship to the land, and Gandhi's explicit focus on the material conditions of life as a precondition for a more nonviolent world. But by and large the field has devolved upon considerations of more anthropocentric matters, such as the prevention of warfare and the establishment of human rights. While some have begun the dialogue to bridge human and "more than human" issues, a fuller articulation of the ecological implications of peace studies—the central premise of peace ecology—has yet to be exhaustively undertaken. This work specifically strives to advance this effort, seeking to spark greater synergy and suggest avenues of critical inquiry and engagement across the social and ecological realms.

Richard Matthew and Ted Gaulin elaborated on these themes shortly after the terrorist attacks of 9/11. They began by pointing out that early environmentalists often opposed war because of its potential for grave ecological destruction, and that some of the key early figures in American peace movements were likewise motivated by environmental concerns in their work. The authors concluded that "it is widely accepted in the environmental community that conservation measures and programs geared towards sustainable development may reduce the likelihood of violence and help preserve conditions of peace" (2002, 36). Similar notions have been articulated in the area of "environmental peacemaking," initially in Ken Conca and Geoffrey Dabelko's influential 2002 book by that name, asserting that environmental cooperation can be a driver of peaceful relations in general. In his work on "peace parks," Saleem Ali (2007, 6) further emphasized how "positive exchanges and trust-building gestures are a consequence of realizing common environmental threats," and that "a focus on common environmental harms (or aversions) is psychologically more successful in leading to cooperative outcomes than focusing on common interests (which may lead to competitive behavior)." Likewise, Christos Kyrou (2006) has argued that peace studies and environmental studies share many common assumptions and affinities including a belief in diversity, interdependence, nonviolence, and the importance of "place."

Drawing upon these insights, it becomes clear that peace scholars and practitioners have been consistently concerned with what has more recently come to be known as "sustainability." Implicit in the field's efforts to transcend warfare and establish human societies based on egalitarian and empathetic principles, there has also been critical engagement with concepts such as "structural violence" that include a focus on the distribution of resources and opportunities alike (see Barash, ed. 2010). This fits quite well within the sustainability literature that often seeks to envision a world in which everyone has access to basic goods including food, shelter, education, health care, meaningful work, creative diversions, a healthy environment, and the capacity to take part in decisions that impact them (e.g., Evans 2012). In the foundational volume *Peace and Conflict Studies*, leading figures in the field David Barash and Charles Webel included a section specifically on "ecological well-being" that looks at a spate of contemporary environmental issues and challenges in the context of building peaceful alternatives:

> A world at peace is one in which environmental, human rights, and economic issues all cohere to foster sustainable growth and well-being. Ecological harmony cannot realistically be separated from questions of human rights or economic justice. The right to a safe and diverse environment, clear air, and pure water is no less a human right than the right to freedom of expression or dissent, equal employment opportunity, and participation in the political process. (2009, 413)

Deepening the point, the impetus toward sustainability suggests that social systems are only viable in a longer-term sense when they promote just and peaceful relations with ourselves, each other, and the biosphere itself. As such, sustainability may be comprehended as personal well-being in a socially just society existing in the context of a healthy environment. Peace educators in particular have done much to advance this synthesis of peace as a sociopolitical and ecological phenomenon (e.g., Wenden, ed. 2004), informed by the basic recognition that "peace will require environmental sustainability and environmental sustainability will require peace" (Bajaj and Chiu 2009, 444), as well as the overarching insight that "peace with the planet is seen as inextricably interwoven with peace among and within nations" (Reardon 1994, 28). Likewise, peace movements have long been intertwined with environmental issues (e.g., antinuclear activism), with the history of mobilizations for peace having "a long pedigree within the broad environmental movement" (Ramutsindela 2007a, 35). Taken together, these interlocking spheres form the basis for an emergent ecology of peace.

Strands of this perspective have appeared most directly around the issue of warfare and its implications, resulting in a great deal of scholarship in recent years. "Resource conflict" has often been viewed as both a leading cause and consequence of warfare (Westing, Fox, and Renner 2001; Wagner 2003), and the environmental impacts of militarism have been well documented in cases such as the Vietnam War (Pfeiffer 1990; Tully 1993), the first Gulf War in Iraq (Adley and Grant 2003), Kosovo (Weller and Rickwood 1999), and Bosnia (Clancy 2004), among other conflicts (see generally Hastings 2000; Austin and Bruch, eds. 2007; Machlis and Hanson 2008; Sanders 2009). The 2008 documentary film *Scarred Lands and Wounded Lives* chronicled the devastating ecological impacts of modern warfare, from toxification and desertification to resource depletion and waste. In *The Ecology of War*, Susan Lanier-Graham noted that "the environment has always been a victim in warfare" (1993, 3), dating back at least to Old Testament descriptions of Samson burning the Philistines' crops and Abimelech sowing the ground with salt after a military victory in order to render it infertile—with the former tactic repeated in the Peloponnesian War in 429 BC and the latter by the Romans in Carthage circa 150 BC. Despite often being thought of as "good wars," Lanier-Graham points out that the American Revolution and World War II both possessed elements of "environmental warfare" (the destruction of the enemy's resources as a conscious tactic of war) and "scorched-earth tactics" similar to those described in the biblical narratives. Westing, Fox, and Renner (2001, 4) have also noted the "deliberate degradation ... of the natural or built environment for hostile military purposes," and Ramutsindela (2007a, 37) likewise observes that "the environment could be manipulated for hostile purposes"—sometimes referred to as "weaponizing" the environment.

Specifically, investigations of this sort have looked at issues such as the enormous cost of warfare and its resource-draining tendencies; the resultant despoliation of resources, including infrastructure, water systems, forests, transportation, and agricultural sites; impacts upon animal populations and ecosystems; and the long-term toxifying and disease-causing effects of warfare on habitats and peoples alike. Gary Machlis and Thor Hanson (2008) have developed a framework for integrating diverse studies on these issues, which they call "warfare ecology," conceptually subdividing the taxonomy of warfare based on its ecological consequences at the preparation stage, during actual conflict, and in the post-war period. In even more explicit terms, Vandana Shiva has pointed out the terroristic aspects of Western military and economic policies, noting that in 2001 when she joined myriad others in remembering the victims of 9/11 she "also thought of the millions who are victims of other terrorist actions and other forms of violence," including "World Bank–imposed policies [that] weakened the food economy" and the "carpet-bombing [of] Afghanistan" (2002, xiii). Concluding her section on "The Ecology of Peace" with a hopeful note, Shiva sought to reconceptualize the ways of war into ones for peace:

> The ecology of terror shows us the path to peace. Peace lies in nourishing ecological and economic democracy and nurturing diversity. Democracy is not merely an electoral ritual but the power of people to shape their destiny, determine how their natural resources are owned and utilized, how their thirst is quenched, how their food is produced and distributed, and what health and education systems they have. As we remember the victims [of 9/11], let us also strengthen our solidarity with the millions of invisible victims of other forms of terrorism and violence that threaten the very possibility of our future on this planet. We can turn this tragic and brutal historical moment into building cultures of peace. Creating peace requires us to resolve water wars, wars over food, wars over biodiversity, and wars over the atmosphere. As Gandhi once said, "The earth has enough for the needs of all, but not the greed of a few." (2002, xv)

A powerful example of this quest to transform the devastation of war into the ecology of peace is the Iraqi and American Reconciliation Project (IARP), which focuses on repairing both the cultural and environmental relationships that have been shattered by the US invasion of Iraq that commenced in 2003. The IARP (www.reconciliationproject.org) emphasizes the "common humanity" of the people of Iraq and the United States as a vehicle for promoting understanding, respect, and awareness across areas including education, the arts, and the environment. As to the latter, the IARP has established a "Water for Peace" program based on the premise that "every person deserves clean water [and] every person deserves peace." The essentiality and centrality of water—which will be a recurring theme throughout this volume—can serve as a potent tool for peacebuilding. In the case of Iraq, one of the lingering impacts of the war has been the loss of access to safe water supplies by a significant percentage of the populace. The IARP specifically seeks to ensure access to clean water in schools and hospitals, since education and health care in particular are paramount for rebuilding the country's human capacities—taking the view that water can be "a vessel" for Iraqis and Americans to work together toward a peaceful future.

In the final analysis, it becomes clear that peace scholars and practitioners have already come a long way in terms of cultivating a perspective that is holistic and cognizant of the deep-seated interconnectedness of people and place, of culture and nature, and of societies and their environments. Reflecting this synthesis, Wangari Maathai was awarded the Nobel Peace Prize in 2004 for her groundbreaking Green Belt Project in Kenya which linked women's rights, economic self-sufficiency, resource conflict resolution, and environmental restoration. Maathai's insights into the impetus for her work are instructive, as she related on Democracy Now!:

> We were able to show the linkage between the way we manage our resources, whether we manage them sustainably or in an unsustainable way, [and] also the way we govern ourselves, whether we respect [the] human rights of each other, whether we respect the rule of law, and whether we promote justice, fairness and equity. These issues are very interrelated, because if we do not manage our resources responsibly and accountably, it means we allow corruption, we allow a few individuals to

benefit from these resources, to enrich themselves at the expense of the majority of the people. And eventually, the majority of the people, who are left behind, who are not included, who are excluded, become very poor, and they will eventually react. And their reaction will threaten our peace and security.... There is a link between the environment, which is symbolized here by the tree, and the way we govern ourselves and the way we manage the resources and the way we share these resources. (2007)

Peace ecology encompasses the pragmatics of creating and sustaining human societies in their material as well as their ideological needs. A peaceful society is one in which people possess tools for resolving conflicts and restoring relationships, distributing resources and opportunities in just ways, and promoting the health and wellbeing of all constituents. It is also a society that relates to the balance of the biosphere in positive and healthy ways, that limits its ecological footprint and sees itself as part of nature rather than its superior. As global conditions worsen and resource wars become pervasive, such notions move from the realm of hopeful idealism to practical necessity. Simply put, as the foregoing discussion indicates, if we do not embrace a perspective that integrates ecological thinking into our daily practice, peace will remain but a distant hope rather than a tangible end. In this sense, we see that peace among ourselves is contingent upon and necessarily related to our ability to live peacefully on earth.

What may initially have appeared to be primarily a sociopolitical phenomenon—i.e., the search for peace—has now taken on critical ecological concerns as well, finding resonance with other exemplars of peaceful, collective self-management such as those that have taken hold around what are sometimes called "common pool resources" (Ostrom 1990) and in particular concerning the cooperative sharing of essential resources like food and water. Furthermore, in recent years a deeper understanding of the relationships among climate change, natural disasters, social justice, and human conflict has emerged (e.g., Barnett and Adger 2007; Hoerner and Robinson 2008). Likewise, it is also apparent, as Peter Vintila (2007, 1) points out, that "war is very, very dirty," it "cost[s] a great deal of money," and it "also acts to extinguish the cultural space [needed for] successful climate change treaty making." In documenting "the widespread ecological consequences of warfare," Machlis and Hanson (2008, 734) emphasize that the distinctive traits of war include the "deliberateness, destructiveness, and intensity of its ecological impacts." Barry Sanders, likewise reflecting on the intensely destructive and toxifying aspects of militarism, has accordingly called for "a coalition of no-war and pro-environmental activists" (2009, 147) to tackle these issues at the grassroots level, succinctly concluding that "we will not survive ... without the total and complete elimination of war" (2009, 167).

Peace ecology is not simply content with articulating the interrelated crises in our collective midst—crucial as this process of empirically informed knowledge coupled with expanding societal awareness might be. As one possible point of departure indicating how peace ecology can help us foster workable solutions, consider the Demilitarized Zone (DMZ) between North and South Korea, which has become a massive wildlife sanctuary in the post-war period (Ali 2007). Having remained relatively untouched for more than 50 years, the DMZ is a rich habitat made up of marshes and grasslands, inhabited by many rare and endangered species including Asiatic black bears, leopards, lynx, and "nearly the entire world population of red-crowned cranes" (Lanier-Graham 1993, 73; Machlis and Hanson 2008, 732). The implications of this are eminently clear, namely that demilitarization can serve to promote biodiversity and thriving ecosystems, whereas militarism produces the inverse: desertification, resource depletion, and tofixication. Indeed, when we consider the actual threats faced by many people around the world, the cyclical nature of violence and militarism becomes starkly evident:

> For most of the planet's people there are more immediate terrors than a terrorist attack: creeping deserts that reduce farms to sand; the incremental assaults of climate change compounded by deforestation; not knowing where tonight's meal will come from; unsafe drinking water; having to walk five or ten miles to collect firewood to keep one's children warm and fed. Such quotidian terrors haunt the lives of millions immiserated, abandoned, and humiliated by authoritarian rule and by a neoliberal world order. Under such circumstances, slow violence (often coupled with direct repression) can ignite tensions, creating flashpoints of desperation and explosive rage. (Nixon 2011)

The lessons I have gleaned from the desert are further illustrative of these points. The southern Nevada desert is a particularly stark region, made even more so because of its treatment as a "sacrifice zone" that includes the most heavily bombed place on the planet: the Nevada Test Site (now the Nevada National Security Site) at which over 1000 nuclear weapons have been exploded since the early 1950s. The impacts of such devastation on humans, animals, and habitats alike are palpable; one can almost feel the deadened nature of the landscape there, and the effects of decades of nuclear testing have been experienced throughout the Southwest with "down-winders" manifesting fallout calamities even in the neighboring states of Utah and Arizona. Still, there is a sense of resiliency that is present there as well, including an annual pilgrimage to the test site (undertaken since the 1980s) by peacemakers under the auspices of the Nevada Desert Experience and its "Sacred Peace Walk." Participating in such a journey leads one to recognize how spaces of profound despoliation can also provide moments of hopefulness and inspiration, as people unflinchingly confront destruction with peace embedded in every step.

In this sense, peace ecology can serve to cast a critical light on current issues while simultaneously articulating positive examples that integrate peaceful human efforts with just ecological outcomes. Above all, peace ecology emphasizes the inherent interconnectedness of our existence; as Martin Luther King Jr. famously said, "injustice anywhere is a threat to justice everywhere." While King was referring to social and political concerns at the time, there is little doubt that the ecological principle reflected in his teachings holds true today as we expand our framework and analysis. The road from a war mentality (and economy) to a peace mindset (and ecology) is likely to be arduous initially but will certainly pay great dividends both for ourselves and the future. Peace ecology asks that we embrace this challenge, counseling that a more just and sustainable world is quite literally in our hands—and in what we choose to create with them.

This brings us to a final element that is crucial to a vibrant and fully formed ecology of peace: actions oftentimes speak louder than words. Theoretical and academic expositions from the field are certainly essential to illuminate the central issues involved and to help develop guideposts for concrete actions. Yet sometimes these notions can also serve to reify the current state of affairs by implying that the world's problems can be resolved primarily through more diplomatic entanglement among nation-states and international entities. While such bodies surely ought to play a role in moving the world toward peace and sustainability, it is equally important to remember that individuals and communities also possess the power to promote these changes, as Thich Nhat Hanh (2008, 4–5) has cogently reminded us: "We all have a great desire to be able to live in peace and to have environmental sustainability. What most of us don't yet have are concrete ways of making our commitment to sustainable living a reality in our daily lives. We haven't organized ourselves. We can't only blame our governments and corporations for the chemicals that pollute our drinking water, for the violence in our neighborhoods, for the wars that destroy so many lives. It's time for each of us to wake up and take action in our own lives."

Peace ecology strives to move such calls to action—informed by the deep well of history and theory—from the back pages to the front matter of human consciousness. Representing a confluence of two inherently value-laden fields of inquiry, peace ecology seeks to unite the best practices and insights from both peace and ecology, highlighting fundamental lessons including interconnectedness, holistic thinking, an emphasis on relationships, and the deeply interwoven nature of peace among human communities and peace between humankind collectively and the balance of the environment. Ultimately, through this burgeoning lens of peace ecology, we come to see that the time is ripe to turn theory into practice, crisis into opportunity, and, ultimately, war into peace. In order to accomplish this transformation, we will need to redefine our engagement with one another and with the habitat, reframing our master narratives and breaking out of the mindset of "scarcity begets conflict" toward one that emphasizes the abundance of creative and cooperative capacities inherent in human beings and their social systems. At the outset, it is important to recognize our place in the world as one component among many in a complex ecosystem, one in which humans are seen as part of nature rather than superior to it—and in this moment of reorientation and restabilization, perhaps humankind will finally know peace.

This book invites you to take part in this process, as an active participant in creating the theories, practices, and visions that are essential for our very survival. Peace ecology uniquely focuses on the most basic aspects of human life (e.g., food, water, energy, community, equality, resilience), as well as on our highest aspirations and ideals: peace, harmony, and wisdom. Indeed, the overarching premise of peace ecology is *interconnection*, and perhaps nowhere is this more fundamental than in the nexus of thoughts and actions. In the pages that follow are a series of ideas, offered as an impetus toward active transformation. I have found peace ecology to be an invaluable tool in this regard, and I hope that you will as well.

Chapter One
Scarcity, Abundance, and Structural Peace

When is a resource not a resource? This is obviously a trick question, since we appear to be living in a time when nearly everything is being privatized, commodified, and classified as a potential resource—from food, water, and land to DNA, near-earth space, and the general spaces we move about in our lives. This "Earth for Sale" sensibility opens up the prospect of subjecting a wide range of materials to being harvested, exploited, sold for profit, and consumed by an ever-growing human population. Coupled with the basic math of residing on a finite planet (for most intents and purposes), one can readily perceive the basis for escalating conflict driven by access to dwindling essential resources, and indeed this motif of "resource scarcity begets conflict" is a pervasive one embraced by a surprisingly broad range of contemporary actors. Yet not too long ago, a contrasting perspective was perhaps equally self-evident and widely held: very little of the world around us was viewed as a "resource" in today's parlance, and life's essentials were more likely to spark cooperation than conflict. In this lexicon, items including food, water, medicine, textiles, and the earth itself might have been viewed more so as gifts or blessings, held in a sense of collective reverence, and perhaps even as extensions of ourselves rather than as externals.

While it may be the case that such a view, idealistic as it seems to be, didn't entirely prevent humans from competing over the acquisition of material items—nor did it prevent them from negatively impacting their landscapes and habitats altogether—it does appear to have led to less pervasive and systematized forms of exploitation than those widely in evidence today. Taking this foray into narrative romanticism one step further, such a contrasting view of "nature" as something transcendent rather than as purely a human life-support system may have had the effect of ameliorating the destructive impacts of humankind vis-à-vis the environment as well as mitigating the stratification of wealth and power within human communities. The anthropological record bears out some of this perspective, and while it is tempting to resurrect some bygone "Golden Age" imagery as an antidote to the profound crises we presently face, time's arrow doesn't readily provide the luxury of returning to such a purportedly better world in any event. It does, however, permit us to suspend our intellectual disbelief as we strive to move from an age of conflictual consumption to one of peaceful coexistence.

An object lesson in the implications of these two contrasting ideologies—which we might loosely refer to as *commodification* and *complementarity*—is the case of the San Francisco Peaks that rise between Flagstaff, Arizona, and the Grand Canyon. One of the most prominent geographical landmarks in the region at over 12,000 feet elevation, the Peaks (as they are commonly called) are a critical aspect of the local watershed and are composed of as many as seven distinct ecosystems, rendering them one of the area's most important repositories of biodiversity. The Peaks can be seen for scores of miles in every direction, pronouncing a majestic visage to all who approach these unique "sky islands" in the midst of the desert's unrelenting topography. Not insignificantly, the Peaks are also considered sacred by over a dozen of the area's Native American tribes, holding special significance as the place where *kachina* spirits reside and for the abundance of medicinal capacities contained on the slopes. Yet these same slopes are also coveted for a more mundane reason: recreational skiing. In recent years, the preexisting ski runs on the Peaks have been greatly expanded, with reclaimed sewage effluent being used to make artificial snow as part of the ski resort's expansion. This use of waste water for making artificial snow, coupled with the increased activity from expanding the ski runs, threatens to alter the sensitive ecology of the Peaks. As with many other sensitive zones coming under increasing human pressure, the Peaks issue suggests that we reconsider how wealth is construed, resources are comprehended, and paradigms are constructed.

Modern life is largely conditioned upon the collective enactment of a belief system that posits humankind as distinct from its environment, thus rendering the products of that environment to be consumable and, accordingly, subject over time to being exploited to the point of scarcity. We might call this the "myth of scarcity," representing a self-fulfilling downward spiral in which competition over perceived scarce resources only serves to further deplete them, in turn yielding deeper antagonisms and more rapid degradation. By pitting person against person, community against community, and nation against nation, this deep-seated cycle also pits humankind collectively against the integrity of its own habitat in the process. Contrasting this framework is another perspective, one that dates to antiquity and that refuses to see the world and each other in zero-sum terms. This worldview emphasizes nature's capacity to promote life, provide sustenance, and create abundance. It is faith-based and eminently pragmatic at the same time, emphasizing the virtues of "right relationship" at all levels, from the personal to the global. In the end, the horizon of this vision allows us to trace the contours of a society in which needs are met, conflicts are transformed, diversity is celebrated, and peace prevails.

An Abundance of Scarcity

At the outset, we need to investigate in greater detail the foundational assumptions underpinning the dominant worldview in which the earth is primarily seen as an array of consumables for human growth and expansion. The paradigmatic nature of this "human superiority" ideology is by now palpable, and is at least partly to blame for prevailing current conditions of depletion, degradation, and destabilization of the environmental bases of human habitation. The origins and implications of this perspective pervade Western thought, prompted by the basic and incontrovertible acknowledgment that we all require resources in order to survive and flourish. Such an instrumentalist view relies upon a number of oft-cited observations about human nature and human culture alike—with the most central being the premise that rational humans are self-interested beings who, when left to their own devices, are incapable of sustained cooperation and thus cannot be entrusted to keep the peace in the midst of wealth to be acquired.

This premise remains among the most influential justifications for the existence of modern society. In his foundational tome *Leviathan*, first published in 1651, Thomas Hobbes asserted that the natural disposition of humankind was aggression, brutality, and a "war of all against all," famously characterizing the time before modern society as follows:

> In such condition, there is no place for industry; because the fruit thereof is uncertain: and consequently no culture of the earth; no navigation, nor use of the commodities that may be imported by sea; no commodious building; no instruments of moving, and removing, such things as require much force; no knowledge of the face of the earth; no account of time; no arts; no letters; no society; and which is worst of all, continual fear, and danger of violent death; and the life of man, solitary, poor, nasty, brutish, and short. (1974, 100)

Hobbes argued that the creation of a political state was necessary in order to bind us under a social contract, to impose by coercion the rule of law, and in essence to protect us from ourselves. Hobbes was primarily motivated by fear in his moral and political philosophizing: fear of the other, fear of nature, fear of death, fear of losing his property and privilege, even fear of his creator. While the modern nation-state employs many militaristic methods to maintain the patterns of social control that Hobbes envisioned—including the hardware of weaponry, imprisonment, and surveillance—it is at root the ideological software of *Leviathan* that is the glue holding the system together. Unsurprisingly, then, modern-day Hobbesians will sometimes accentuate fear among the masses as a means of preserving their positions of power.

Notwithstanding its widespread influence, this narrative is based on the most specious of evidence, namely that people living in Hobbes's time (circa 1650) would lock their doors at night or travel armed as an expression of the obvious distrust they felt for the brutish other. But these people already lived under a nation-state that had laws and a social contract, so all that Hobbes really confirmed was that "civilized" people acted aggressively and in the spirit of self-interest. To this he attempted to contrast the purportedly aggressive tendencies of indigenous Americans, but neglected to mention any of the brutal behaviors of those who had ostensibly come to "civilize the savages." Indeed, centuries later, civilization still has not staved off the ravages of warfare and endemic violence, but in many ways has expanded them. What Hobbes thus created has essentially become another self-fulfilling prophecy. In the name of overcoming our fear of the worst traits in humankind, we have institutionalized those tendencies; out of mistrust of ourselves and each other, we have created societal norms that render us even more untrust-worthy by making self-interest and acquisitiveness virtuous—in the process normalizing a social order premised on fear, competition, and the logic of "winners and losers."

Such zero-sum thinking is deeply engrained as part of the "realist" school of thought. It is an old story, yet one that is constantly revised and updated for contemporary application. Charles Darwin's emphasis on competition as the driver of evolution finds resonance today in Social Darwinism and its merit-based justification for widening gaps in wealth and opportunity—both within and among nations. Thomas Malthus reasoned that human popula-tion would eventually outstrip food production and thus contribute to social decay; his basic premise of supply and demand retains particular resonance among many resource theorists today. A neo-Malthusian perspective inte-grates the software of fear, self-interest, and competition with the hardware of resource scarcity to argue for greater securitization of raw materials in a world increasingly prone to resource conflicts. In this view, scarcity is based not only on food production and population, but also on environmental degradation and depletion as well as the potential ravages of climate change and related forms of destabilization. In short, the argument is that conflict is inevitable in a world of finite, dwindling resources where global demand is continually rising.

There is an obvious plausibility to the scarcity-based worldview, as anyone left short on their monthly bills can surely appreciate. Simple math dictates that sometimes there just isn't enough to go around, yielding a "something's got to give" realization from which conflict can arise. In the case of interna-tional relations with regard to essential items, there is a common assumption at work, as described by Giordano, Giordano, and Wolf (2005, 48): "If resources are scarce relative to the demand for those resource, nations are more likely to conflict, since the imbalance will impinge on economic health or basic levels of human well-being. From this argument it follows that international resource conflict will escalate in the future, as human populations and their demands continue to expand while supplies of many basic resources decline in both quantitative and qualitative terms." Dire predictions of food shortages, water scarcity, and dwindling energy reserves have been issued, resulting in the widespread belief that "resource scarcity would serve to increase poverty and migration, stretch institutional capacity to its limits, and deepen social cleavages, all of which would increase the likelihood of violent conflict" (Bhavnani 2009, 66). Indeed, as far back as 1974, Edward Goldsmith wrote on "The Ecology of War," exploring the connection between resource shortages and conflict, and predicting the centrality of commodities such as oil and water in potential future conflicts.

Perhaps the most nuanced articulation of the neo-Malthusian perspective was rendered by Thomas Homer-Dixon in his 1999 book, *Environment, Scarcity, and Violence*. Homer-Dixon defined scarcity broadly to include various forms of environmental depletion and degradation, positing that such could indeed contribute to violence in many parts of the world: "Environmental scarcity has often spurred violence [and] in coming decades the incidence of such violence will probably increase as scarcities of cropland, freshwater, and forests worsen in many parts of the developing world" (1999, 177). Scarcity, in this view, can be either supply-induced (i.e., depleted or degraded), demand-induced (i.e., population growth or rising total usage), or structural (i.e., disproportionate use or maldistribution). The effects of scarcity can be exacerbated by what Homer-Dixon refers to as "resource capture" (the impetus of powerful interests to shift resource distribution in their favor) and "ecological marginalization" (the systemic stresses that cause people to migrate to ecologically fragile regions), but can also be mitigated by ingenuity and innovation as well as the presence of democratic governance and institutions. As Homer-Dixon concludes, not only have scarcity and degradation often led to internecine conflicts (such as civil wars), but moreover "as global environmental damage increases the gap between the industrialized and developing worlds, poor nations might militarily confront the rich for a fairer share of the planet's wealth" (1999, 3).

This formulation at least rejects the bare determinism of the scarcity-conflict school by acknowledging the fundamental mathematics while crediting political and social factors in the process. While ensuing empirical research has cast doubt on the linearity of the neo-Malthusian argument, Homer-Dixon's introduction of intervening criteria has broadened the discussion in important ways. For one, it suggests that scarcity is a product of stratification and inequality perhaps even more so than simple aggregates of volume and quantity. It also counsels that scarcity can be exacerbated, if not caused, by the machinations of powerful interests that could use the plausibility of resource depletion to secure more for themselves at the expense of the overwhelming majority of the planet's population—and with an urgency of extraction that comes at the expense of the environment as well. In this sense, we come to see scarcity as equal parts practice and perception, based equally on how we procure the resources in our midst and what their use and control signifies in modern society. Resource scarcity generally exists within a context of great abundance; those who have a lot tend to need more and are more prone to notice a lack. In fact, a hunger for more in the midst of plenty can itself become a driver of conflict.

The Scarcity of Abundance

Whereas the neo-Malthusians embrace scarcity and competition as a virtual *fait accompli*, their modern counterparts—often referred to as "economic optimists" or Cornucopians—point out that such dire predictions have not come to pass largely due to human innovations in technology, self-regulating market mechanisms, and the functions of social institutions that promote more equitable resource allocation. This school of thought emphasizes the potentially non-finite capacities of the earth to support life, coupled with the unbounded possibilities of human ingenuity and technological advancement. Cornucopians highlight our inherent adaptive capacities, and point out that in fact humankind has continually staved off the spate of apocalyptic projections issued by neo-Malthusians for decades. This is considered an optimistic, open-ended, solution-oriented perspective that stands in contrast to the grim pessimism of the neo-Malthusians. In essence, it prioritizes a spirit of abundance and plenty that is limited only by the capacity of human imaginations and intellects to push the frontiers of science and economics.

Unfortunately for the Cornucopians, their paradigm hasn't fared much better than that of the neo-Malthusians when subjected to empirical scrutiny. While often couched in terms of ingenuity and adaptation, at the core of this "abundance mitigates conflict" perspective are a series of market-oriented assumptions about the self-regulating nature of supply and demand as well as the alleged virtues of development schemes. Cornucopianism is actually quite consonant with neoliberalism and corporate globalization, and generally cloaks its contributions to degradation and impoverishment behind a facade of opportunity and plenty. While innovation is a positive attribute, its application in the context of a profit-driven world also leads to more effective means of exploitation, and requires continual interventions in order to keep up with the rapacious growth that it engenders. Cornucopians cannot plausibly deny that many of the crises predicted by the neo-Malthusians have indeed come to pass for many of the world's inhabitants, nor that the reliance on technological fixes for degradation and destabilization can potentially yield unintended consequences including new crises and escalations of existing ones. Prominent examples of such "doubling down" include the widespread use of genetically modified foods, plans to begin harvesting minerals and resources from near-earth asteroids, and proposals to avert the catastrophic effects of climate change through geo-engineering on a planetary scale.

Putting aside science fiction scenarios, the fact remains that the Cornucopian worldview has largely not delivered on its promise. Global poverty and insecurity persist, the environment is rapidly destabilizing, and conflicts (especially internecine warfare and imperialist interventions) remain omnipresent. Scholars have even coined the phrases "resource curse" (Le Billon 2001; de Soysa 2002) and the "paradox of plenty" (e.g., Bhavnani 2009, 70), contending that resource abundance and not scarcity can be a driver of conflict, and that it almost always works to the misfortune of people to be in proximity to a resource coveted by global markets. Resource abundance has been cited as a factor in numerous civil wars (as rivals battle for control of valuable materials including oil, diamonds, gold, gems, timber, and minerals), insurgencies, and other forms of social unrest. Still, the "abundance begets conflict" perspective, like its ecoscarcity cousin, has likewise received a mixed review in the literature; while there is some evidence, for example, that oil abundance in particular can contribute to the onset and/or prolongation of hostilities (e.g., Di John 2007), other studies have found that resource-rich countries actually have a lower tendency toward civil wars (e.g., Brunnsch-weiler and Bulte 2009).

Nonetheless, the inquiry is not ended there, and explanations are still due to the millions killed in Congo in recent years, as well as those who have suffered in places like Iraq and Afghanistan, and moreover to those multitudes rendered homeless and destitute in the developed nations as a result of severe economic recessions. The problem with the "scarcity versus abundance" dichotomy is that both sides are partially correct and partially false, rendering it difficult if not impossible to discern the true drivers of global conflict. The situation in Darfur, for instance, at times has been attributed in part to issues of resource scarcity and degradation (see Leroy, ed. 2009), as has the ongoing violence between Israel and Palestine (see Weinthal et al. 2005). At the same time, the dynamics of power and profit are undeniably at play, with issues of differential internal access and external political influence contributing to hostilities in many such scenarios. The economic optimist perspective does not fully account for the privatization of resources, the displacement of peoples, or the effects of interposed austerity in its market-oriented calculus. In short, neither the neo-Malthusian nor Cornucopian perspective alone can adequately explain the origins and perpetuation of conflict—unless we view them as conjoined.

Too Much, Too Little, Too Late?

There are other perspectives on the scarcity-abundance dynamic, but thus far they have mostly received relatively scant attention from scholars and practitioners. Perhaps the primary third option in the mix is what Homer-Dixon alluded to as a Distributionist school, contending that the overarching problems are poverty, inequality, and the maldistribution of resources and wealth. Whereas the neo-Malthusians and Cornucopians may view these issues as a set of mitigating factors among many others, the Distributionists highlight the ways in which political institutions and socioeconomic arrangements in a given society (or even in global society as a whole) generate unequal patterns of wealth distribution, thus comprising a critical underlying impetus toward conflict and potential violence. Such a formulation could apply both within and among nations, and probably held its greatest salience as a form of neo-Marxism in the 1980s. A contemporary version of this perspective is sometimes expressed as "the political ecology of war" (Le Billon 2001); in this view, "resource wars" are seen partly as a manifestation of competition over valuable materials as well as a symptom of commodities being controlled and maldistributed, oftentimes to the disadvantage of poor people in resource-rich locales. Crucially, neither scarcity nor abundance exists as an absolute, but they are relative terms based on "the socially constructed nature of valuable resources" and thus need not drive conflict (Le Billon 2001, 565).

There is also a Threshold-oriented view that holds greater salience as environmental scientists have sharpened their understanding of the earth's systems, particularly with regard to anthropogenic climate change and the prospect of catastrophic (and perhaps unpreventable) outcomes once certain limits are exceeded as to atmospheric carbon concentrations, nitrogen levels, ocean acidification, biodiversity loss, freshwater utilization, ozone levels, and other critical planetary metrics (see Rockström et al. 2009). Distinct from the neo-Malthusian emphasis on supply and demand and from the Cornucopian predilection toward perpetual innovation and inherent abundance, this burgeoning Threshold perspective considers the conflict-inducing potential of environmental destabilization to be of paramount concern. For instance, a significant body of recent literature explores the concept of "climate violence" as a key issue in the twenty-first century (e.g., Parenti 2011). At the same time, however, some in this emerging camp also observe a marked tendency toward cooperative outcomes in the face of more frequent and impactful "natural" disasters, which will be explored further in Chapter Five.

Interestingly, this parallels a significant body of literature around the issue of water scarcity in particular that finds cooperation rather than conflict or competition to be the most frequent outcome between nations sharing water resources. This strand (let us call it the Interdependency school) cites empirical data from the world's 260-plus shared river basins to paint a picture of cooperative tendencies that even transcend open hostilities between the parties on other fronts. The takeaway from this line of reasoning (considered more deeply in Chapter Six) is that too little or too much as to a given resource can lead to conflict, whereas a moderate amount (coupled with other factors such as the parties' history, the nature of the resource, and the local topography) can serve as a basis for cooperation based on the implicit or explicit recognition of the parties' mutual reliance on the resource (see, e.g., Dinar 2009). Like the Threshold view, the Interdependency position is one that urges a consideration of structural, environmental, and humanistic factors in concluding that conflict need not dominate at all, suggesting the utility of a *peacemaking* framework that we will explore in subsequent chapters.

The central question is whether these suppositions have come too late in the game to effectively change the paradigm. For decades, the neo-Malthusian and Cornucopian camps have given the appearance of a vigorous debate that has largely kept other views out of mainstream and policymaking conversations—even as it has become evident that the neo-Malthusians and Cornucopians are merely two sides of the same coin constituting the dominant perspective on global politics and international affairs. These respective neo-conservative and neo-liberal analyses trace their roots back to the same historical forebears (such as Hobbes), and both presume for their starting point that human beings are rational, self-interested actors who will (both individually and collectively) respond to cost-benefit calculations in their decision-making. Where the two theories seem to diverge—over the inevitability of supply and demand versus the capacity for technology to skew the equation—is actually a point of synergy. Consider for a moment how the global economy works through a combination of force (militarism, sanctions) and persuasion (marketing, incentives), or how social control within a country is also maintained with equal parts coercion (laws, police) and comfort (consumerism, convenience). The union of neo-Malthusians and Cornucopians is indeed quite potent, as reflected in the dual biblical injunctions to "be fruitful and multiply" and "obey the king's command."

In fact, many scholars of late have made such assessments. In *Water Wars*, Vandana Shiva (2002) expounds upon the concomitant privatization of water supplies and the centralization of power that both accompanies and enables these processes to run rampant. Philippe Le Billon (2005) has discerned that neither "too much" nor "too little" can fully explain the persistence of resource conflicts, and that the root cause may be the overarching tendency toward "resource exploitation" itself and the skewed power relations that it often entails. The literature on environmental security, exemplified by the critical insights of figures such as Jon Barnett (2007), acknowledges the potential for scarcity and degradation to spur violence while recognizing the general alleviation of local environmental conditions as the primary benchmark of security in the era of globalization, thus uniting the neo-Malthusian and Cornucopian perspectives. Yet, as Barnett (2007, 7) contends, other factors are equally if not more crucial to the occurrence of violent conflict, including "poverty and inequities between groups, high levels of military spending and/or high availability of weapons, external indebtedness, poorly developed conflict resolution institutions, a history of violence, state illegitimacy, weak or no democracy, an abundance of lootable resources, and poor leadership."

These formulations trace the boundaries of the dominant paradigm while asking us to reconsider its efficacy. As Henrik Urdal (2005, 419, 426) has observed, while often depicted as competing, "the scarcity and abundance hypotheses are not theoretically mutually exclusive and may in fact coexist," despite studies regularly indicating "limited, and not very robust, support for both neo-Malthusian and Cornucopian propositions." Considering the mixed findings from the substantial body of research on these issues, Ravi Bhavnani (2009, 66) focuses instead on "how the two may interact: abundance breeding scarcity; scarcity breeding abundance; and how, in a complex new world in which abundance and scarcity coexist, we should craft policies that take these interdependencies into account." Indeed, as Bhavnani (2009, 72–73) concludes, "abundance and scarcity are two sides of the same coin," and we are now residing in an age typified simultaneously by "unprecedented wealth and unrivalled poverty." Likewise ruminating on scarcity and abundance and "the irony of their co-existence," Anne Murcott (1999, 305–306) has assessed their impact on food in particular, noting the rising rates of obesity *and* anorexia in a world where people are "either starving or stuffed."

It is a paradoxical time, to be sure. Like Coleridge's ancient mariner, we often seem to be awash in resources like water (due to rising sea levels triggered by climate change), but of the wrong sort: "Water, water, everywhere, nor any drop to drink." Climate change is also poised to potentially unearth valuable resources by melting arctic ice, evidencing a recurring theme in which the world's powers extract greater profit from disaster. Advocates of "peak oil" contend that there will be a precipitous drop-off in global fossil fuel energy production as supplies dwindle and eventually reach their finitude—yet this realization seems to have triggered greater degrees of resource exploitation instead of more sensible conservation efforts. As with the obesity/anorexia, stuffed/starving dichotomy, there is a widening wealth gap in evidence globally, steadily marking out a "two-tiered society" of haves and have-nots around the world. We experience profound scarcity in the midst of plenty, with maldistribution being the norm and its inherent inequities enforced through legal and military apparatuses alike. Meanwhile, time—perhaps the most precious resource of all—seems to be running out as thresholds are being approached and converging crises mount in their frequency and intensity. Communities oscillate between droughts and floods, and the question remains whether it is too late to right the ship.

From Structural Violence to Structural Peace

As with the struggle for the preservation of the San Francisco Peaks noted at the outset of this chapter—and indeed, as with nearly every social or environmental movement—there is an aura of inevitability presented by the "other side" that must be resisted if change is to occur. Living in an era where the fate of humankind seemingly hangs delicately in the balance is challenging, to say the least, yet it is not without its virtues. Perhaps the main benefit is that today we are keenly aware of the deep-seated interconnectedness of the issues before us, and in particular how social and ecological processes are intertwined. On some level this serves to explain the utter contradictions in the studies examining both the resource scarcity and resource abundance rubrics, in the sense that a complex integrated system with many feedback loops and potential intervening variables is likely to yield different results in different places, at different times, and through the eyes of different observers. This may well be as it should: complex problems require complex insights, and we are still taking baby steps on the whole.

Nevertheless, there are some important planks already set in the foundation. One is the recognition that militarism and violent conflict can serve as both causes and effects of environmental degradation and resource maldistribution, thus creating a potential feedback loop "between war and environmental insecurity" (Barnett 2007, 10) that mirrors the resource feedback loop "in which the pursuit of material goods at all costs merely renders those materials more elusive, thus requiring even more relentless pursuit" (Amster and Nagler 2010). As noted in the Introduction to this volume, we also know that the war system in its full dimensions is a leading driver of environmental change through its consumption of vast energy resources, the massive toxic wastes it produces, the effects of combat on landscapes and habitats, its impacts on climate systems, and the diminution of human capital through economic drains and productivity loss. And further, we have come to comprehend that human-human violence is part and parcel of existing in a larger frame dominated by violent conflict at the human-environment interface. As Shiva (2010) observes, "the bigger war is the war against the planet," and thus "making peace with the earth . . . has now become a survival imperative for our species."

In the end, we come to see that "the longing for peace and the yearning for a sustainable environment are inextricably linked" (Amster and Nagler 2010), and likewise that "peace and environmental security are therefore intimately related, and neither can be achieved without the other" (Barnett 2007, 12). Amid conflicting empirical studies and contrasting data sets, "what is clear is that the well-being of societies and the environment . . . are mutually dependent" (de Soysa 2002, 30), providing not only the benefit of keener insight into the nature of the challenges before us but also the opportunity to run the society-environment feedback loop in the direction of peace and sustainability rather than war and despoliation. As Shiva (2010) concludes, "Sustainability is based on peace with the earth." Creating peace thus requires the development of a "social system that at all levels produces abundant life and justice, a system in which . . . basic human needs are met, including the right to life, to food and clean water" (Shifferd 2011, 111). As with a healthy ecosystem, such a social system must be "layered, redundant, resilient, robust, and proactive. Its various parts must feed back to each other so the system is strengthened and the failure of one part does not lead to systems failure" (Shifferd 2011, 173). These insights reside at the core of a robust and potentially transformative peace ecology.

The task thus becomes one of moving from a paradigm characterized by violence at all levels to one distinguished by an equivalently multilayered impetus toward peace. In terms of understanding the problem, we have already looked at forms of "direct violence" that devolve upon militarism, resource control, and the use of force to secure advantages. More subtly, modern societies are also marked by "structural violence" (Galtung 1996), which entails the inequitable distribution of opportunities, freedoms, and resources necessary for individuals and communities to reach their full potential in exercising their autonomy and influencing the collective course of action. Structural violence is a social, political, economic, and ecological phenomenon, and exploring the full dimensions of its relationship to land, food, water, energy, environmental stability, present and future security, and other essentials will be part and parcel of the following chapters. At this juncture, it would be most fruitful to consider the utility of structural violence more so for the prompt it gives us to envision its inverse, "structural peace." In essence, the goal will be systemic *peacebuilding* to mitigate the presence of violent conflict.

At the outset, both scarcity and abundance can contribute to structural violence, with the former yielding poverty and deprivation and the latter contributing to stratification and inequality. These outcomes are not inevitable, yet as the rough consensus of the extant studies indicates there may be a correlation between resource levels at the extremes and violent conflict. We need not view this formulaically, but merely consider how the matter of *quanta* is relevant to conceptions of structural peace—both as to how much *in toto* humans are extracting from nature and as to how those resources are distributed. A stable, healthy society would be one that drew what it needed from its environment so as not to "overfish the pond" or otherwise hinder the carrying capacity of the habitat to continue supporting life. Likewise, a structurally peaceful society is one that distributes its wealth and opportunities in an egalitarian fashion that, at a minimum, provides the essential bases for all of its members to survive and thrive. This is neither altruism nor communism—it simply makes good sense for a society to maximize its human potential in the context of maintaining sustainable relations with the balance of its environment.

This is about self-preservation more than being saviors of the world. Eco-movements have perhaps too often led with a "Save the Environment" ideology suggesting that human opportunities and progress should be forsaken in the name of saving other entities—seemingly oblivious to the fact that most people in modern society are deeply inculcated with a cultural mythos of human superiority. This way of getting at the issue could actually foster the very sense of a "humans versus nature" rift that frames the problem in the first place. A more apt concept would be to "Save the Humans," since it is sheer hubris to believe that the world needs saving from human interventions; the earth and its life-giving capacities are resilient and will almost certainly (at least on a geological time scale) survive whatever we throw at it short of total nuclear pulverization. In fact, many other life forms would flourish without us here, with nature rapidly re-wilding even the concrete jungles we have created. It really is about saving ourselves, which is a more realistic aim and one that is consistent with our actual place in the web of life.

Let me illustrate the point with a brief recounting. A few years ago I asked the students in a course on ecology and peace whether water was a scarce or abundant resource. Being good environmentalists, they mostly reflected upon the hard-to-deny fact that water is scarce and getting scarcer—it is the "new oil" and "blue gold," as various outlets continually suggest. There is certainly a truth in this perspective, and yet water can also be seen as an abundant resource that is continually renewed by the planet's evaporation-rainfall cycle. We can actually quantify the amount of water it takes to maintain a local aquifer or the flow of a river at healthy levels; this is sometimes known as the "recharge rate" of how much it would be necessary to put back in to keep the water flowing. Swimming pool owners in hot climates, for example, often fill their pools a little bit each morning to compensate for evaporation, and thus perform a low-tech version of recharging their water levels in this manner. Filling a pool is not exactly a conservationist endeavor, but it indicates at least some recognition of the overall water cycle.

In fact, every resource has an inherent recharge rate, in the sense that an overall balance can be expressed by relating all inputs and outputs for a given system. Recharge rates are estimable if not outright calculable in most locales, suggesting that in practice we can find the balance point between output (i.e., what we consume) and input (i.e., what gets replaced) for any given resource. On some level, everything has a potential rate of renewal and can thus be sustained over time. We usually think of this in terms of renewable and nonrenewable resources, but the addition of the recharge rate to the mix adds a temporal element that accounts for gradations of renewability and is more consonant with a sustainability framework that seeks stability over time. Resources like air and water that have faster recharge rates are among the most basic for survival and are also the most vulnerable to disruptions in their renewal cycles. Food sources recharge fairly quickly as well, as do soils for growing; timber resources take a bit longer but can still renew within human time spans. Coal, oil, uranium, precious metals, and natural gas recharge very slowly and should be consumed with caution—not to mention that their extraction is often associated with significant environmental degradation and in many cases with human suffering as well. Solar radiation, geothermal energy, wind power, and tidal cycles renew continuously, making them suitable for regular utilization.

Thinking about what and how much we consume are critical to promoting peace at both the human and environmental levels. We can of course make use of the materials in our midst, as we must, with those being essential for survival factoring more heavily into our resource base. Thich Nhat Hanh (2008) refers to something along these lines as *mindful consumption*, which he contrasts with widespread practices that are doing violence to the earth and that have yielded a pervasive sense of societal violence as well. Reflecting on the obesity/anorexia dilemma of modern life and our relationship to food in particular, Hanh (2008, 20–21) illustrates the potential for sustainable alternatives with the story of the vessel of *appropriate measure*: "Since the bowl is exactly the right size, we always know just how much to eat. We never overeat, because overeating brings sickness to our bodies.... Mindful consumption brings about health and healing, for ourselves and for our planet." In this light, mindful consumption is far more than a dietary practice or New Age trend; it is, rather, a substantive *peacekeeping* initiative that seeks to place our own ability to attain sustenance on a par with others' capacity to do the same, thus tamping down a critical driver of potential hostilities and contributing to peace with the earth.

Obviously we must consume in order to survive, but if we do so outside the bounds of an "appropriate measure" our survival is placed in grave jeopardy.

If someone who is cold burns down an orchard to stay warm for a night, they will likely have to cope with hunger the next day; in this manner humanity often seems to find itself cascading from one crisis to the next, as each quick-fix intervention leads to a new (and perhaps more intractable) problem. People inclined to get rankled over any sentiment that encourages us to do with a bit less of some particular item might consider what it would be like if we were forced to try and survive with less (or none at all) of *everything*, which may be in store if we fail to act. Consuming within recharge rates is one way to ensure not only our short-term but also our long-range existence on this remarkable, self-renewing world that sustains us. Finding that balance point between too much and too little is the key for being mindful consumers, and thinking about renewal rates likewise calls upon us to be producers and sustainers in the process. We will look more at practices such as mindfulness in Chapter Eight; for now, the key point is that structural peace begins with conscious consumption.

Implicit in this perspective is the concomitant notion that structural peace devolves upon a *subsistence perspective*—not merely bare survival, but existence within the context of sustainability. The hallmarks of subsistence-oriented systems are production for need rather than profit, shared labor to produce essentials, and shared fruits of that labor among participants. Such societies also tend to mitigate dependency by (a) promoting *interdependency* and (b) preventing vast power and wealth differentials between producers and consumers. In this manner, we surmise that more egalitarian sociopolitical outcomes are connected to more balanced human-environment relations; the more reciprocal the latter are, the less stratified the former will be. In pursuing such aims, we see that "the issue of environmental quality is inextricably linked to that of human equality," and further that "a sustainable society must also be an equitable society, locally, nationally and internationally [since] social justice and environmental sustainability are inextricably linked" (Agyeman et al. 2003a, 1; Agyeman et al. 2003b, 323–325). Again, these items will be explored more deeply and concretely in the following chapters—particularly with regard to common pool resources, food and water, and free economy systems. Here, the focus is to build up a working vision of a structurally peaceful society to illustrate what a coherent alternative to a dominant order based on imposed scarcity and false abundance might look like. It is a complex vision (after all, it is a complex problem), yet one that is urgently needed.

2020 Vision

Let us conclude this chapter with an unflinching call for embracing the tenets of structural peace in short order, lest our well-meaning interventions and impassioned diatribes go for naught. As Chapter Five will chronicle, time is running out, and it is incumbent upon us to turn crisis into opportunity at every turn. The good news is that we already possess the knowledge to accomplish such a transformation; all we need is the will, and a vision to help guide us. In this chapter we have begun to map out the basic values for a structurally peaceful society: mindful consumption based on appropriate measure; a subsistence perspective based on shared labor and shared fruits; interdependency; sociopolitical egalitarianism; reciprocity at both the human-human and human-nature interfaces. These may seem like abstractions, but they are all based on excruciatingly concrete practices. The aim, again, is to simultaneously resolve the conjoined issues of endemic warfare/violence and environmental degradation/destabilization. It is a monumental task—a generational crucible—and we already know what needs to be done.

There is good news to be found in all of this. The very same processes that create feedback loops of conflict-degradation in our economic and political arrangements can also be made to yield mutually supporting positive results as well. Greater appreciation for the environment lessens our rampant consumption, and transcending our imposed identities as consumers opens up the prospect of becoming co-creators instead. Being purveyors of peace creates fewer conflicts around us, and fewer "hot spots" in turn promotes greater feelings of peaceableness. Experiencing relationships based on trust and mutual aid cultivates instincts toward greater trustworthiness and adduces behavior motivated beyond the narrow confines of acquisition and unbridled self-interest. In this sense, a potential self-fulfilling apocalypse can just as likely become a self-fulfilling utopia. It won't be easy, and it will require a reinvigorated spirit of sacrifice and collective responsibility. In the end, we can either choose to alter course and turn crisis into opportunity, or have the same imposed upon us. The former seems preferable.

So let us add a few more potential planks to this nascent foundation. Structural peace addresses our basic material needs, allowing people to meet as relative equals and thus to cultivate levels of opportunity and participation on that basis. It involves a holistic view premised on mutualism, interdependence, and the sense of a common future—yet it is also intensely localized in terms of the scale of our communities and the patterns of our consumption. Structural peace entails the reconciliation of self-interest and other-interest, valuing our differences as strengths but rejecting the divisiveness of dichotomies like us/them and nature/culture. It prioritizes qualities such as resilience and reciprocity in our dealings with one another and the environment, and utilizes these attributes as the basis for establishing healthy societal processes for resolving conflicts and building durable relationships over time. A structurally peaceful society would remove from the realm of competition and control the essentials of a full human life: food, water, energy, health, education, meaningful work, political voice, personal autonomy, community, environmental stability, and sustainability. This is merely a cursory list, but the basic concept is evident.

Occasionally, we may catch glimpses of such a society in our mind's eye. People work for sustenance and pleasure; education and labor are intertwined lifelong pursuits; children are reared collaboratively and joyfully; wealth is measured in relationships and one's willingness to share. The basics of life are firmly entrenched as the collective assets of humankind, and in even more enlightened terms are no longer seen as resources to be consumed but rather as blessings for which to be grateful. Tools replace technologies, actual people supplant abstract politics, conflicts are welcomed as teachable moments and learning opportunities, and the virtues of meaning supersede the value of money. The planet's inherent regenerative processes are celebrated, as mechanistic and dichotomous thinking falls into disrepute. Humans willingly take their place among the vast web of life, not in relegation but in celebration. Violence in any manner is an extreme aberration, and is treated restoratively so as not to beget more. People look forward to the future rather than dreading what lies ahead, and collectively take as their highest priority creating a peaceful world for those yet to come.

This may seem idealistic, but consider that it is no more so than continuing on our present course and hoping for a happy ending. Rather than a world of winners and losers, we can cultivate win-win scenarios; rather than zero-sum thinking, we can embrace a sense of the whole as greater than the sum of its parts. Humankind has struggled with these issues for millennia, and by most accounts it appears that we are rapidly approaching a proverbial "tipping point" in our relationships at all levels. The neo-Malthusians posit that competition in the face of scarcity is inevitable, while the Cornucopians assert that growth is good and that we can always find clever ways to continue expanding. Both dominant worldviews are plausible, and together they form the essential basis for the "human superiority" paradigm in which we have been living. What is most disconcerting is how the pendulum swings so seamlessly between these two perspectives, and how they bring together the forces of militarism and corporatism as two sides of the global coin. But more military conquest will not save us; nor will an expanding techno-capitalism.

It is up to us to imagine and implement another way of being in the world that mitigates the endemic violence of warfare and exploitation. We need a system that is durable, resilient, and sustainable. It should reconsider our histories, revamp the present, and preserve the future. The current paradigm of fragility, dependency, and entropy provides an object lesson in what *not* to do. Fortunately, there are many examples of what a coherent alternative looks like in theory and practice. Investigating the common roots of such examples is the subject of the next chapter.

Chapter Two
The Triumph of the Commons

In the middle of the seventeenth century, a major change in the relationship between people and the land was institutionalized under the laws of England. These new laws turned what had previously been common land—utilized by peasants, pastoralists, and farmers for grazing animals and growing food—into private property, thus bringing with it rights of the landowner to exclude others from having access. Known as the Enclosure Acts, this transformation from collective use to individual control of vast swaths of the countryside was backed by the military might of the state, which served to enforce this new exclusionary regime. Public lands were literally enclosed by fences and walls, prohibiting open access by commoners and interrupting the natural exchange of ecosystems and patterns of wildlife migration. (In Chapter Seven we will look more deeply at the human and ecological consequences of interposing border walls between nations.) From today's vantage point, the early enclosures appear as a harbinger; their initiation nearly half a millennia ago provides an opportunity to consider the relationship between common access to resources and the prospects for building peaceful and socially just communities.

Recognizing the implications of the enclosures on what were previously "the commons," small bands of radicals and visionaries attempted to reclaim the common lands for the public's use. Notable among these early activists were the True Levellers (named as such due to a belief in the common heritage and equal rights of all people), represented by pamphleteer Gerrard Winstanley, who took over vacant lands for cultivation and grazing, providing food and distributing crops free of charge. More colloquially known as the Diggers in light of their penchant for tilling and farming, the group was disbursed in 1650 when local landowners used hired thugs to violently drive them from the commons. While their intervention was short-lived, the Diggers did leave a legacy that includes these intriguing historical footnotes: being credited with one of the first modern socialistic community experiments; inspiring a legendary 1960s US-based radical sect by the same name; being sympathetically depicted in a 1975 feature film called *Winstanley* that sought to bring the saga to life in a historically accurate manner; and yielding a 1999 uprising on their 350th anniversary that included a march and reoccupation of the original Diggers' site (which, like its predecessor, was quickly disbanded).

Three centuries after Winstanley and the Diggers revolted against the enclosure of the commons, one of the great neo-Malthusians of the modern age penned a tract that would have repercussions for decades to come. In 1968, Garrett Hardin published an essay in *Science* titled "The Tragedy of the Commons," arguing that the rapid expansion of human population coupled with an entitlement to necessary resources was pushing the world to the brink, and that access to the commons thus had to be mitigated or eliminated in the name of preventing imminent tragedy. Hardin's thesis—which included an explicit call to curtail human breeding—was roundly criticized by many contemporaries, even as its influence continued to grow. While Hardin's foundational text leaves much to be desired as a piece of cogent scholarship, it did serve the purpose of setting forth the basic terms of a critical debate over the present and future of the commons, including spawning a spate of subsequent literature and a plethora of case studies on the use of the commons by people and communities around the world. What Hardin ultimately argued, problematically, is that patterns of social injustice are preferable to the thoroughgoing tragedy that he surmised was in the offing, reflecting a Hobbesian sensibility (akin to that noted in the previous chapter) whereby people will revert to unbridled war and violence to survive.

In this light, it becomes apparent that while modern society is built upon structures of power and systems of inequality, at root it may be even more so constructed upon a foundation of untenable allegories. The "tragedy of the commons," like its cousin the "state of nature" from Hobbes's time, depicts humankind as inherently incapable of managing resources cooperatively and sustainably. This narrative, in essence, counsels that we must destroy the commons in order to save them, by privatizing all aspects of our shared world lest they be despoiled by greedy, self-interested actors. By now, however, it appears that we have done little more than deliver upon ourselves that very result, flying in the face of logic and common sense. In actuality, the commons represent a powerful venue for reinvigorating basic human processes of cooperation, sustainability, and self-regulation. Examples from around the globe illustrate the potential of reclaiming and restoring the commons to literally remake the map of the world. One particularly durable model is the *acequia* from the southwestern United States, a centuries-old common pool system of self-governance for the sharing of limited water resources in an arid region. In this chapter, we will develop these themes and highlight the peacemaking potential of the commons.

Beyond Institutionalized Injustice

In the time since Hardin's landmark essay, there has been an effort worldwide to privatize resources in the name of more effective extraction and exploitation. Resting on the notion that someone (i.e., powerholders and/ or corporations) needs to be "in charge" in order for resources to be properly utilized, this view has taken hold as a major underpinning of both globalization and militarization in the modern era. Today, with resources dwindling and the global economy plainly unable to deliver on its false promises of prosperity, there is even greater elite urgency to exploit the remaining commons in the name of "national security" and "progress." The problem, however, is that the tragedy of the commons has become a self-fulfilling prophecy, and it is actually the privatization of the shared wealth of humankind that has led to environmental degradation and structural violence in society. It is not the maintenance of the commons that is tragic, but rather the loss of them that is such; for many social and environmental advocates, it is precisely the restoration of the commons that represents an antidote to the tragedy of enclosure.

As Vandana Shiva (2005, 2) writes, "In contrast to viewing the planet as private property, movements are defending, on a local and global level, the planet as a commons." In the contemporary milieu, concepts such as *peace* and *justice* are often deployed specifically against the privatization, corporatization, and militarization of common resources; these processes are largely built on the mythology of private ownership as the only means of spurring innovation and hard work, comprising an emerging global system that steadily eliminates contrary formulations and alternative visions (cf. Kahn and Minnich 2005, 202). In addition to basic resources like land and water, modern processes of privatization and enclosure extend to erstwhile commons ranging from public airwaves and the internet to biodiversity and DNA. Public services such as education and health care are increasingly privatized, as are urban centers and rural pastures alike. Resulting from the enclosure of these material realms, there are also concomitant impacts on social, political, and psychological levels. As Shiva (2005, 20) has observed, the loss of the commons carries with it (a) the exclusion of people from access to resources; (b) the creation of "disposable" people who are denied access to essentials; (c) the replacement of diverse socioeconomic systems with a monocultural commodity-based system; and (d) the enclosure of "minds and imaginations" by associating privatization with progress and privilege.

Interestingly, Hardin himself foresaw much of this, even as he helped usher in its realization. Nearly a decade after his infamous essay, Hardin (1977a, 46) characterized the Enclosure Acts as unjust, noting that "it would be hard to find a justification for this under any acceptable definition of social justice." Hardin went on to quote an anonymously coined rhyme that was popular in the 1600s during the time of the rampant enclosure of England's commons:

> They clap in gaol the man or woman
> Who steals the goose from off the common;
> But let the bigger knave go loose
> Who steals the common from the goose.

Still, Hardin (1977a, 46) insisted that though the Enclosure Acts were unjust, they at least "put an end to the tragedy of the commons" as to the aspect of agriculture. This is actually consistent with his initial formulation, where injustice is preferred to the prospect of tragedy:

> An alternative to the commons need not be perfectly just to be preferable. With real estate and other material goods, the alternative we have chosen is the institution of private property coupled with legal inheritance. Is this system perfectly just? As a genetically trained biologist I deny that it is.... We must admit that our legal system of private property plus inheritance is unjust—but we put up with it because we are not convinced, at the moment, that anyone has invented a better system. The alternative of the commons is too horrifying to contemplate. Injustice is preferable to total ruin. (1968, 1247)

Injustice is preferable to total ruin. This is the false choice we have been presented with for centuries, the one that is holding the future hostage to the ravages of the past and present. This prevailing narrative essentially states that since we cannot have perfect justice in society, it would be better to create a system of "controlled injustice" rather than risk the potential ruination that would come with unbridled competition and the lack of coercive authority to enforce rules in a finite world. Simply put, this story suggests that humans cannot be trusted to self-manage the commons or to work cooperatively with others, and that people will only pursue their self-interest and thus ruin the commons for all concerned unless forcibly prevented from doing so. This coercion is unfortunate, as Hardin laments, yet it is deemed necessary in order to keep us from destroying ourselves and everything around us, as was prophesied from time immemorial. Hardin refers to this system as "mutual coercion mutually agreed upon," updating the *social contract* theories popularized by Hobbes and others (notably crafted at the dawn of the era of enclosure), though it is not clear precisely who has "agreed" or given consent to such a system.

This is a seductive story, and is one that gets great buy-in—at least from those who are predestined to be on the winning side of the ledger, i.e., the side that gets to aspire to "justice" vis-à-vis the unfortunate multitudes who bear the disparate burdens of violence, inequality, and injustice. After all, if everyone was afforded true equality in terms of access to life's essentials and a share in the collective wealth of humankind, it would only lead to "total ruin" since there would be no limit to our unbridled, ruthless competition with one another over resources and power alike. The antidote, consciously chosen, is to adopt an inherently unjust system that skews its benefits in one direction and its burdens in another, in order to keep the entire operation afloat at all. As many have observed, however, Hardin's formulation makes a number of presumptions that are philosophically, pragmatically, and/or empirically dubious. First, it is not the case that people sharing common resources act merely in their short-term self-interest; indeed, numerous examples exist that indicate precisely the opposite. Second, Hardin conceives of the commons as a "free for all" system where anyone can simply come in and extract gross resources at any time; in fact, most commons-oriented systems are managed by collective norms of behavior, requiring shared burdens along with mutual opportunities to reap benefits. Finally, and perhaps most significantly, Hardin assumes (without supplying evidence) that sharing the commons will lead to a Hobbesian war of each against all, thus destroying the bounty of nature for everyone.

Even if we take Hardin's "unregulated access by self-interested actors" scenario at face value, he still reaches the wrong conclusion. Consider the case of outer space (a commons in principle if not practice), where recent decades have seen a "space race" for the colonization of desirable vantage points (e.g., stable satellite orbits) and the exploitation of valuable resources (e.g., plans to mine near-earth asteroids). The international sphere is said to be similarly plagued by an untenable "anarchy" (Kaplan 1994), due to a lack of regulation and actors pursuing their own pecuniary and strategic interests—an ethic that is further reified by the presence of so-called free trade agreements that install minimalist regulatory frameworks while opening up new markets and potentialities for resource extraction. Or take the case of public lands mining, ranching, and logging in the United States, or that of off-shore oil and gas drilling in ocean waters, where private entities are granted nearly unfettered access to extract resources from common areas, oftentimes with disastrous effects on communities and the environment. In each of these real-world scenarios, the actors responsible for looting the commons to further their own interests—to wit, nation-states and corporations—are in fact precisely (and perversely) those that Hardin proposes we designate to "manage" the commons through coercive force and privatization.

What we thus come to realize is that it isn't sharing the commons and existing within the delicate balance of natural systems that bring ruination—exploitation and inequality do. It is actually the prescribed antidote to "total ruin" that foments devastation; that which we have been told will forestall our demise actually hastens it. Civilization didn't save us from the scourge of violence and the impetus toward self-destruction; it merely institutionalized these qualities and rendered them endemic as tenets of an emerging system of globalization that is steadily working to achieve enclosure (of both habitats and societies) on a planet-wide scale. A genuine solution to the problems that Hardin's formulation has engendered might in fact devolve upon the reclaiming, reinvigorating, and restoring of the commons—the very alternative that Hardin says is "too horrifying to contemplate." With the benefit of hindsight, we can surmise that the real tragedy is the loss of the commons and the social architecture that accompanies their management. Notwithstanding enclosure, it remains the case in many locales that "the principle of cooperation, rather than competition, among individuals still dominates" (Shiva 2002, 27).

As Shiva (2005, 53–55) concludes, what we are really faced with today is the "tragedy of privatization," with its impetus to break down community structures that have preserved shared resources while increasing wealth disparities and environmental destabilization. At this juncture, many of those struggling to survive might well trade the grim reality of immiseration and despoliation for the hypothetical horror of equal access and the uncertainty of negotiation among peers. The dominant "solution" of privatizing the commons in order to "save" them is nonsensical (eerily reminiscent of the discredited logic from the Vietnam War arguing that we had to "destroy the village in order to save it"), even as it claims the mantle of rationality. Rational beings simply do not practice self-interest to the exclusion of their communities and at the expense of the habitat that sustains them. In the end, we come to realize that the self-proclaimed "realists" are in fact the most quixotic ones of all, insisting despite all evidence to the contrary that more of what has pushed us to the brink will somehow guide us away from it.

Performing CPR

We thus find ourselves in a serious predicament that requires immediate intervention. While we cannot go back in time to prevent the emergence of enclosures, we can work in the present to challenge their continuance and present counterexamples that illustrate the viability of alternative approaches. The task is one of historical import, and its outcome may in large measure help to determine the future existence of human societies on this planet. It serves no purpose to either understate or overstate the matter; it simply is as it is: Humankind appears to be rapidly approaching a point in our evolution where the very things that have enabled us to thrive and expand are now imperiling our capacity to survive at all. I would characterize this notion as equal parts shocking and mundane—to wit, a great many people are blissfully (perhaps even intentionally) ignorant of this situation, even while nearly as many see it so clearly as to render it almost axiomatic. As Jay Walljasper writes in *All That We Share: A Field Guide to the Commons*, we are in a time of great urgency and the requisite transformation will be substantial:

> To deliver us from current economic and ecological calamities will require more than administering a few tweaks to the operating system that runs our society. A complete retooling is needed—a paradigm shift that revises the core principles that guide our culture top to bottom. At this historical moment, the commons vision of a society where "we" matters as much as "me" shines as a beacon of hope for a better world. (2010, 6)

When we think of the commons, we need to move beyond bucolic images of pastoralists grazing livestock on shared grasslands or villagers sharing the catch from local fisheries. Compelling as these traditional examples are—and not to disregard their utility as sustainable alternatives—there is more to the commons in a complex modern world. Consider the following spheres, as identified in *All That We Share* (Walljasper 2010, 7–8): air and water; parks and sidewalks; libraries; human and non-human DNA; cultural trends and linguistic evolutions; public services and social security programs; the airwaves and the internet; traditions and folklore; biodiversity; open-source publications; taxpayer-funded research; education and transportation systems; the oceans; Antarctica; and outer space. In *Sacred Economics*, Charles Eisenstein (2011, 187) further adds the surface of the earth and the minerals under it, as well as "the centuries-long accumulation of human knowledge and technology." Unfortunately, all of these spheres are under direct threat from privatization and enclosure, plainly transgressing Thomas Paine's famous dictum (quoted in Walljasper 2010, 61) that "Nature's gifts are the common property of the human race." As Walljasper (2010, 25) ultimately discerns, the commons are "creations of both nature and society that belong to all of us equally and should be maintained for future generations."

For millennia human communities have collectively managed shared resources without resorting to widespread privatization and continually expanding apparatuses of coercion. Rather than constituting a free-for-all such as that imagined by Hardin, the commons throughout recorded history have actually been characterized by concomitant *rights* and *responsibilities* attendant to their utilization (cf. Rowland 2005, 702). Building a bridge between theory and practice, these living exemplars are sometimes referred to as *common pool resources* (CPRs), and taken together they constitute a "proven, effective method" for equitable resource sharing as well as a "viable alternative" to strictly legalistic approaches based on coercive methods (Rowland 2005, 703–705). Such systems are found everywhere around the world and at multiple scales of engagement, from the intensely localized to the international; indeed, the extant case studies demonstrate that "the number of resource users in a common pool resource management system does not have to be small for the system to be sustainable" (Rowland 2005, 703).

Perhaps the best-known exponent of the CPR model was Elinor Ostrom, who won the 2009 Nobel Prize in economics for her work in establishing a comprehensive set of "design principles" for the sustainable, collective management of shared resources. In her landmark 1990 book *Governing the Commons*, Ostrom set forth a number of related notions that have informed subsequent research on and treatments of CPRs around the world. Crucially, Ostrom concluded that social systems were just as important as infrastructural design in terms of sustaining a CPR, and that it is largely the presence of reciprocal relationships among users (based on trust and accountability) that determines whether a CPR will be successful. Based on systematic case studies of diverse CPRs (e.g., riparian rights in Spain; Alpine grazing in Switzerland; old-growth Japanese forests), Ostrom (1990, 21) asserted that in many situations people sharing resources have found that "working rules" existing in a climate of communication, respect, and the sense of a common future are more useful than the "rule of law" and its coercive mechanisms. As Ostrom (1990, 213) noted, once external officials become involved, individual ability to self-regulate is abated, reciprocity and trust are diminished, the sense of mutuality and a common future is undermined, and rewards are skewed to the benefit of the external officials.

There is no magical solution to the dilemma posed by Hardin—only actual people working out equitable, sustainable arrangements in concrete settings where their livelihoods are interdependent. People living in mutual reliance upon a CPR often implicitly (if not explicitly) recognize that there is no advantage to overusing the resource or fighting over it, and that self-interest to the exclusion of community and conservation is illogical. What Ostrom's work asks us to consider is that we are not constrained to make an illusory choice between Hardin's ruinous "tragedy of the commons" and Hobbes's coercive "leviathan" in order to sustain our societies and ecosystems alike. Indeed, as Ostrom (1990, 1) contended on the first page of her influential tome, "neither the state nor the market is uniformly successful in enabling individuals to sustain long-term, productive use of natural resource systems," counseling instead that "communities of individuals have relied on institutions resembling neither the state nor the market to govern some resource systems with reasonable degrees of success over long periods of time." Ostrom may have couched her conclusions in cautious rhetoric, but the implications resound loudly.

Despite the careful language, Ostrom's body of work is inherently radical in its full implications. Her basic premise is that the "tragedy of the commons" is actually an inversion of logic and reality, and that in fact the most sustainable forms of resource management are collective, cooperative, egalitarian, and decentralized in nature. In short, she demonstrated how people in localities everywhere have crafted and maintained elegant solutions to what might otherwise become conflict-ridden scenarios involving competition over either scarce or abundant essential resources. Ostrom's genre-defining work provides an impetus to include within the terrain of *economics* those visions of human discourse and practice that exist largely outside of commonplace touchstones such as supply and demand. By conceptualizing the commons as a locus of resource management rather than one of exploitation, Ostrom not only focused on the hardware involved in such systems but on the software as well, adducing the myriad non-hierarchical forms of decisionmaking and non-reified authority that pervade the administration of many CPRs. When people resist externalization of control over their resources and instead decide to take on the challenges of collective self-management—thus rejecting both the state and the market—not only is the resource base preserved, but the spirit of democracy is also bolstered.

Such systems necessitate not only rough political equality, but also a strong undercurrent of mutualism that is often masked in competition-based frameworks. Still, Ostrom was careful to resist concluding that people in common pool systems are somehow nicer or more culturally predisposed toward cooperation and mutual aid. In fact, her examples and cases reflect the essential notion that people can and will inculcate the virtues of concerted action and common humanity not only because it is morally imperative but perhaps even more so because it actually works in practice. Cooperation and egalitarianism, it turns out, are viable and sustainable practices both socially and ecologically—and the solution to the purported problems of the commons is neither more nor less than that. What emerges is a set of principles that demonstrate the viability of collective resource management, emphasizing the need for egalitarian human-human relationships based on reciprocity and mutuality coupled with similar mechanisms for promoting enduring systems at the human-environment interface as well. And the hallmark of these longstanding regimes lies in the delicate balance of what is taken *from* and given *to* them.

Balancing Rights and Responsibilities

Almost universally, treatments and studies of common pool systems have emphasized that their success involves reciprocal relationships at three distinct but related levels: between users of the system; between the resource system and the ecosystem of which it is a part; and between the rights of users and their responsibilities to the community and environment alike. The argument presented in this volume for the efficacy and desirability of peace ecology as a viable paradigm of thought and action is largely contingent on these same reciprocities, premised on the notion that patterns of both human-human and human-environment engagement are necessarily interrelated in a healthy system. The CPR model, based on the historical vitality of the commons, encapsulates not only a system of resource allocation but also a set of social and political structures for existing in balance with one another and the larger habitat. In this sense, we can view the commons as geophysical locations (e.g., forests, pastures, river basins) *and* the sociocultural structures created for their utilization and maintenance. Indeed, this concept of the "social commons" may be taking on even greater salience in the digital age, as virtual communities and divergent geographies are steadily supplanting traditional physical ones.

Critically, it has been observed that shared resources have been sustained over time rather than degraded in scenarios where "common users agreed on the nature of the problem and established and adhered to responsibilities, rights, and other rules" (Burger et al. 2001, 1). The conventional CPR model (such as those in Hardin's formulation) presumes a simple system composed of homogeneous users seeking to maximize their short-term gains in the context of a predictable resource supply. In the real world, CPRs are actually much more complex and are often characterized by heterogeneous users (perhaps cognizant of the impacts of their actions on others and on the resource base itself) who draw resources asynchronously from a non-linear system. In such settings, empirical studies conducted by Ostrom and others indicate that "many more local users self-organize and are successful than is consistent with the conventional theory" that led Hardin to his conclusion that a tragedy would ensue absent coercion and control (Ostrom 2001, 17). Hence, there is actually a high likelihood that CPR users will organize themselves in many instances, by specifying "rights and duties" in an environment where communication, trust, and reciprocity are allowed to take hold (Ostrom 2001, 20–22). Significantly, cooperation in this context is more likely when CPR users enjoy relative *autonomy* in the sense of managing the system "without external authorities"; in this manner, large-scale CPRs are workable when they are rooted in the autonomous self-governance of local units (Ostrom 2001, 22–23).

These formulations defy the leviathan-tragedy paradigm that dominates the discourse about resource utilization and the sociopolitical systems that are possible. Indeed, Ostrom (1990, 183) specifically counterposed her conclusions to those presuming that "universal institutional panaceas must be imposed by external authorities," instead conceiving the self-management and sustainability of the commons as feasible even in light of "complex, uncertain, and difficult problems." It is not the advocates of just and sustainable resource systems who should bear the burden of proof here, but rather those presenting false "solutions" (steadily being imposed worldwide) that "are themselves based on models of idealized markets or idealized states" (Ostrom 1990, 216). We live in a world marked by perpetual conflict and a rapidly destabilizing environment—precisely what the advocates of authoritarianism and privatization have claimed their systems were designed to prevent. At this point, it appears that "conservation is not enough," and that in order to avert a global disaster "we must change the way we think" about resource use and governance equally (Tang 1992, xiii). The CPR model, based on a "complex web of reciprocal relationships," represents a workable, time-tested alternative (Tang 1992, 130).

As we have noted, the range of the commons extends from the oceans and the atmosphere to the internet and cultural products, and the range of their use spans the gamut of geographical scales and encompasses a multitude of diverse users (Dolšak and Ostrom 2003, 5). Each of these points on the scale represents a potential locus for either competition or cooperation, since "the interests of resource users at these multiple levels are often in conflict" (Dolšak et al. 2003, 338). To an extent, Hardin himself seemed to be aware of the stakes regarding which path we choose to pursue, observing in his essay on "lifeboat ethics" that "no generation has viewed the problem of the survival of the human species as seriously as we have" (1977b, 261). Unfortunately, Hardin's analysis of potential solutions remained fixed in zero-sum logic, arguing against food aid programs and human reproduction as being incompatible with a finite world in which "complete justice" inexorably leads to "complete catastrophe" (1977b, 263). At root is his basic view of humans as burdensome, unconditionally self-interested, and destined for ruination: "Every human being born constitutes a draft on all aspects of the environment" (1977b, 271). To this we might offer another perspective: every human being born is *part* of the environment.

Extending this argument, we can begin to articulate a cohesive vision of humankind as necessarily embedded in reciprocal relationships with the environment and one another. It is in reality the myth of separation—plied by Hobbes, Hardin, and their scions—that makes cooperative, just, and sustainable resolutions appear unworkable. The CPR case studies diligently assert the efficacy of reciprocity within and among human communities; drawing that fundamental lesson toward the human-environment interface asks us to consider our place in a complex web of exchange that we are simultaneously *part of* and *dependent upon*. As Shiva points out, "The commons are where justice and sustainability converge, where ecology and equity meet" (2005, 50). We live in a world defined by new challenges and opportunities alike, with rapid changes evident in technology, consumption, population, global linkages, and ecosystem impacts (Burger et al. 2001, 2). There is also a temporal element involved, yielding a burgeoning awareness of sustainability as part of an "intergenerational commons" that cannot be attained through self-interest but must instead be "shared as a common responsibility" (Burger et al. 2001, 9). We are inextricably linked, spatially and temporally, and that is indeed a good thing.

Peacemaking and the Shadow of the Future

One of the critical lessons gleaned from an interconnected system is the inevitability of what are referred to as "unintended consequences" or, alternatively, the principles of "chaos theory" that are better-known colloquially as the "butterfly effect." The basic concept is that small actions in a nonlinear system can yield large impacts, and that we are not always capable of knowing beforehand what the results of our actions will ultimately be. We have seen this play out most directly in the context of climate change and the loss of biodiversity, and in turn each of these effects will become the cause of further outcomes as the cycle continues. These phenomena are sometimes collectively termed "cascade effects" to indicate their branching, escalating nature. In the context of CPRs, we are essentially dealing with nested systems of local resource use that are agglomerated into regional and ultimately global scales; in short, we are part of a single planetary ecosystem that is made up of many interlinked smaller systems. Before the modern era, the linkages between individual systems were far less pronounced, but in the age of global transportation and communications there is a greater propensity for action anywhere to impact systems everywhere. The same occurs temporally, in terms of our capacity to impact the future.

Thus, when one set of users in a specific locality overgrazes a pasture or overfishes a pond, it can impact other users remotely in both distance and time. The loss of even a single species can crash an entire ecosystem, a regional water table can be contaminated by even one major polluter, and the planet's climatic regulatory systems can be disrupted by the wholesale consumption of a solitary fuel source. In the ensuing chapters, we will see that all of these outcomes can spark potential conflicts, violence, and even warfare in some instances. But there is another side to the story of interconnection that often goes unacknowledged, namely that positive actions in one sphere might contribute to beneficial results in the balance of the system, arguing for the practicability of localized responses to global problems. Peace ecology is an approach that seeks to maximize this potential "positive cascade effect" by linking sociopolitical practices and environmental processes, suggesting that steps toward peace can promote sustainability, and vice versa. This is not an algebraic formula, but more so a sensibility that strives to connect the various spheres of human existence in a positive, proactive manner.

These synergies have begun to reveal themselves in the commons literature. Michel Gelobter (2001, 294–295) refers to institutions, ideologies, and cultural norms as "social pool resources" (SPRs) that exist as a corollary commons to CPRs, arguing that each influences the other and that "the stability of resources and human institutions are deeply interwoven." Looking in particular at the Americas as a case study on the linkages between justice and ecology—both for the relative recency and the overall rapacity of change throughout the hemisphere—Gelobter (2001, 298–299) reflects upon the "whirlwind conversion from the most communal to the most commercial geography in the world," surmising that, at root, "the domination of nature led to new forms of domination and injustice among people." The prevailing instrumentalist view of the colonizers, in which nature exists merely as a resource for human use, failed to account for non-commercial aspects of the commons such as those reflected in historical, cultural, or spiritual formulations. Built upon the genuine tragedies of slavery and genocide, the Americas were forged through practices of privatization and resource exploitation that turn Hardin's thesis on its head: the commons were destroyed by institutionalizing injustice and violence.

While the colonization of the Americas (which continues today) represents a negative example, various theories of cooperation have been propounded that offer positive alternatives. Consonant with the literature on CPRs, Robert Axelrod posited in *The Evolution of Cooperation* that cooperation (even among purely self-interested actors) could develop and sustain without the presence of a central coercive authority by promoting reciprocity and "enlarging the shadow of the future" (1984, 124–141). The central notion advanced in this and subsequent works is that when people exist in communities where their mutual interdependence is acknowledged, coupled with their joint reliance on shared essential resources, the result is more likely to be cooperation than competition. As Gelobter (2001, 315) concurs, justice in a commons depends on "evolving shared norms for the present and the future," and the implications of this can be profound:

> The strength of our social commons lies in no small measure in how its members come to see each other and the resources they must depend on as part of an integrated whole. The question is thus no longer which injustices are necessary for the survival of the commons, but instead which to remedy first to alleviate suffering and to promote a sustainable future for our societies *and* our resources. (2001, 321, emphasis in original)

In a similar vein, one of the more trenchant and literate critiques of Hardin's inverted thesis was delivered contemporaneously by Kenneth Boulding, who was also a central figure in the development of peace studies as an academic discipline. Noting at the outset (with all due irony) that "Malthusian species actually seem to be rare in nature, perhaps because they do not develop enough redundancy to have survival value," Boulding (1977, 284–285) more soberly affirmed that the prevailing solution to the tragedy of the commons—namely appropriating and privatizing the commons—has resulted in "the segregation of misery through a class structure." Such a social order can remain stable for a time, "if the class structure can be preserved, [and] if the fences hold through a combination of the threat system, the police and the military," but even its ostensible success "undermines its acceptability" before long (Boulding 1977, 286). Against the fictitious tragedy of the commons, Boulding presents "the comedy of community" as an imperfect, long-term, learned endeavor that calls upon us to develop peacemaking and conflict resolution skills in order to survive—based in large measure on our innate capacities for empathy, compassion, and love. In the best tradition of peace ecology, Boulding surmised that such a system must by necessity include "the whole human race *and beyond* as a potential community" (1977, 293, emphasis added). What follows is a living example of this ethos.

Water: The Ultimate Common Pool Resource

Life in the desert Southwest is richly complex and oftentimes a great challenge. A hint of frontier culture remains even as rampant growth and homogenization take hold at breakneck speed. People love the landscapes and the history, but can still sit and watch both disappear in the name of progress. At times it seems as if a strange double consciousness exists, nowhere more prominently than in the relationship to water. The trouble is, as many already well know, there isn't much of it left in the region. Or, more precisely, due to unbridled development schemes and unsustainable resource policies, nearly every drop of river water is allocated and groundwater aquifers are being pumped faster than they can be replenished. Most significantly, the water laws instantiated in the West reflect the sensibilities of "manifest destiny" and cultural conquest brought by the settlers, defined by the doctrine of "prior appropriation" that simultaneously sets up private ownership over water and allows it to be severed from the land for use elsewhere. This doctrine is also problematic since the first users were native people whose rights were discarded.

Patterns of water commodification and consumption in the American Southwest are potential harbingers of a looming global water crisis. The earth's surface is about two-thirds water, and humans are made up of roughly the same percentage. Water is the lifeblood of the planet, and of ourselves as well. While abundant in a general sense, much of the planet's water is in the oceans, and desalination takes large energy inputs (generally from non-renewable sources) in order to yield any net benefit. Global climate change is melting arctic ice and playing havoc with the water cycle, creating disastrous floods and relentless droughts alike. As this essential resource dwindles, two related phenomena take hold. First, military strategists overtly cite "resource control" as a principle aim of national security, blithely observing that conflicts to attain it will dominate the coming decades. Second, multinational corporations are pumping water as fast as possible, turning a previously common resource into one that is privatized and engendering a global commodity trade that gives new meaning to "liquidity." In both cases, the aim is to wrest water supplies away from localities and set up a distribution system that simultaneously turns a profit and forces people into a dependent posture to meet a basic need.

We inhabit a world where public goods such as energy, education, health care, and the airwaves are increasingly privatized—but when these processes reach the level of water, the situation is vastly different since water is one of the few substances (along with food and air) that no one can do without under any circumstance. This raises the stakes considerably and threatens to tighten the sense of dependency that often pervades the machinations of the global commodity system. For many of us in the developed world, our sense of self-reliance has atrophied as powerful forces take what once belonged to all of us and sell a watered-down version (pun intended) back to us. Companies marketing bottled water brands capture this diminishing common resource at the expense of communities around the globe, often without paying for it, and we wind up purchasing from them that which ought to be free and which no one should ever own. The common law actually comprehended this fact, going back to Blackstone's 1766 treatise on the laws of England that later helped to form the basis of many modern legal systems:

> There are some few things which, notwithstanding the general intro-
> duction and continuance of property, must still unavoidably remain in
> common, being such wherein nothing but an usufructuary property is

capable of being had.... Water is a moveable, wandering thing, and must of necessity continue common by the law of nature; so that I can only have a temporary, transient, usufructuary property therein.

In plain terms, Blackstone opined that water could only be used but never owned as property, harkening back to the earlier formulation codified in the Institutes of Justinian (circa 535 AD): "By the law of nature, these things are common to mankind—the air, running water, the sea." American frontier law turned this on its head through the doctrine of prior appropriation (sometimes colloquially understood as "first in time, first in right") but conveniently ignored the rights of the continent's prior inhabitants (cf. Shiva 2002, 23). To make a bad situation even worse, frontier laws required water to be used to be subject to the forfeit of one's property rights, creating an incentive not to conserve but rather to exploit the resource as much as possible (cf. Anderson and Hill 1977, 213; Shiva 2002, 22). Prior appropriation laws also rendered the rights of senior users as superior to those of subsequent users, meaning that in times of shortage senior users can draw their water share even if it forecloses the water rights of junior users (Schlager and Blomquist 2001, 144). This is a zero-sum, competitive system that stands in stark contrast to the many collaborative, cooperative models found around the world.

In this regard stand numerous examples of people and communities still managing scarce resources collectively and sustainably. In the desert Southwest, in fact, one of the last great CPR systems in North America provides irrigation water to farmers and pastoralists. Derived from the imported culture of Spanish settlers (via the Arabic Moors, who previously brought the concept to Iberia) and combined with the best practices of the native peoples of the region, the *acequia* system is a powerful example of how people can sustainably work together not only with each other but with the land itself. In this model, water is viewed as sacred and not subject to private ownership. Instead, local communities manage the resource together through a collective self-governance system whereby everyone using the water gets what they need and also contributes their labor to maintain the entire operation. A non-authoritarian *mayordomo* administers the resource equitably, resolves conflicts, and guards the overall integrity of the structure before passing the baton to someone else and thus rotating the role of facilitator. Devon Peña

(2005, 82–83) thus refers to the acequia as a "watershed democracy," in the best tradition of the commons.

The acequia is a low-tech solution to a complex modern problem. Water is moved through ditches and channels (primarily earthen), and everyone takes only as much as they need. It works because, over time, people engaged in such an enterprise come to see themselves as interconnected with their neighbors in a meaningful way, so that their own prosperity is bound up with that of their fellow community members. Mutual interdependence replaces corporate dependence, and in a feat of old-school sustainability people in the Southwest have been cultivating this way of life for over four centuries. Mirroring patterns found worldwide, the acequia system demonstrates that people confronted with resource scarcity have the capacity to create and maintain stable, cooperative, and non-authoritarian common pool systems. Today, people around the world are facing severe and growing water shortages, and nearly everywhere this vital resource is ceasing to be a right and instead becoming a commodity. The acequia model offers a compelling commons-based alternative—grounded in reciprocal relationships between water users, their communities, and nature itself—arising out of a conservation-oriented tradition of sharing that merits emulation in an age of increasing competition for scarce resources.

Institutionalized Justice in the Commons

Coming full circle, then, the acequia represents a powerful alternative to the tragedy of the commons and the self-fulfilling nature of its preference for injustice as against the false specter of "total ruin." Among all natural resources, water stands apart as a quintessential commons "because it is the ecological basis of all life" and due to its free-flowing, border-crossing, communal qualities that require collaborative efforts in order to maintain the resource for all concerned (Shiva 2002, 24). Moreover, water also exists as part of a temporal commons in which sustainable management systems such as the acequia are "passed on from generation to generation" (Shiva 2002, 28). The acequia—which refers to both the physical delivery system of canals and ditches as well as the social structures that have developed around their collective management (Rodríguez 2006, 2)—is more than the sum of its parts, and at its core the system represents "a way of life that is in balance with the land" (Gallegos 1998, 242). Among others, Sylvia Rodríguez (2006, 75, 115) has written poignantly on the "moral economy" of the acequia as a system based on equitable distribution, self-regulation, community control, cooperative practices, interdependence, and above all the "common principle that water is always shared."

As such, the acequia is a working model of institutionalized justice. All users are bound to contribute labor to keep the ditches operating, the management of each ditch is directly democratic (one person, one vote—rather than voting by shares, which could privilege larger landowners), and conflicts are resolved through mediation and an ever-present ethos of reciprocity and mutualism (Rivera 1998, 34–35). As acequia farmer Joseph Gallegos (1998, 237) has observed, "The acequias work only because the farmers depend on each other for the water." José Rivera (1998, 38, 52) has likewise characterized the acequia system as one built on a foundation of "need, noninjury, equity, and a concern for the common good," cultivating at every point in the process a sense of shared ownership and responsibilities coupled with an overarching desire to promote the "welfare of the entire community." Despite local variations and diverse practices among the specific ditches in the network, "the common thread among acequias is the community value of water," which is continually reinforced by the reciprocal nature of the "*right to participate* in the collective governance of the acequia and the *duty to contribute* to the maintenance of the acequia" (Garcia 2000, emphases added). As we have seen, this duality of rights and responsibilities is the hallmark of CPRs as models of justice-in-practice.

Stanley Crawford, author of the book *Mayordomo*, escribing his time serving in that role in an acequia community, is careful to point out that these are far from utopian visions. Conflict persists and human nature does not radically change—but human culture can, and in doing so it tends to accentuate people's better instincts. Crawford (1989, 88–96) in fact recounts a scenario that is framed by "countless disputes" between irrigators sharing a particular ditch and among the network of ditches as a whole, yet indicates that such disputes are positively resolved due to the cooperative, egalitarian processes at work throughout the system, and due to the nature of the interconnections being "close and local and among near equals." This "remarkable tradition of self-governance" has evolved a "complex social fabric" of conventions and traditions that creates a "sense of common purpose" that works to prevent "inevitable disputes" from escalating into deeper forms of divisiveness or even violence (Crawford 1989, 177, 223–224). Indeed, water is a "substance that can inspire passion like no other," and only blood relationships are deeper than those surrounding water in the acequia communities (Crawford 1989, 23–26). As such, water issues are not merely economic, but are about "cultural identity, social welfare, and political self-determination" (Rodríguez 2006, xiv), rendering the stakes for all concerned are enormously high.

In this light, the desert Southwest is a microcosm of larger global forces. Without question, "the landscape tells of the finite nature of water," and this finitude means that "the region must deal with the reality of an extremely limited and increasingly variable water supply" (Garcia and Santistevan 2008, 111–112). More and more, we are coming to realize that "scarcity and the preservation of clean freshwater supplies are global and transnational issues," and that we are now in the midst of a "world-wide conflict over who owns what water" (Rodríguez 2006, 128). At root, the contest between global viewpoints centers on the commons and whether they will remain viable in an age of wholesale privatization. On one side of the ledger we have the "hegemonic zero-sum, winner-take-all ethic of global capitalism" in which water and other resources are taken as commodities that are "separated from the earth in a manipulative relationship with nature" (Rodríguez 2006, 128); on the other is the vision of water and other essential resources as a human right, "best shared in a community of mutually responsible and account-able stakeholders" (Rivera 1998, 200). As Peña (1998, 274–275) cogently discerns, "this is a battle of paradigms: a bureaucratic model of state and capitalist control of nature as a commodity and the indigenous model of sustainable local stewardship of the homeland"—and at stake is "the future of the commons" and its living legacy of a vibrant "ecological democracy."

Unfortunately, the acequia system and other resource-sharing models like it around the world are imperiled by modern-day practices of enclosure, commodification, and legal adjudication that seek to break down community structures and "convert what has been held in common to that which can be owned privately" (Crawford 1989, 176). As Gallegos (1998, 247) laments, "the common land has been taken from us," yet there remains a sense that the long view may prevail if given space to do so: "In the end, no one owns la Sierra. The mountain owns us: She cares for us and makes our livelihoods possible." Despite persistent threats to their existence, the acequias "remain and function as common-property resource systems," transmitting the conjoined social and ecological ethos of participatory democracy and sustainable subsistence from "generation to generation" (Rivera 1998, 201). While such notions may sound quaint or even naïve to those inculcated with a more technocratic, rationalistic perspective, they actually represent quite eloquently what has become the leading edge of contemporary thinking about how to manage the escalating sociopolitical and environmental crises in our midst. Indeed, from climate change activism and food justice movements to alternative economies and peacebuilding initiatives, there has been a reprioritization of values such as localism, community, and equity.

In particular, the tenets of peace ecology suggest that the way forward on issues such as militarism and degradation is precisely about how we negotiate the human-environment nexus. The concept of sustainability is both social and ecological, composed equally of how we manage our relationship to resources and among one another alike. The acequia model teaches us that "resource sustainability" is intimately connected to the "social fabric" of our communities; for acequia users, "the resource base of land and water have knitted the community together," constituting a democratic model of sustainability "with global implications" (Rivera 1998, xviii, 171–172). The earthen-ditch, communal-labor, cooperative-management ethos of the acequia system strives to promote the renewability of our natural resources and social relationships all at once. In the true spirit of the commons, it becomes apparent that we cannot attain justice in one sphere without it being present in the other. The acequia system, as representative of the continuity of the commons, emphasizes ecological regeneration and intergenerational justice, rooting our lives in a collective past while pointing toward a shared future. Losing all of this would indeed be a tragedy, especially regarding those items essential for human survival. The next chapter considers further how people and communities are engaging in this vital struggle.

CHAPTER THREE
BACK TO BASICS

RECLAIMING LIFE'S ESSENTIALS

In the Introduction to this volume, the impact of warfare on the environment was mentioned in two related contexts: as an ancillary casualty of war and as an intentional tactic of war. In the case of the former, the most vulnerable and essential resources are often impacted, such as food supply lines and water treatment facilities; as to the latter, history itself recounts episodes including fields being salted, orchards burned, and wells poisoned as a deliberate tool of warfare. In both instances, collateral or intentional, the outcome is equivalent for people living in war-torn areas as the basic elements necessary for their survival are impinged. While the problematic of *war* represents an acute case, it can also obscure the deeper realization that even outside the "theater of combat" our food and water supplies are increasingly militarized—and our capacity to access them thus rendered less secure. A stark example of these challenges is posed by the multinational corporation Monsanto, which pro-duced the herbicide Agent Orange that was used to decimate food supplies during the Vietnam War in the 1960s, and today is one of the dominant companies holding numerous patent rights on seed supplies and genetically modified foods. In this light, control of basic resources can be recognized as a tactic in times of war and peace alike.

In the peace-themed courses I teach, I have periodically posed this question to students: What are the absolutely essential resources that you must have in order to survive? Being clever young people with good senses of humor, I have occasionally received responses such as "pizza," "beer," and "coffee." Yet most have seriously given consideration to what actually constitutes the basis for human existence, and even when factoring in the appurtenances of a complex modern life, the list of true essentials is fairly minimal. Paramount among these requisite *basics* are of course food, water, and air; next in the queue generally come shelter, an energy source of some sort, and access to healing techniques or medicinal substances. Following these are the more emotive invocations of community, interpersonal relationships, meaningful work, and creative outlets. Next we arrive at societal and structural notions of political voice, human rights, economic equity, security, and education, as well as technological concepts such as transportation and communications. More metaphysically, we generally conclude the list with items such as a sense of personal well-being, the opportunity for a spiritual practice, and a capacity to sustain authentic hope for the future and continue to improve humankind's existence.

This isn't exactly parallel to Maslow's famous "hierarchy of needs," but it does reflect a good deal of sophistication about what it takes to make a meaningful human life. Consider, however, just how many of these items are presently under direct pressure from forces of militarization or privatization, and what the implications are for ourselves and our communities. Increasingly, the myriad spheres of our lives are reliant upon the whims of governmental bureaucracies and multinational corporations, from the hardware of technology and energy to the software of relationships and entertainment. This situation, which has become especially pointed in the era of globalization, tends to include a concomitant transfer of power to those remote actors who control the conveyances and conveniences that make up the baseline of our lives. In light of this realization, we have seen in recent years a burgeoning set of movements relating to reclaiming some of that power at the level of individuals and communities. Often bound up with a strong sense of localism or regionalism, these efforts have begun to strip away the layers of external control by grounding themselves in the essentials of life and seeking to reclaim relative autonomy over them. Yet these movements are still in their infancy, and the challenges are great.

One of the primary ways that people are constrained to work against their own interests is through the sense of imposed dependency that comes with the external control of basic resources such as food, energy, and water (for an overview of the centrality of these basics, see FEW Resources, www .fewresources.org). When these essentials of survival are privatized and commodified, it sets in motion a sequence of increasingly alienating conditions that pit sustenance against sustainability, success against society, values against values, and wealth against well-being. Conversely, when people work to reclaim the capacity to satisfy their basic needs cooperatively, the quality of their environments and societies improve—thereby serving to mitigate the drivers of conflict at both the human-human and human-environment interfaces. Looking at examples of localized systems and burgeoning movements—from free farms and urban gardens to food justice and energy alternatives—this chapter highlights the positive nexus of community-based collaborations and sustainable cultivations steadily taking hold in an increasing array of locales as to the production and maintenance of life's essential elements. Here, we will emphasize in particular those experiments expressly connecting the principles and practices of *peace* with their actions and visions, thus yielding an even more bountiful harvest. But first we need to articulate more deeply how interdependency has yielded to dependency.

Webs of Dependency

It would not be an overstatement to suggest that humankind is fast approaching a technological tipping point. Particularly in the so-called developed world, a thoroughgoing dependence on high technology for life-sustaining materials and activities is evident in all spheres of modern society. The hardware of our lives, from food and energy to transportation and shelter, is entirely bound up with the workings of a highly mechanized and digitized global economy. And no less so, the software of our existence—communications, relationships, entertainment, education, media, politics—is equally entwined within that same technocratic system. To describe this state of affairs as a *fait accompli* or to conspiratorially suggest that it is all part of some process of orchestrated inevitability misses the larger point that it merely constitutes what *is* at this point in history. The utter dependency of our collective lives on the intricate workings of a hyper-technical web makes the perpetuation and evolution of that network a survival strategy for a significant portion of the species. In relatively short order, many of us have come to believe (at least implicitly) that we *need* this technological grid in order to survive. And in this sense, we begin to realize the double-edged meaning of "the web" as something that simultaneously interconnects *and* ensnares. Our habituation to this web traps us even as it connects us.

Consider the implications from the perspective of a typical modern life. First and foremost, our entire financial being—and with it the capacity to procure almost everything else—exists almost exclusively due to a computer's ability to recognize and recall our credentials to transact. More and more of our work activities and labor energies are expended on digitally based tasks that likewise rely upon computerized repositories and retrieval mechanisms of which we are scarcely knowledgeable. A substantial portion of our political, educational, and health care opportunities are similarly enmeshed in remote databases and personal delivery devices. And increasingly, our social interactions are coming to be dependent upon equivalent circuits of electronic exchange. We store our treasured family photographs in "the cloud," establish "paperless" office practices in the name of environmentalism, listen to songs and watch movies by "streaming" them (rather than sharing them in community settings), update our statuses throughout the day to our circle of virtual "friends," and coordinate our personal and professional calendars through digital servers. Almost seamlessly and without much critical analysis, we have become quite nearly symbiotic with these expanding technological networks.

What would transpire if this web suddenly was to disappear? As noted in previous chapters, I am not inclined to view humankind through a Hobbesian lens of aggression and ruthlessness, and thus resist the idea that if the "grid goes down" people will turn on one another in a brutal competition over scarce resources. We might actually find surprising ways to reconnect to people and place that stave off the worst forms of behavioral descent, and even open up new pathways for sustainable and just living arrangements both among ourselves and with the balance of nature. There may be enough farmers, builders, teachers, and artists among us with old-school skills sufficient to sustain communities, if not cultures, on some level. Perhaps there yet remains an atavistic thread of time-tested humanity still within us that recalls the basic ways the species survived for the overwhelming majority of our existence. Such a vision could indeed come to pass for some—but in a more "realist" rendering, it might also be reasoned that many will perish or otherwise suffer in the process of any such rapid technological demise. Similarly, it might be tempting to suppose that people in the "developing world" could somehow escape the worst outcomes should the techno-web "crash" precipitously, yet the lives of people in those locales are rapidly becoming conditioned upon the existence of that same overall system.

In the near term, we might surmise that there is a paradigmatic "point of no return" just up ahead. There is a threshold of dependency that, once crossed, may be irreversible in terms of our basic humanity, as essential survival skills are bred out and replaced with capacities suitable for application to the global web. Consciousness and desire will likewise adapt to the pervasive technologies in our midst, as even emotions and sensations become approximately replicable. Our very identities steadily become reflexively intertwined with this grid, just as our bodies are increasingly dependent upon its workings. At a certain point in time, if not already realized by now, there comes into existence a new line of human: *homo technologicus*. We can all too easily envision a near-future society where everyone bears on their person a device that carries with it real-time locational and data-streaming capabilities in a fully wired world. Wherever we move in this landscape, our precise whereabouts are logged electronically and our economic credentials are verified biometrically. We can simply take items from store shelves and stroll out with them, with each purchase automatically tabulated. Status updates of our movements and interactions will be uploaded instantaneously to our personal profiles for remote friends to share. And in fact, whether in physical or virtual space, the likes and preferences of our circles of association will be with us, helping to guide our choices as to basic goods and points of information alike.

Such notions suggest the tenuous nature of our capacity not only to provide for ourselves but to exist at all without recourse to a web of technology that few of us can operate, repair, or even completely understand; in this light, it becomes apparent that "dependence creates profound vulnerabilities" (Fettweis 2011, 203). This burgeoning worldwide integration yields a remarkable lack of resiliency and a frightening degree of fragility if you stop using it for a moment to consider the full implications. How many of us are still in a position to procure food and water without the workings of this web? Are we content simply to turn over to remote, inaccessible, and largely unaccountable forces the provision of the basic items we require to survive? Is a life filled with ostensible "creature comforts" that are available on demand even tenable when access to essentials is thoroughly co-opted? Vandana Shiva (2000) wrote eloquently on "the hijacking of the global food supply" even before its full dimensions had manifested, Maude Barlow (2009) has starkly warned of the impending corporate control of water resources on a global scale, and Tina Evans (2012) has poignantly highlighted the sense of "enforced dependency" that pervades modern life in terms of our increasing reliance upon multinational corporations and their governmental sponsors for access to life's basic needs. As Thich Nhat Hanh (2008, 2) succinctly concludes: "We have constructed a system we can't control. It imposes itself on us, and we become its slaves and victims."

In this volume we have looked at patterns of resource control and allocation as a function of social justice and the prospects for peace both among humans and with the environment. The argument has been that humankind is beset by a bevy of intersecting crises, primarily of our own making, but that these crises are also profound opportunities for envisioning and implementing another way of being in the world—one that is just, sustainable, and more peaceful at all levels. The task is complicated by the realization that we are increasingly dependent upon a web of control that is pervasive yet often unnoticed in its operation—and somehow we must disentangle this web even as we are reliant upon it to provide life's essentials. In order to create a safe operating space to accomplish this monumental task—metaphorically akin, perhaps, to building a new ship out of the pieces of a rusted, decaying one while we are still kept afloat by it—many individuals and communities around the world have begun to develop new systems for producing and distributing essential resources apart from the dominant web of control, oftentimes grounded in the values of community and sustainability. We will explore the potential of these models with particular regard to essentials such as food, water, and energy, beginning briefly with the latter.

New Clear Energy

As the foregoing suggests, it may plausibly be argued that humanity is on a collision course with reality, and the window of time in which to act may be rapidly closing. This isn't a product of "dismal science" or political posturing, but merely a reflection of the hole we have steadily dug for ourselves. If we don't make wholesale societal changes immediately, irreversible thresholds are likely to be crossed and our very existence will be a tenuous prospect at best. And the alarm bell rings out with one key word: *energy*. Societies are defined in large measure by their energy inputs, which also bear directly upon how a given people will relate to the world around them. Energy is embedded in corollary issues including food, economics, population, pollution, and even politics. It works as a force both literally (e.g., calories and kilowatts) and metaphorically (e.g., capacity and capital) alike. Human development through-out history has been keyed to the available energy sources at hand, and in the past two centuries the advent of highly exploitable and relatively cheap fuel resources has literally remade the map of the world (Heinberg 2010).

The rise of the petroleum economy since the mid-1800s has triggered technological progress and economic expansion in the industrial era; in this time span, humankind has likewise seen its population increase sevenfold, and has had to find ways to keep pace with the production of food supplies that are also dependent in large measure upon the same fossil fuel sources. Also in this time frame we have seen the birth of the "anthropocene" as the era in which humankind has significantly impacted the regulatory systems and carrying capacity of the biosphere—with notable episodes including the breakup of arctic ice that is the planet's thermostat and weather initiator, an unprecedented loss of biodiversity, the steady erosion of arable soils, and an ongoing depletion of freshwater supplies. The toxification of our environment has been generated to such a degree that it can be measured in the rising incidence of industrial-era ailments and diseases. So-called natural disasters have increased in their frequency and severity, ostensibly as a result of rapid climate change. The cycle thus expands exponentially as the quest for more of the very resources that feed the problem only exacerbate it through warfare, waste, and wanton consumption.

Socially and politically, the fossil fuel era has increased the unequal distribution of wealth, power, and privilege along racial, ethnic, and gender lines. It has yielded foundational shifts in our military strategies, political campaigns, and mass communications systems. Family units have been redefined in the carbon-based period, and the moral sentiment of individualism has ascended. Transportation in particular has seen a quantum leap both forward and backward with the pervasiveness of the automobile as an obvious outcome of the petroleum economy, and with jet flight opening up the world for those wont to utilize it despite the carbon footprint. "Oil is one of those few commodities whose significance has a cognitive or perhaps even visceral dimension," writes Christopher Fettweis (2011, 204)—suggesting why we make war over it. Undoubtedly this has been an exciting and even prophetic period in the history of the species, yet the limits of its wisdom and utility may be fast approaching. In addition to the realization of potentially apocalyptic scenarios, there is also the growing apprehension of the fact that the availability of easy access to abundant energy sources may have reached its peak. While this is a matter for geologists and hydrologists to debate as to the science involved, a nuanced reading suggests that more than just the availability of oil has seemingly reached its proverbial tipping point. Peak Oil may already be here—with Peak Food and Peak Water perhaps not far behind (cf. Gleick 2010; Brown 2012). Indeed, Peak Everything is a distinct possibility before long.

The truly intriguing aspect of all of this is that a not-insignificant percentage of the populace is aware of it on some level. While resources decline, ideas are abundant, even if political will remains stagnant at best. Unfortunately, most of the en vogue notions have their own limitations, and in any event no one has yet conceived a viable energy substitute at the scale of fossil fuels that could power a global economy without further degrading the habitat in the process (Hiscock 2012; Ehrenfeld 2005). Many of the leading contenders merely replicate the same centralization of power and wasteful consumptive patterns of the present moment (hydrogen, natural gas), whereas others substitute new problems for each one they claim to solve (nuclear fission, biofuels). Some are extremely water-intensive (large-scale solar), and others are just thoroughly ill-conceived (tar sands, hydraulic fracturing or "fracking"). A few hold promise (wind, tidal power), but the scale of their applicability and capacity remain questionable. "Now the world has an energy choice," as Geoffrey Hiscock (2012, xvii) observes, "but what a choice. The remaining oil is too political, coal's too dirty, nuclear's too dangerous, wind's too fickle, solar's too expensive, hydro's too dislocating, geothermal is too hard to wrangle, and fracked gas is too divisive." As Michael Klare (2012a, 210–214) unfortunately concurs, we are rapidly nearing "the end of 'easy' everything," from energy resources to available food and water supplies.

The road ahead will be difficult, and perhaps that may be a restorative balance to the era of Peak Leisure and Peak Apathy in which we have recently resided. Something has to give, and who better than those of us who have taken so much? This may be the greatest challenge humans have faced in our tenure on this planet, outstripping times of widespread deprivation for the simple reason that we have gotten so used to being above that sort of thing, and concomitantly our very survival skills have waned in the process. Can we voluntarily and collectively decide to place our lives at a level that does not openly court extinction? In some ways, the social and political implications of such questions are even more daunting than navigating the grim resource scenarios in our midst, as it becomes more evident that we will either have to make hard choices on our own terms or have them imposed on us by the realities of finitude. Still, whatever else we may be guilty of doing to ourselves and the planet, humankind has generally found the capacity to "dig deep" when we have needed it the most. Taking this encouragement literally, myriad communities have rediscovered the art and science of collective food production as a beacon of hope-in-action in difficult times. Movingly, these experiments have not only revamped food and sustenance but have also rekindled a communal ethos that is essential to peace.

Let It Grow: Back to the Garden

In an interconnected world, action in one sphere has implications in manifold others, and, as argued above, the realm of energy production in particular is filled with speculative alternatives and patently false solutions. For instance, nuclear energy (presently based on fission reactions, with their corresponding wastes and environmental calamities such as with Fukushima and Chernobyl) is sometimes touted as a potential "clean energy" solution to the problem of carbon emissions that is driving climate change (see LaDuke 2009). Similarly, plant-based fuel sources such as ethanol (derived from corn) or biofuels (from soy, canola, or palm oils) are put forth as cleaner burning and environmentally friendly, even as they require vast fossil fuel inputs and chemical fertilizers in order to produce—leading Lester Brown (2012, 36) to term biofuels "one of the great tragedies of history." As others have observed, "Biofuelling for a continued rise in the living standards of people in the west can hardly prevent poor people from hunger and starvation" (Hanjra and Qureshi 2010, 368). Thus, while millions around the world go hungry, and in the midst of an era marked by soaring prices and food riots (Klare 2012a, 213), arable lands and dwindling water supplies are consigned to the production of automotive fuel sources and the perpetuation of a top-down, centralized economic system whose chief product is captivity.

Indeed, it has been observed that by now "there are more prisoners ... than farmers in the United States" (Magdoff and Tokar 2010, 17). The food market is increasingly dominated by a handful of multinational players—from seeds and crops on the production side to supermarkets on the retail end, as detailed by Wenonah Hauter in her 2012 book *Foodopoly*. From Walmart to Monsanto, global agribusiness is expanding its reach and oftentimes presenting its machinations as the only viable solution to fomented crises including a plateau in the production of staples, major crop failures due to extended droughts, the diversion of grains to meat production, and patterns of "depeasantization" that force farmers off their lands (Magdoff and Tokar 2010, 10–11). The neoliberal "fixes" to these and other pressing issues is generally to double-down further on supersizing corporate farms and markets, yielding a world in which "supermarkets have seized control of their supply chains and standardized food selection" (Gottlieb and Joshi 2010, 45). These processes of consolidation contribute to a system in which people are increasingly "overfed but poorly nourished" (Gottlieb and Joshi 2010, 68), where there is "hunger amidst plenty" (Magdoff and Tokar 2010, 15), where "half the world starves while the other half wastes enough to feed the first half" (Eisenstein 2011, 19), and where a large percentage of the substances consumed are in actuality highly processed "non-food" items with little nutritional value (Murcott 1999, 307). As Raj Patel (2012) succinctly puts it, we are "stuffed and starved."

All of this indicates an emerging food crisis, one that is intimately related to crises over water and energy (cf. Boaz and Berger 2010; Hiscock 2012). In fact, food represents embedded water and energy, and the relationship between these human essentials is like a tightly woven tapestry (cf. Hauter 2008). Moreover, the conflicts of the modern era often devolve upon these basic resources, with numerous predictions of "water wars" (Shiva 2002) being rendered and the reality of energy wars impossible to deny (cf. Klare 2002). Hunger and food insecurity have likewise been noted as causes of conflict and even civil wars (Allouche 2011, 54), and grim forecasts of near-future "food wars" have been issued (Klare 2012a)—along with the concomitant realization that it is not the overall quantity of food supplies that is the problem, but more so the structural factors that yield inequitable patterns of allocation and distribution (Allouche 2011, 57; Hanjra and Qureshi 2010, 366). These are symptoms of living amidst "an economy based on waste," as Wendell Berry (2001, 9) has observed, which at root is "hopelessly violent, and war is its inevitable by-product." As Shiva (2005, 109) likewise laments, "a nonsustainable economic system based on principles of free trade, greed, and imperialism is creating vicious cycles of violence from which there seems to be no way out."

This globalized system centered on the control of essentials seeks to eradicate viable alternatives—yet at the same time, perhaps paradoxically, there is a vibrant global movement to democratize the production of food. In the United States alone there are thousands of community gardens in public spaces or on reclaimed lands, serving as a reminder that growing food for ourselves, our families, and our communities is an important step toward reclaiming power that we have steadily ceded to remote agribusinesses, and likewise that genuine "security" comes through the capacity to produce essentials like food without being beholden to outside interests (cf. Letman 2010a, 2010b). Beyond food production, another critical aspect of security is the cultivation of strong community ties. When people work in concert to acquire, restore, and cultivate land for both nutritional and aesthetic purposes, they begin to develop mutual respect, bonds of trust, cooperative instincts, and the sense of a shared future that figures so prominently (as argued in the previous chapter) in commons-based alternatives. By doing all of this through the medium of environmental engagement, an additional notion of being part of something larger than oneself can steadily emerge. In this spirit, communal food systems bring people together across race, class, gender, and other lines in ways that serve to promote solidarity and forestall conflicts.

There are many inspiring examples to consider. Frances Moore Lappé, who has been a leading voice on food issues since her classic volume *Diet for a Small Planet* was released in 1971, has more recently (2009) written about Belo Horizonte—Brazil's fourth largest city with 2.5 million people—as "the city that ended hunger." The city established a council charged with conceiving a new food system, which declared a "food-as-a-right policy" that emphasizes universal food security coupled with highly participatory public processes. The initiative included everything from supporting small-scale farmers in securing space to grow and sell food to subsidizing "People's Restaurants" around the city that serve healthy food at low prices. The project has also included extensive community and school gardens, coupled with widely available nutrition classes and free meals for early-age schoolchildren. The overarching idea is not to foster another version of dependency, but rather to "create channels for people to find solutions themselves" by moving the "social mentality" from one of food as a commodity to "food as a right of membership in the human family" (Lappé 2009). And the results have been inspiring, with infant mortality substantially reduced and nutritional outcomes vastly improved.

The case of Missoula, Montana, is also intriguing, due to the relatively harsh climate (mountainous, arid plains, cold winters) and a growing season that averages fewer than 100 days each year (J. Smith 2010, xi). The city has about 70,000 residents, with nearly one-fifth living in poverty; nevertheless, an ambitious project was launched that interconnects seven neighborhood farms and community gardens, supplying fresh locally grown food not only to those farming but to area food banks, homeless shelters, and youth homes. The project, called Garden City Harvest, also includes an explicit educational and therapeutic component, opening the farms and gardens to at-risk youth and community events such as concerts and lectures. The attendant benefits have included more than 100,000 pounds of healthy food being placed into the community, students learning invaluable farming skills, and in general the development of a framework in which "strangers participating in community gardens to grow their own food form unexpected new friendships and enlarge one another's sense of neighborhood" (J. Smith 2010, xii). These neighborhood-based gardens are designed to be "peaceful places" that seek to provide the "right environments" for people to heal through "therapeutic, service-oriented" agricultural work (J. Smith 2010, 76, 148, 166). The project also includes a CSA (community-supported agriculture) program where members can subscribe for a weekly share of the seasonal harvest, and with its focus on youth and children ties into initiatives such as Edible Schoolyards and Youth Harvest.

Another compelling example that likewise integrates the social architecture necessary for growing not only food but more peaceful communities as well is the network of urban community gardens in Seattle, Washington. As part of an even larger agglomeration of such projects—the American Community Gardening Association (www.communitygarden.org) includes data on thousands of community gardens across the United States and Canada alone—the Seattle model has evolved a sophisticated peacebuilding perspective. Paramount among the lessons gleaned there, in addition to the relational and therapeutic aspects noted in the Missoula case, are the connections people cultivate with open/public spaces, the opportunities for dialogue and cooperation that come from sharing common resources, greater social equity among a diverse range of users, and an increased capacity for resolving disputes by strengthening social ties (Hou, Johnson, and Lawson 2009, 3, 25–27, 156). The Seattle community gardens are not problem-free, as with those in other urban settings, yet the interpersonal and intercultural conflicts that sometimes manifest there "also create opportunities for dialogue"—not only about the gardens but as to wider community issues at the same time (Hou, Johnson, and Lawson 2009, 171–172).

The overarching aim (in Seattle and other similar projects) is to encourage participation and collective action among residents by revitalizing the neighborhood commons and bringing people into direct interaction within shared public spaces. Such efforts link the ways in which people procure food and share resources (including land and space) with the social bonds and common concerns that enable wider peacemaking potentials. In Chapter

Six we will look more closely at *environmental peacemaking* as a global phenomenon; community gardens are an important local example of such processes that bring together the social and ecological components of peace. As longtime Bay Area garden advocate Karl Linn (2005, 43) observed just before his passing: "Community gardening not only produces healthy food close to home but also cultivates community among neighbors.... The growing sense of community fostered by these modern-day commons empowers neighborhood residents and strengthens their social, physical, and mental health. This increasingly widespread network of grassroots gardeners working together contributes to the building of a more democratic society." Linn (2005, 49) concluded that community gardening projects can in fact yield greater compassion, empathy, respect, and caring—which are all powerful indicators of peace and justice.

Just Food: Growing Peace and Building Communities

I was reminded of these lessons when my oldest son "graduated" from preschool and the children were asked what they wanted to be when they grew up. His response was, "I want to be a farmer like my dad"—and I couldn't have been prouder. To be sure, I am hardly a "farmer" in any real sense of the word, even though I worked hard over the years to scratch out a good-sized family garden in our high-desert habitat. Notions of cultivating food in the desert, relearning essential skills, becoming more self-sufficient, and staying close to nature are all important—yet the essence of these pursuits, at root, devolves upon the lessons being taught to the children. In a society that tries to breed out any connection to the natural world and mostly teaches young people that food comes from the supermarket, my son's preliminary aspirations are heartwarming and encouraging. My wife and I have sought not only to connect our family to farming and gardening, but also to think more broadly about where things come from as well as the embedded social and environmental ethics contained within the basic items we rely upon in our lives.

Disturbingly, some have come to define this emerging sensibility over food ethics as a potential pathology. There is even a term bandied about to encapsulate it: "orthorexia," which is defined as an obsession with "healthy

or righteous eating"; according to the website Eating Disorders (www
.eatingdisordershelpguide.com), the term was coined by Steven Bratman,
MD, in 1997 and refers to "people who create severely limited diets in the
name of healthy eating." A popular-media article (Cool 2011) that received
over forty thousand Facebook recommendations further noted that "going
to extremes in an effort to eat only healthy foods can also be socially isolating and can undermine personal relationships." The *Journal of the American
Medical Association* (JAMA) ran a review in May 2001 of Bratman's book
Health Food Junkies, in which he emphasized the typical orthorexic's "self-
righteousness" in denigrating fashion: "As orthorexia progresses, a day filled
with wheatgrass juice, tofu, and quinoa biscuits may come to feel as holy as
one spent serving the destitute and homeless." And an article in *Psychology
Today* (Strand 2004) further observed that "sufferers devote excessive attention to their own strict rules and often spend hours each day worrying about
tomorrow's meals. Such a person may find himself socially isolated because
he doesn't indulge in everyday dishes."

While a critique of certain "green" obsessions is not without merit, one
can also see how this perspective could provide a pathway toward continued
complacency when it comes to the production and consumption of the food
in our midst, with potentially disastrous implications for both personal and
planetary health. Ultimately, if we are going to turn that long-overdue corner
toward a sustainable and just society, there will need to be a lot of people with
the awareness and skills to manifest life's essentials of food, water, and energy
in a healthy way. The pathology isn't in knowing too much and trying to take
immediate action; it lies in consciously avoiding the knowledge and lapsing
into socially affirmed complicity and corporate-imposed dependency. There
is no future in that for people or the habitats that sustain us. What we need
desperately are visions and actions that bring food issues to the fore, while
linking them with larger concerns over the drivers of conflict, violence, and
militarism—from marginalization and divisiveness to loss of the commons
and resource wars. In short, we need to bring more peace into our meals.

Indeed, this is the mission of the PeaceMeal Project (www.peacemealproject
.com), whose slogan is "cultivating peace through food." The project was
founded by Stephanie Knox Cubbon and Hannah Renglich, who met while
studying at the United Nations–mandated University for Peace in Costa Rica.

PeaceMeal incorporates research and writing, educational workshops, online courses, and networking with like-minded organizations as part of its overall effort to highlight the deep-seated connections between food and peace. The project is still in its early stages, but the basic framework is in place for educating people through hands-on workshops and courses about the ways in which food is often co-opted (ethically and economically) and how reclaiming its essence can serve as a tool for building relationships, communities, and, ultimately, peace. In mid-2013, I asked Cubbon about the project's vision:

> Peace and food are connected at every level, from the personal to the international. At the level of inner peace, the very act of eating can be meditative and a source of connecting with our calm inner center. At the interpersonal level, meals can serve as an opportunity for bonding and community, a way to cultivate peace in relationships. At the international level, our ability to cultivate food depends on ecological peace, taking care of our planet.... [Food] provides this amazing lens through which you can look at peace issues and realize the inherent interconnectedness of life on this planet.... I believe that this realization of our interconnectedness is what it will take for us to wake up and solve the problems that humanity is facing today. Each time we eat, we have the opportunity to be reminded of this vast interconnection and interdependence (should we pay attention). Thus the very act of eating has a huge role to play in our understanding and promotion of peace.

Putting these ideas into practice is one of the most prominent global peace-food initiatives: Food Not Bombs (FNB), a decentralized international movement grounded in the free distribution of healthy food in public places. Founded in 1980 in Cambridge, Massachusetts, by anti-nuclear activists, FNB promotes nonviolence, vegetarianism, and positive social change with food sharing as the linchpin. As detailed by co-founder Keith McHenry in the 2012 book *Hungry for Peace*, the FNB movement highlights the ways in which warfare and violence produce hunger and poverty, and likewise how reclaiming food as a human right and making it freely available presents a profound challenge to the persistence of militarism. FNB provides free meals in public spaces and parks—oftentimes to impoverished and/or homeless people—as well as at many protests and demonstrations, and in the context of post-disaster relief situations. By occupying public areas and sharing food, FNB simultaneously reinvigorates the core ideals of the commons while contesting the privatization and commodification of the food supply. As a growing movement with chapters all over the world, FNB has cultivated an engaged ethos of nonviolent intervention that integrates the best practices of community, solidarity, and resiliency.

There is an emerging food-based movement afoot, and it is squarely located within the context of growing our peacebuilding and community-organizing potentials. For instance, the Food Recovery Network (www .foodrecoverynetwork.org) reclaims food that would otherwise be wasted at college and university dining centers, instead having student volunteers bring it to local food banks and shelters, thus providing food to people in need and avoiding more methane-producing buildup in landfills. As we have seen, human essentials such as food and water have become increasingly compromised by forces including industrialization, privatization, and an unsustainable agribusiness model that controls much of the planet's sustenance. This has fostered a pervasive condition of dependency that negatively impacts fundamental values of sovereignty, autonomy, and security. In response to this burgeoning co-optation of the world's life-sustaining capacities, local movements have begun to emerge literally everywhere, oftentimes linking the virtues of community and small-scale subsistence with a broader critique of the processes of corporate globalization. The result is a widespread, decentralized, and potent global movement for peace and justice that remains largely overlooked in many treatments of nonviolence and peacebuilding. This movement goes by many names—including "food sovereignty," "slow food," "locavorism," and (the one I prefer for its peace-oriented nomenclature) *food justice.*

As the Seattle-based Food Justice Project (www.seattleglobaljustice.org /food-justice) proclaims: "Food Justice is the right of communities everywhere to produce, distribute, access, and eat good food regardless of race, class, gender, ethnicity, citizenship, ability, religion, or community. Good food is healthful, local, sustainable, culturally appropriate, humane, and produced for the sustenance of people and the planet." Similarly, the Community Food & Justice Coalition (www.cafoodjustice.org) "promotes the basic human right to healthy food while advancing social, agricultural, environmental and economic justice," envisioning a food system "in which all activities, from farm to table, are equitable, healthful, regenerative and community-driven." Expanding on these concepts, Gottlieb and Joshi (2010, 6–7) conceive of food justice as a tool for simultaneously addressing inequities in society and seeking to reformulate the workings of the food system in general; in essence, food justice represents the union of sociopolitical analysis and environmental action from the local to the global scale. Indeed, we are operating within a globalized system, but in the end it comprises myriad unique localities.

Living La Vida Local

Among scholars and activists across a wide range of social and environmental issues, there is something of an emerging consensus as to the efficacy and desirability of local initiatives. This may be reflective of the reality of living in a world in which we are able to *interact* globally but for all intents and purposes can only *act* locally. Despite the increasingly globalized nature of modern life, with its concomitant issues of technocracy and dependency, the day-to-day existence of most people remains circumscribed within relatively narrow geographical bounds. Perhaps this is as it should be, given the challenges attendant to a global frame that is dominated by multinational corporations and militarized nation-states. Pragmatically and philosophically, local engagement is not only a potential antidote to abstract and repressive global forces, but also constitutes an effective domain for rethinking our practices and reclaiming our autonomy. As E. F. Schumacher presciently argued in the influential volume *Small Is Beautiful* (1975), inspired by studies of village-based economies, growth is not always good and bigger is not better. Indeed, James Gustave Speth (2010) has called our fixation on growth "the world's secular religion." Embracing this spirit of natural limits and appropriate scale, it is not a coincidence that many of the movements centered on food and water have exalted the virtues of *localism*—which, as David Suzuki (1999, 7) asserts, will in all likelihood be "the key to human survival."

For instance, Berry (2001, 28–30) urges that people reconstruct a "local food economy" in order to "shorten the distance between producers and consumers," and to ground these localized systems in the conjoined principles of "neighborhood and subsistence." Starting from the premise that "eating is a political act," Gottlieb and Joshi (2010, 184, 219) highlight the myriad ways that "food justice and alternative food advocates are trying to reinforce the social justice basis for local, sustainable food production and consumption," reflecting an expanding "desire for an alternative farm-to-table approach." Proponents of "real security" have cited the need for re-localizing agricultural and food processing systems, energy production, water distribution, waste disposal, and building materials, in conjunction with greater community control over such initiatives (Letman 2010b). Following this line of reasoning, Sandra Postel (2010, 13) observes that "the more a community lives on water, energy, and food produced locally, the more options arise for solving multiple problems simultaneously, building resilience through resourcefulness, and preparing for future uncertainties." Shiva (2005, 17, 82) accordingly calls for the reinvigoration of a "sustenance economy" in which "people work directly to provide the conditions necessary to maintain their lives," with localization as the necessary cornerstone.

Advocates of *food sovereignty* have likewise embraced the virtues of localism, focusing in particular on "local autonomy, local markets, local production-consumption cycles, energy and technological sovereignty, and farmer-to-farmer networks" (Pimentel 2010, 255). Early manifestations of food sovereignty movements appeared in the 1970s, seeking to establish local farming systems and develop agricultural cooperatives to promote land conservation and prevent the loss of agrarian-oriented peasant livelihoods (Gottlieb and Joshi 2010, 114–115). In the early 1990s, just as the era of globalization and so-called free trade was emerging, food sovereignty activists from around the world came together to form the basis for what soon became La Vía Campesina, "a new global food network of small farmers and peasants in the developing world" (Gottlieb and Joshi 2010, 115–116). Today, La Vía Campesina (www.viacampesina.org) counts among its network about 150 organizations from 70 countries, comprising 200 million farmers in total, all working to resist the corporatization of food supplies and to defend small-scale agriculture as a pathway toward social justice and sustainability. Significantly, associations like La Vía Campesina do not view themselves as anti-global, but more so as advocates for an alternative globalism rooted in local food and water systems (Gottlieb and Joshi 2010, 116–117).

An inspiring example of the penchant for local food alternatives was the Free Farm (www.freefarmstand.org), an urban farm founded in January 2010 by a constellation of nonprofit organizations in San Francisco. Located on a one-third-acre lot loaned by St. Paulus Lutheran Church, the Free Farm grew and gave away thousands of pounds of fresh organic produce, convened gardening and urban homesteading workshops, and hosted community, school, and religious groups. Its mission included notions of "creating a microcosm of mutualism," promoting food justice, cultivating community, and practicing hospitality. In April 2013, I asked one of the project's founders ("Tree") to offer his thoughts on these concepts, as the news was being disseminated that the Free Farm would be closing by the end of the year:

> If we try to do good in our own lives it will have a ripple effect and inspire those around us. So as the Diggers of San Francisco said, we can be life actors. We can run a Free Farm and grow food and give it away at a Free Farm Stand.... What we hope to do is inspire people to make radical/root changes in their own lives—to embrace what in the old days was termed "voluntary simplicity," living below one's means, to move away from money transactions, to practice generosity and compassion, to make all we do beautiful and wondrous.

The Free Farm and other efforts like it strive to localize the production and consumption of food, making it possible for communities to reclaim their conviviality and promote peace all at once.

Seeds of Construction and Zones of Peace

Without relative resource autonomy at the communal, regional, and/or national level, globalization can become a form of corporate neo-feudalism, bringing with it the dual factors of dependency and vulnerability that make conquest more probable and peace more impracticable. One of the landmark interventions against these looming prospects was launched by Mahatma Gandhi in the struggle for Indian independence from British colonization. While he is known, of course, for his nonviolent theories and practices,

Gandhi's life and work were also deeply rooted in environmental issues and the cultivation of autonomy as to essential items. To take a prominent example, the famous Salt March of 1930 centered on the defiant reclamation of people's ability to make their own salt from the ocean rather than remaining beholden to the British monopoly (and concomitant taxation) over this basic element of life. Gandhi also advocated the wearing of *khadi* (homespun cloth), and would often use a *charkha* (spinning wheel) in public as a demonstration of self-sufficiency (*swadeshi*) and nonviolent resistance (*satyagraha*) to oppression. "Gandhi did not bring the British Empire down with cannons or armies," writes Shiva (2005, 183), but did so "with a pinch of salt and a spinning wheel."

Articulating a philosophy grounded in *swaraj* (self- or home-rule), Gandhi's legacy includes a potent combination of local autonomy, community building, and freedom from dependency. Often overlooked in historical remembrances that highlight his active resistance to and principled defiance of the British Empire, Gandhi actually emphasized what is known as a "constructive program" grounded in the creation of sustainable, cooperative alternatives. One of the most inspiring examples informed by this legacy is the Canticle Farm in Oakland, California. Located in a section of the city plagued by urban problems ranging from gang violence to environmental toxification, this peace and nonviolence community includes a large organic garden situated between four connected houses. Core values include the local production of food, promoting justice and peacemaking in the neighborhood, teaching nonviolence and conflict resolution skills, and building community relationships through food sharing. One of the project's core participants is Pancho Ramos Stierle (internationally known for his arrest while meditating at Occupy Oakland and facing deportation proceedings as a result), who observed (in Dear 2012) that local food is "Gandhi's twenty-first century spinning wheel." The project emphasizes the constructive program, as articulated by co-founder Anne Symens-Bucher:

> We want to take down the physical fences in the neighborhood and the fences in our hearts, because we know our real security is not in our fences or the bars on our windows, but in our relationships. This is the way to peace.... [We] try to help each other to get ready for the future

by growing our own food and taking care of one another.... We could go to the neighbors and say, "The end is coming, so start growing your food and get ready," or we could say, "Let's grow our own food now because it's fun, we can share it with one another, get to know one another and build a safer and beautiful community." (Dear 2012)

Such notions have resonance in an increasing array of communities. A quintessential case is that of Detroit, Michigan, where mid-1990s post-industrialization resulted in a depressed economy and the loss of access to supermarkets across the city (Solnit 2007). The city also found itself plagued by urban violence issues, including a spate of police-initiated shootings of mostly African American males. Rather than descending into further forms of decay and despair, local residents—inspired by long-time justice advocates such as the indefatigable movement matriarch Grace Lee Boggs—began reclaiming vacant land abandoned by fleeing businesses and torn-down homes, planting hundreds of urban gardens and small farms throughout the city (Bonfiglio 2008). Associated with this urban agricultural renaissance has been the equally important task of rebuilding communities through the establishment of neighborhood cooperatives and "peace zones" to stem violence and provide spaces for conflict resolution practices (Flores 2010). These "Peace Zones for Life" (often located in open, green areas) were initiated by the Detroit Coalition Against Police Brutality, whose mission statement advocates a holistic approach to achieve "real security" through the "development of independent self-sustaining economic/social institutions." In the end, these efforts have resulted in "more than just food production" (Bonfiglio 2008), comprising nodes for people to reconnect to themselves, one another, and the earth itself. As Boggs observed (in Bonfiglio 2008), "you can bemoan your fate or ... you can plant gardens."

At the outset of this chapter, the question was posed: What are the absolutely essential resources that you must have in order to survive? To the list of basic items such as food, water, and energy, we might also add peace as a fundamental component of life. This does not entail a conflict-free existence or one in which all challenges have been resolved, but rather (as the examples here indicate) a state of being that includes healthy relationships and communities, mechanisms for addressing conflicts and promoting social justice, and a sense of self-sufficiency when it comes to producing life's essentials. It is not mere happenstance that many of the most inspiring community-based models for accomplishing this devolve explicitly upon equal parts food production and peacebuilding. Examining the revolutionary potential of urban agriculture movements, Rebecca Solnit (2012) asks whether peace may also be a crop, observing that "a lot of people hope to overcome the wars of our time more indirectly through their own gardening and farming." Through the production of food in local settings, people around the world have rediscovered a "means of producing understanding, community, social transformation, and catalytic action" (Solnit 2012). These attendant benefits constitute another harvest, one that rekindles the best aspects of the commons as described in the prior chapter—and that likewise nourishes a spirit of empathy, solidarity, and compassion that will form the basis of the next.

CHAPTER FOUR
FREE AT LAST

EMPATHY, SOLIDARITY, AND THE GIFT ECONOMY

In many cultures, one has a responsibility to provide water and/or food to those in need. The acequia system detailed in Chapter Two is derived in part from an Arabic model based on the "right of thirst" and in recognition of the basic fact that all living things require water (Peña 2005, 83). Food sharing among humans has been the overarching norm throughout our existence, with expressions like "breaking bread" coming to symbolize conviviality and positive exchange. Many people today still practice forms of charitable giving in their lives, even to the degree of structured tithing that is part of some faiths. Without thinking about personal gain, people will often react to a crisis in their midst by rushing to the scene and offering assistance, including acts of heroism as we have seen on display in nearly every disaster in recent years. Additionally, utilizing the internet and social media, a vibrant system based on the provision of free items can be found in most cities across the United States and, increasingly, worldwide. While perhaps these activities have not been named as such, taken together there is evidence to suggest the beginnings of a working *gift economy* premised on the non-monetary exchange of goods and services as well as on the implicit recognition of our responsibility to aid others as part of a healthy society. We might even say that these nascent Golden Rule–like efforts comprise a *shadow economy* with empathy, solidarity, compassion, and mutual aid as its dominant currency.

There are a plethora of examples of this phenomenon, which we might also refer to as an emerging *free economy*. Reflecting the pervasiveness of the mindset (but in an altogether perverse manner), some years ago a cellular phone company ran a national ad with the image of Martin Luther King Jr., and a voiceover from one of his famous speeches proclaiming "Free at Last," in reference to an offer of free weekend minutes. But despite such attempts at the corporate co-optation of the concept, there is actually a growing grassroots effort toward creating and sustaining an alternative economy where things are mostly, or even always, free. From the Really Really Free Market and local Free Boxes to Food Not Bombs and the Karma Kitchen, there are myriad inspiring exemplars of this emerging economy premised not on profit and control but on people and community. The resonance of a free economy is increasing as the reality of a permanently depressed "unfree" economy begins to set in worldwide. Seeking to manifest this positive alternative, cutting-edge theories of peacebuilding suggest that humans may be "wired for peace" in the dualistic sense of peace among ourselves and with the earth.

This is the essence of the argument we will explore here, namely that human beings possess an inherent sense of other-orientation that exists in stark contrast to the dominant construction of self-interested, egocentric actors often plied in Western societies. While it is certainly the case that people can be competitive, aggressive, and even warlike, to promote these attributes as a form of "rationality" or "realism" is to disingenuously ignore the equally rational behaviors associated with attributes of empathy and compassion. It is entirely plausible that self-interest and mutual aid can exist simultaneously, and that the idea of freely giving to others also conveys benefits upon oneself. Indeed, if we take the core ecological idea of interconnectedness seriously, anything done to support the systems in which we reside (and the other people living in them) supports us as well. This is almost tautological in its self-evident nature: If I am part of a system, and if I work to maintain that system, then I am also maintaining myself. There is nothing mystical or idealistic about any of this—and even in a time rife with the pressures of competitiveness and conspicuous consumption, people increasingly "get it" on some level.

Many of the free economy projects in existence include a strong environmental aspect that adds another dimension and closes the loop in an even more inspiring manner. If we take our ecosystemic thinking to its logical conclusion and include the non-human environment in our calculus, we begin to conceive it as an extension of ourselves (and vice versa) and thus find individual gain through our stewardship of the whole; in other words, we can recognize our mutualism with everyone and everything around us, without denigrating our unique selves in the process. "If a person perceives their self to be connected to the entire whole," Mark Boyle (2013) writes, "then to act in your own self-interest would involve making decisions where looking after yourself would mean protecting the rivers, atmosphere, soil and forests." What we will explore in this chapter extends and bolsters the thread of the argument we have been constructing thus far, from structural peace and the commons to localism and resource sharing. The concepts introduced here round out the architecture of a dynamic, evolving peace ecology that connects person to person and people to place. And the cornerstone of it comes through understanding how our interdependence actually sets us free.

Really Really Free at Last

Increasingly, communities are looking to non-monetary forms of exchange as a mechanism for resisting patterns of commodification, privatization, the loss of the commons, and the erosion of the public sphere. Around the world, a host of alternative currencies have appeared in recent years, from "hyperlocal" substitute dollars bearing the likeness of figures including W. E. B. Du Bois to "time exchange" systems where services are offered through a network that allows providers to build up credits (Ward 2013). The nation of Bhutan has gone so far as to replace Gross National Product as the measure of quality of life with Gross National Happiness instead, focusing on factors including social and environmental wellness. The common thread among these alternative formulations is that they deemphasize monetary exchanges as the central locus of social interchange, calling upon people instead to reconsider the nature of their relationships to others in their communities—and to the overall health and stability of the biosphere as well. Many such alternative systems are formed expressly as a reaction against "the global monetary economy's relentless drive to convert our social, ecological, cultural and spiritual commons into cold, impersonal numbers" (Boyle 2013), and with due regard to the looming realization that "limitless economic growth as a measure of human well-being is inconsistent with the continuity of life on earth" (Blue River Quorum 2011). As Charles Eisenstein (2011, xi) elaborates: "Money seems to be destroying the earth, as we pillage the oceans, the forests, the soil, and every species to feed a greed that knows no end."

Indeed, the Western lexicon is replete with references to money as "the root of all evil" and parables such as Jesus throwing the moneychangers out of the temple. Despite these cautions, however, the equation of wealth with money is dominant in modern society. There seem to be contrasting ideologies at work, whereby "the pursuit of happiness" (as enshrined in the Declaration of Independence of 1776) is really, at root, about the pursuit of property; in fact, the subsequent US Constitution of 1789 used the phrase "life, liberty, or property" in the Bill of Rights. In making this move from happiness to property, there is a concomitant move from the well-being of the collective to the wealth of the individual—with money representing this process of conversion and thus standing as "the corpse of the commons" (Eisenstein 2011, 79). In this view, money is the result of common resources (e.g., land, water, minerals, forests) being turned into private ones; an alternative formulation could involve money being based on common wealth which would further entail "a general devolution of financial and ultimately political authority to the local level" (Eisenstein 2011, 195). Such a "localization of money" could work to reclaim not only the commons but community as well (Eisenstein 2011, 293).

An extension of these ideas is the localized gift economy, which has seen a stark resurgence since the global economic recession of 2008. Some of the most inspired examples center on the production and provision of food, such as the Free Farm noted in the previous chapter. Accompanying this effort is the Free Farm Stand (www.freefarmstand.org), which has given away 40,000 pounds of local produce in the San Francisco area (circa April 2013). Its mission is to "help make locally grown, fresh and nutritious organic produce accessible to all, especially those families and individuals on low incomes and tight budgets [and] to help empower people who have the space to grow their own food and become more self-reliant." Another Bay Area food-centered project is the Karma Kitchen (www.karmakitchen.org), an ephemeral restaurant concept that first appeared on Sundays in Berkeley, California, and that has now spread to cities including Tokyo, Japan. The premise of this gift economy experiment is that healthy food is provided to anyone free of charge—with a "check" for $0.00 delivered at the end of the meal and a note explaining that it was a gift from someone else who ate at the restaurant earlier, and asking guests to continue the "pay it forward" process in whatever manner or amount they wish (including volunteering in the kitchen). In this way, "the generosity of both guests and volunteers helps to create a future that moves from transaction to trust, from self-oriented isolation to shared commitment, and from fear of scarcity to celebration of abundance."

Beyond these locally rooted efforts, there are a host of decentralized networks that exist macroscopically, and even globally, while manifesting in concrete locales at the same time. The basic process inherent in these initiatives is to provide a forum for connecting people together through the free exchange of goods and services. While critics (e.g., Eisenstein 2011, 323) contend that these "free economy networks" tend toward more of a "mile wide, inch deep" quality in that they are less robust at building community due to their transience and transaction-oriented nature, a working list of such systems from recent years is nonetheless impressive:

> Couchsurfing (www.couchsurfing.org) is a network of people in local communities who make their homes available for free to visitors, numbering 6 million users in over 100,000 cities and making placements "in every country on earth"—all based on the vision of "a world made better by travel and travel made richer by connection [and] fostering cultural exchange and mutual respect."
>
> Freeconomy (www.justfortheloveofit.org) involves the free exchange of skills, tools, and space, seeking specifically "to help reconnect people in their local communities through the simple act of sharing," and is based on the premise that "not only is sharing our resources better for the environment, it saves you money and builds friendships with those people who live closest to you."

Freecycle (www.freecycle.org), whose motto is "changing the world one gift at a time," consists of a network of over 5000 groups with nearly 10 million members around the world, constituting an "entirely nonprofit movement of people who are giving (and getting) stuff for free in their own towns"—all done so that items are reused and kept "out of landfills."

Freegle (www.ilovefreegle.org), a United Kindgom–based network of nearly 400 local groups and over a million users, similar to Freecycle in its ethic of reusing items and preventing more waste from accumulating, is explicitly based on the premise that such a system "helps to develop local community networks and friendships in the process."

Recyclebank (www.recyclebank.com) is a company that seeks to "bring together communities, waste haulers, and local and national brands to help us realize a world where nothing is wasted," allowing users to register for free and earn points and other rewards for engaging in sustainable and "green" behaviors such as recycling, reducing consumption, and making donations.

Warm Showers (www.warmshowers.org) is a worldwide network for traveling bicyclists seeking lodging, based on the notion of "reciprocal hospitality" and touting tens of thousands of hosts and members in its circle of affiliation, promoting not only a free place to stay but also the interpersonal dynamic in which people can "share great stories and a drink."

This small sample of networks is indicative of the range of actors—from radical activists to sustainable entrepreneurs—rethinking the reliance on monetary exchange as the dominant method of producing and procuring essential resources. Many cities and towns have less-networked examples of this ethic, from Free Boxes and Free Stores (giving items away) to Food Not Bombs and Freeganism (reclaiming discarded food). One of the early innovations along these lines is the Really Really Free Market (RRFM), initially conceived in 2003 as part of the demonstrations against neoliberalism and corporate globalization. The RRFM is a temporary marketplace of free items, often in a park or other public setting, in which a gift economy is practiced as an alternative to capitalism and in order to build communities based on resource sharing. Today, the RRFM exists as a loose, decentralized network with regular or occasional manifestations in cities across the United States and around the world. Unlike the networks noted above, the RRFM lacks any central coordination even sufficient for a website, but like the foregoing it takes as its operative principle the idea that *economy* should unite rather than divide people, and that the essence of a healthy community lies in the giving rather than the taking.

The Gift of Service

Throughout human history, the dominant form of exchange (if it can even be defined as such) has been the giving of gifts. The classic treatment of the subject was rendered in 1925 by anthropologist Marcel Mauss in *The Gift*, where it was observed that gift giving has been used to create reciprocal bonds of exchange, and that these bonds formed the basis for social solidarity. Contemporary scholarly explorations often retain this logic of gift-exchange-bonds (e.g., Eisenstein 2011), even as some practitioners have begun to move away from exchange-based formulations in favor of ones grounded more in the spirit of "what goes around comes around" (as with the Free Farm Stand and Karma Kitchen noted above). The exchange-based models retain some of the contractual indicia of commodity exchange (e.g., obligations, indebtedness, witnessing), yet still emphasize the ongoing relationship between the participants to the gift-giving dynamic rather than the pursuit of profit (Eisenstein 2011). In this context, it is apparent that gift giving is more than mere altruism: It benefits the giver by inuring to the overall benefit of the society as a whole. Beyond this, even grander visions and experiments are to be found.

ServiceSpace (www.servicespace.org) is an all-volunteer organization built on the virtues of generosity, service, and love for ourselves, one another, and the world. The model is unique in that it is intentionally non-commercial, made up of a diverse range of service-oriented projects under its umbrella (including the Karma Kitchen and a Daily Good newsletter highlighting positive news), and based on a "pay it forward" ethos in which small acts create ripples of kindness and positive change. Its mission ("Our Model") integrates the gift economy with peacebuilding, including an emphasis on solidarity and relationships, as well as a specific call to move beyond the scarcity-conflict paradigm in favor of one based on abundance and sustainability:

> ServiceSpace projects are built within a gift-economy system, an economic system in which goods and services are given freely, rather than traded. In a traditional market economy, one's wealth is increased by saving. In a gift economy, giving leads to increase: an increase in connections and relationship strength. Our services are given freely, without asking for anything in return. Instead of scarcity and fear for an uncertain future, our second principle roots us in abundance and trust. We have realized that over time, if you serve with pure intentions, people's cups of gratitude overflow. They don't give to fulfill a need, they give as an expression of their own solidarity and joy. These genuine gifts, no matter how small or large, are what sustain us.

The founder of ServiceSpace, Nipun Mehta, is a skilled organizer and dynamic visionary who was named one of the "Breakthrough 15" by *YES! Magazine* (Kaye 2011). Mehta (2012) characterizes his philosophy and practice as a form of *giftivism*, which he defines as "the practice of radically generous acts that change the world." For Mehta (2012), this works "by transforming the heart of the change maker, even more than the impact on its external beneficiaries," further observing that giftivism "has no enemies [and] is unconditionally kind to everyone." For those unaccustomed to thinking this way, such notions can appear naïve or impossible. But for those such as Mehta who practice them on a daily basis, there is a profound sense of obvious joy and sophisticated ethics at work. As Mehta (2013) describes it, the act of giving without condition or expectation of reward (i.e., "radical generosity") is as much about challenging our own perceptions and limitations as it is about being of service to others: "Connecting one's inner transformation to the external world in this way changes everything." Mehta (2013) insightfully posits that an act of kindness or generosity "creates an endless ripple of positivity that could change the world," while at the same time yielding moments of transformation that "ultimately shift our relationship to situations that previously might have felt adversarial."

In this light, giftivism is simultaneously a form of personal transformation, interpersonal generosity, and societal conflict resolution. Mehta (2013) sees the agglomeration of gift-giving moments as constituting a gift economy "ecosystem," which he contrasts with the dominant "tragedy of the commons" motif we often experience in society, observing that "acts of transformation-driven Giftivism have a much longer afterlife [in which] each kind act creates an external ripple effect and an internal one; *both* are required to create a gift [economy]. If you reduce generosity merely to its external impact, it naturally will decay into the tragedy of the commons." As an example of this inner-outer nexus, Mehta (2013) cites the Karma Kitchen, one of the projects he helped inspire through ServiceSpace, noting that more than simply giving away free food it "creates an ambiance where people's innate empathy blooms" and invites participants to experience a "profound interconnection" with those who come to the space before and after. If we take such lessons and apply them at the level of communities, societies, and cultures, we can see the inherent transformative power at work in this model. And if we take it a step further and include the environment in the framework, we come upon what may be the essence of peace ecology—which Mehta (2013) sums up as the need to "keep trusting Nature."

Another key figure in the emergence of communities based on compassion, service, and peace is Pancho Ramos Stierle (mentioned in the previous chapter as part of the Canticle Farm), who is affiliated with ServiceSpace as well. He is also a core member of the Casa de Paz in Oakland, California, which includes among its operating values: Service (direct engagement with the local community), Community (practicing kindness and the principles of the gift economy), Nonviolence (communicating and addressing conflicts restoratively), and Regeneration (simple living, healthy food, respecting the earth). Pancho is widely regarded as an inspiring figure, both for his political work and personal ethics. He was pursuing a Ph.D. in astrophysics at the University of California at Berkeley, but when the university announced it was developing "safer nuclear weapons" he decided to stop participating and has been living "undocumented and unafraid"—including risking deportation when he was arresting while meditating at Occupy Oakland in

November 2011. His activism and life's work focus on issues of human rights, environmental sustainability, nonviolence, peacebuilding, urban agriculture, restorative justice, and the development of a vibrant gift economy—citing influences ranging from Gandhi to the Possibility Alliance, an "educational homestead" centered on radical simplicity, unconditional service, social and political activism, inner transformation, and gratitude (Martin 2011).

Taking these insights and principles to heart, there is a palpable sense of expanding concepts of *community* and *solidarity* to their widest possible limits—incorporating all peoples, all living things, the environment, and creation itself. This is not a pat formula for suddenly revamping human nature or ushering in an era of perpetual peace; indeed, proponents of such an expansive definition of community are often among the most deeply engaged activists in terms of addressing concrete social problems and conflicts. Such actions and visions are reminiscent of those of Dorothy Day, co-founder of the Catholic Worker Movement and widely known for her tireless efforts on behalf of the poor and downtrodden. On the constructive side, Day strove to manifest authentic communities where mutual aid was the dominant form of exchange, and in which people lived in a sustainable manner upon the land (Solnit 2007, 69). Day's vision of interlinked, egalitarian, non-commercial farming communes presaged the solidarity-based ethic that often emerges in contemporary social and environmental activism. What we glean from these teachings is that shared burdens not only lessen the load, but can increase the peace as well.

Solidarity Not Charity

In the wake of many so-called natural disasters (a subject we will explore further in the next chapter), there is often a strong impetus to help coming from people across a wide range of persuasions and perspectives. This is generally a good thing, yet even empathetic intentions can go awry when they foster conditions that can leave vulnerable people in a permanent state of dependency. As is often the case with crucial matters of peace and justice, the words of Martin Luther King Jr. serve as a potent and prescient reminder of the core issues involved:

A true revolution of values will soon cause us to question the fairness and justice of many of our past and present policies. On the one hand we are called to play the Good Samaritan on life's roadside; but that will be only an initial act. One day we must come to see that the whole Jericho road must be transformed so that men and women will not be constantly beaten and robbed as they make their journey on life's highway. True compassion is more than flinging a coin to a beggar; it is not haphazard and superficial. It comes to see that an edifice which produces beggars needs restructuring. A true revolution of values will soon look uneasily on the glaring contrast of poverty and wealth. (1967)

All too often, the lessons of authentic gift-giving, being of service to others and our communities (even the global community), and emphasizing root issues rather than symptoms remain elusive. In Chapter One we thus explored the concept of "structural peace" as a potential antidote to the commodification and control of resources, and likewise as a path toward engaging the societal "edifice" (as King's words suggest) by promoting interdependency rather than dependency.

This is the intrinsic conundrum with focusing primarily on *charity* as a vehicle for justice, namely that it can serve to maintain an inherently unjust edifice. As an alternative, we might strive to express our compassion in terms of *solidarity* instead, by building "a movement in which we're not acting on behalf of one another" (Moore and Russell 2011, 15). As Lila Watson (in Moore and Russell 2011, 15) famously said: "If you have come to help me, then you are wasting your time. But if you have come because your liberation is bound up with mine, then let us work together." An essay following the disastrous 2010 earthquake in Haiti reflected upon the essential character of this task to move from charity to solidarity-producing efforts:

We must demonstrate our solidarity, and not just in the short term, when the emergency requirements are so crucial. We can all ask ourselves what might be the best ways that we can each offer meaningful support, now and in the longer term.... But the language of charity is not the model, for it springs from pity and is not based on a principle of equality. It ends up enhancing the generosity of the giver and—ironically—emphasizing the distance and disconnection between the giver and the receiver. (Trotz 2010)

Unfortunately, as Benjamin Dangl (2010) observed in the earthquake's aftermath, expressions of solidarity are oftentimes relegated and marginalized in the popular discourse. Despite the fact that a great many people in post-disaster Haiti, for example, were "working together to pull their neighbors, friends and loved ones from the rubble, [it was not] this type of solidarity … that most corporate media in the U.S." focused on in the ensuing analysis and depictions (Dangl 2010).

Drawing parallels from other recent crises, we come to see the ways in which disasters continue to evolve and enlarge the scope of oppression over the long term, years after the large portion of aid operations have been concluded and the world's attention has moved on to new concerns. In post-Katrina New Orleans, grassroots activists at Common Ground Relief (www .commongroundrelief.org) and elsewhere explicitly took up the mantra of "Solidarity, not charity" to express the view that any relief efforts must be about helping people to help themselves, or they would merely be another form of disempowerment, even if well-intentioned.

There are some well-known charity and aid organizations that constitute part of what has been called the "disaster industrial complex" (e.g., Lewis 2008); such mainstream charities often partner with multinational corporations to create "synergies" such as handing out Walmart gift cards. (This was the case following Hurricane Katrina; activists in Waveland, Mississippi, took it upon themselves to open a makeshift "Wall-less Mart" that provided free resources and served as a statement against disaster profiteering and disempowerment.) Even in cases where these entities perform charitable works in good conscience, they often find themselves in the position of perpetuating a marginal existence for the "victims" rather than addressing the root causes of impoverishment and imposed vulnerability that made the disaster possible in the first instance.

The critical aspects of any true relief effort, whether in response to an acute disaster or to the perpetual crises in our midst, are empowerment and solidarity—both of which are based on the active sense of compassion that King was referencing half a century ago. In post-Katrina New Orleans, thousands of grassroots activists have been to the city, with a great many seeking to practice—albeit imperfectly, at times—this spirit of solidarity. The aim has been to help people maintain the capacity to decide how to rebuild their own lives and communities, and also includes the struggle to preserve meaningful political opportunities for people to be able to influence their local decision-making structures. Solidarity efforts, akin to the free economy and gift economy examples cited above, also necessitate forms of economic self-reliance in which people can produce and share the resources necessary for their livelihoods without having to resort to outside profiteers. Contrast this sensibility with the remarks of former president George W. Bush, which reinforced the "imposed dependency" approach by focusing on remote aid, monetization, and a top-down infrastructure of relief led by external actors (Phillips 2010):

> The challenges down there are immense, but there's a lot of devoted people leading the relief effort, from government personnel who deployed into the disaster zone to the faith-based groups that have made Haiti a calling. The most effective way for Americans to help the people of Haiti is to contribute money. That money will go to organizations on the ground and will be—who will be able to effectively spend it. I know a lot of people want to send blankets or water—just send your cash. One of the things that [we] will do is to make sure your money is spent wisely.

Evident here is the tendency to replace compassion with cold cash, to write a check rather than directly checking in with ourselves and others. This is a path to subjugation, not empowerment.

Against this dominant and distinctly disempowering approach stand the efforts of many grassroots entities. The Haiti Emergency Relief Fund (www .haitiemergencyrelief.org), which was formed in 2004 as an acknowledgment of the ongoing sense of "emergency" there, has worked specifically to support "Haiti's grassroots movement—including labor unions, women's groups, educators and human rights activists, support committees for prisoners, and agricultural cooperatives"—by funneling any aid received directly to these entities. The Batey Relief Alliance (www.bateyrelief.org) likewise has partnered with grassroots organizations in Haiti as part of its mission to "help create a safe, productive and self-sufficient environment, through health care, food security, education, disaster relief, and community development programs, for children and their families severely affected by extreme poverty, disease, and hunger." Partners in Health (www.pih.org) had a presence in Haiti for many years before the 2010 earthquake, in light of its larger mission to provide medical care and help assuage despair "based on solidarity, rather than charity alone." Another group working in Haiti even before the earthquake has been SOIL (www.oursoil.org), which helps build composting toilets in water-scarce, illness-prone areas, thus "protecting soil resources, empowering communities and transforming wastes into resources" as part of an integrated approach "to the problems of poverty, poor public health, agricultural productivity, and environmental destruction."

All of these examples suggest the utility of small but crucial steps that are viable in any context—from the unfathomable devastation of earthquakes and hurricanes to the ongoing crises of worsening economic immiseration, perpetual warfare, and rampant environmental degradation. It is indeed a challenge for the well-meaning among us to know how to help others (even ourselves) in an effective and worthwhile manner. By focusing on people and entities working at the grassroots with long-term perspectives, we can be part of the essential process of creating structures through which people can take action to help themselves. This is, in short, an expression of solidarity that reflects the best sense of our common humanity. It is representative of the spirit of *ubuntu*, an African philosophy grounded in the tenets of interconnectedness, generosity, spontaneous community, collective prosperity, and warmth. The notion of *conviviality* seeks to go even "beyond solidarity" (e.g., Convivial Research and Insurgent Learning, www.cril.mitotedigital .org/cril) as a pathway "to address community struggles, reclaim commons, regenerate culture, facilitate intra/inter-cultural encounters, and promote direct democracy." In this spirit, an ancient Mexican greeting translates to "you are my other self," based on the idea that "real happiness comes by seeing ourselves in others" (Escamilla 2005). Appropriately, cutting-edge theories of human behavior confirm that this is indeed so.

Radical Empathy: Are Humans Wired for Peace?

What does it take to make a happy life? Can personal happiness be had at the expense of others—or of the non-human environment upon which our existence depends? Is happiness conditioned more upon what one receives or what one gives? What responsibility does a happy individual have to the well-being and integrity of the whole? And is there something in particular about the nexus of peace and ecology that suggests a tendency to promote such a holistic version of happiness? These are the sorts of questions that keep philosophers busy, drawing back to landmark works such as Aristotle's ethical assessment of happiness as both a state of *being* and a condition of *doing*. It will not be apropos here to pursue this much further than raising the issue about how we might balance the needs of the individual with the needs of the community, and further how we can reconcile collective human needs with the maintenance of a healthy environment. From a peace studies perspective, we might take for a point of departure on these issues the human capacity for cooperation, mutualism, compassion, caring, and love. In so doing, we will avoid self-help invocations, focusing instead on how we can conceive of *empathy* as a radical practice that works at both the human-human and human-environment interfaces.

The notion of developing a radical form of empathy calls upon us to manifest nonviolence and to cultivate awareness in the daily practice of our lives. The concept also includes as part of its underpinnings some of the cutting-edge theories of human capacities for compassion, such as *mirror neurons* and *epigenetics*. Part of the aim involves fostering an authentic "ethic of care" that applies equally to the self, our societies, and the balance of the biosphere as well. This task is more critical now than ever, and is likely to become increasingly so as the very concept of well-being (or, by extension, happiness) steadily loses its ethical foundations in favor of a mass-marketed form of hedonism posing as an antidote to widespread signs of alienation, burnout, apathy, overconsumption, and aggression. What we will invoke here as a vision of *radical empathy*—i.e., the conscious deployment of our capacity for empathy as a tool for positive social and ecological change—can serve as a pathway toward mutuality, solidarity, and the realization of a sustainable peace at all levels of engagement. As Alistair McIntosh (2004, 284) asserts,

"If humankind is to have any hope of changing the world" and averting environmental cataclysm, we must learn the lessons of empathy, respect, and love.

In recent years, scholars and practitioners alike have begun to address the nexus between well-being, sustainability, and the cultivation of compassionate and empathetic relations. The core concept is that by recognizing the interrelated nature of our existence, we come to see the welfare of the other as intimately bound up with our own welfare. As Mehta (2012) has observed: "When we engage at the cusp of our own evolution, we can't help but broaden from self orientation to other orientation. We then serve from a place of abundance, which means we serve with joy and gratitude. We honor our profound interconnection, and as we align with a natural unfolding that is greater than us, we continue to transform ourselves." The one and the many have always been thus connected, and it is by now considered a *sine qua non* of social justice that the well-being of the individual is intimately bound up with that of the whole, as King (1963) famously wrote in his *Letter from a Birmingham Jail*: "We are caught in an inescapable network of mutuality, tied in a single garment of destiny. Whatever affects one directly, affects all indirectly." King drew upon a wide range of sources and inspirations in his essays and speeches, and in many ways this vision of interconnection was central to his overall thesis.

When we extend this logic further to include the environment upon which we are all (inter)dependent, these themes come into even sharper focus. "Our liberation is bound up with that of every other being on the planet," wrote Aurora Levins Morales (1998). In this sense, the practice of empathy becomes the keystone of sustainable well-being as it creates a positive feedback loop among interconnected components of a whole system; in other words, caring for others and for the habitat in an essentially closed cycle *is* taking care of oneself, and vice versa. Cutting-edge insights from social psychology and neurobiology likewise indicate that we are not merely passive consumers of remotely decided outcomes, but rather that we possess the inherent power to shape our realities and relations as we engage them. *Mirror neurons* (sometimes also referred to as "Gandhi neurons") provide a biological basis for understanding that when we observe others' (re)actions, it stimulates a similar response in ourselves on both a biophysical and emotional level; thus, well-being begets well-being, and suffering begets suffering (cf. Acharya and

Shukla 2012). Or as Peace Pilgrim once said colloquially, "the world is rather like a mirror—when you smile at it, it smiles at you." In essence, cutting-edge neuroscience indicates that "compassion and empathy, feeling the experience of another, is not just something we're capable of, it is woven into the fabric we are cut from" (Slack 2007).

Where mirror neurons provide a potential biological basis for empathy between humans, the burgeoning field of epigenetics posits that environmental factors can influence the expression of DNA in future generations, adding both ecological and temporal factors to the mix. Emerging out of research on societal-level traumas such as famine and war, epigenetics focuses on the ways in which external conditions can influence how our genes express themselves—in essence, why certain genetic switches are flipped on or off—apart from any specific alterations to the genetic code itself. In other words, epigenetics demonstrates "the power of the environment over gene expression," without permanently affecting the baseline genes (Cloud 2010). Whereas evolution is the process of producing genetic changes over long periods of time, epigenetics indicates that responses to environmental stimuli "can be inherited through many generations via epigenetic marks, but if you remove the environmental pressure, the epigenetic marks will eventually fade" (Cloud 2010). This provides a basis for extending our senses of empathy and symbiosis beyond humans and, to the larger environment, further suggesting another potential impetus for turning crises into opportunities—yielding immediate *and* intergenerational benefits.

As humankind rapidly approaches an apparent turning point in our capacity to sustain and survive, we directly confront the critical questions of the era. Can we emphasize self-care, care of others, and care of the environment in our lives and work? What are the new challenges and opportunities that will arise as conditions likely continue to worsen around the globe? Can we become reintegrated with the world in time to save it—and ourselves? Far from mere academic exercises, engaging these queries can inform our daily practice by promoting personal happiness, mutual well-being, and ecological sustainability all at once. As it turns out, humans possess a remarkable array of attributes for embracing this ethic creatively and constructively. While it would be foolhardy to deny our tendencies toward competition, aggression, greed, and violence (i.e., the dominant Hobbesian narrative), it would be equally so to overlook our counterbalancing capacities for empathy, compassion, solidarity, and giving. As we saw in Chapter One with the concepts of scarcity and abundance, the task is not so much to replace one with the other but more so to see the potential in the intersection of the two. Too much of either can lead to conflict, whereas it is in the balance of opposing tendencies that we are able to flourish.

This chapter has looked at fundamental concepts of solidarity and empathy as they apply to both human-human and human-environment interactions. A critical moment where these notions play out is in our economic arrangements, which call into question sociopolitical processes of wealth creation and distribution, as well as ecological issues over resource extraction and patterns of consumption. The nexus here becomes apparent, as we consider alternative economic arrangements (such as gift giving, local currencies, and free networks) that simultaneously address human needs in an equitable manner while lessening our collective strain on the environment. These practices provide another set of illustrations of peace ecology in action, bringing together previously discussed concepts of resources (Chapter One), the commons (Chapter Two), and basic essentials (Chapter Three), while adding another dimension: the inherent human capacity for empathetic and compassionate relationships among ourselves and with the balance of the habitat. In the next chapter, we will explore these themes in the context of "post-disaster" scenarios, which are often viewed as bringing out people's worst behaviors—even as research continually suggests that such moments can bring out our best.

CHAPTER FIVE
FLIRTING WITH DISASTER

COMMUNITY RESILIENCE IN TIMES OF CRISIS

In the aftermath of Hurricane Katrina in late 2005, the city of New Orleans came to resemble an occupied territory, with tens of thousands of military troops on patrol and entire neighborhoods cordoned off with razor wire. Residents already besieged by floodwaters were subjected to roadblocks and checkpoints, and some were even "threatened with eviction at gunpoint" (Harnden 2005)—leading some locals to begin referring to the area as "Baghdad on the Bayou." Katrina represented an acute case of what has now become a normalized occurrence: the militarization of post-disaster relief efforts. Numerous critics observed the presence of this phenomenon in Haiti following the devastating earthquake there in 2010 (Democracy Now! 2010). When issues along the US-Mexico border reach a crisis point, such as during times of a perceived increase in cross-border violence, National Guard troops have been deployed by both federal and state authorities. Following the Boston Marathon bombings, army soldiers were stationed at locales around the city including subway stations, ostensibly "to provide security and ensure public safety" (Broughey 2013). In each of these representative instances, the operative premise on the part of authorities is that militarism can serve as a positive response to crisis.

This is problematic on a number of levels, not the least being that the military "does not have great tools for building things, for creating things, for bringing hope and dignity" (Matthew 2010, 41). Yet just as militarization is an inappropriate and ineffective tool for remediating crises, equally so is the other dominant sphere of disaster response: *privatization*. Increasingly, the global "security" apparatus is coming to be defined by the presence of private companies, sometimes of the militaristic sort (e.g., the erstwhile Blackwater) but more often of the service-oriented profiteering variety (e.g., Halliburton). (Notably, both Blackwater and Halliburton were quickly on the ground in post-Katrina New Orleans.) Where militarism is the blunt edge of crisis management, corporatism is its friendlier face, often coming under the guise of "opportunity" and "redevelopment" for disaster-ravaged populations. These top-down forms of intervention, however, only increase a sense of dependency and helplessness, as people who have suffered a calamitous event sometimes find themselves re-victimized upon the realization that whatever rebuilding occurs will not inure to their benefit. In short, the paired spheres of militarization and privatization are the *cause* of crisis, and neither is even remotely effective at remediating it.

As we saw in the previous chapter, some of the most authentically effectual responses to crises have been engendered by ordinary people working together in a spirit of solidarity and mutual aid. While grossly underreported in the mainstream media, this inspiring resurgence of post-disaster communitarianism is actually a more productive version of the "new normal" that often takes hold in the aftermath of calamitous events. In this chapter, we will explore some of the innovations that have developed as people around the world are increasingly exposed to the impacts of "natural disasters" and other grave challenges. These microcosmic efforts to restabilize stricken communities reveal consistently cooperative impulses, as well as providing insight into longer-term strategies of coping with a rapidly changing environment. By now, it is becoming evident that the patterns and processes often associated with *climate change* can contribute to rising sea levels, extended droughts, and the intensification of hurricanes; as the US Environmental Protection Agency has concluded, "These changes will impact our food supply, water resources, infrastructure, ecosystems, and even our own health" (EPA n.d.). With each successive storm—or now, *superstorm*—we are realizing these impacts. The lessons can be profound, even as the frequency and ferocity of the crises are disconcerting.

A Rising Tide . . .

Humankind stands at the cusp of its gravest challenge, and the prospective survival of the species itself hangs in the balance. While there is an attempt on the part of some invested in the status quo to depict the climate crisis as debatable or even false, the reality is that an unprecedented and near-unanimous consensus exists among credible sources that indeed thew predicament is real and the window for action is rapidly closing. Against this backdrop of denial and the disempowering potential inherent in grim projections, a global movement has arisen to meet the challenges of climate change in all of its dimensions—from the social to the ecological, and as to both its short- and long-term impacts (Tokar 2010). One of the salient points of climate change is that those who contribute the least to it often bear its consequences disproportionately. Another is that the feedback loop we have seen between environmental degradation and violent conflict may be exacerbated by the ravages of climate change, with the leading edge of these processes already in evidence. Yet every crisis contains within it genuine opportunity, and the generational crucible of climate change has yielded inspiring examples of people reclaiming power and promoting peace—notwithstanding the complexity and magnitude of the challenge before us.

Climate change is interlinked with a number of related phenomena, including the loss of arable lands, desertification, ocean acidification, food and water scarcity, and resource depletion. Part and parcel of environmental change in general, climatic shifts and the escalating disasters spawned by them are also linked with the potential for increased conflict and violence. Indeed, the United Nations Environment Programme (UNEP) includes an explicit "Disasters and Conflicts" node (www.unep.org/disastersandconflicts) focusing on the interlinked nature of these challenges, noting that "the environment can play a pivotal role in human security and well being" and emphasizing "the role of healthy ecosystems and sustainably managed resources in reducing the risk of disasters and conflicts." UNEP also maintains a specific node for climate change, referring to it as "the major, overriding environmental issue of our time." In recent years, a notable body of literature has arisen looking specifically at the link between climate change and violence (e.g., Lee 2009; Parenti 2011), including dire predictions of "climate wars" either already in the offing or just around the corner (Dyer 2010; Welzer 2012). Rather than realizing the benefits of the free-market dictum that "a rising tide lifts all boats," there is instead a growing recognition that rising waters will more likely serve to flood cities and sink people's hopes.

Changes in climate have historically been associated with the potentials for war and/or peace (Vintila 2007), most significantly in that the ostensible prosperity associated with the advent of civilization has been partly enabled by a period characterized as a "climate sweet spot" (Matthew 2010, 44). That "sweet spot" now appears to be souring, in large measure by our own hand, with scholars (e.g., Barnett and Adger 2007, 640) noting the unparalleled nature of the challenge: "There is now widespread agreement that the changes underway in the earth's climate system have no precedent in the history of human civilization." As Richard Matthew (2010, 46) similarly concludes, "We are on the threshold of a set of changes that will put us outside of where humankind has ever lived." Significantly, the combined potential impacts of climate change and environmental degradation pose an existential threat to humankind that is perhaps "second only to nuclear war" (Kane 2007, 536), with some believing that "there is a probability of wars, including nuclear wars" if global temperatures continue to rise at predicted levels (Dyer 2010, xii). The net effect of these sobering assessments is to forthrightly suggest that "the second half of this century will not be a time you would choose to live in" (Dyer 2010, xiii).

Unsurprisingly, given the grave implications, climate and environmental issues have begun to move to the fore in security discourses, including militaries themselves explicating scenarios in their documents and strategies alike. As Christian Parenti (2011, 13) observes, "The Pentagon is planning for a world remade by climate change"—which of course also has the effect of shaping events, since "planning too diligently for war can preclude peace." Gwynne Dyer (2010, 11) likewise asserts that "the American military and intelligence communities are now fully committed to playing a leading role in the struggle to contain the negative effects of climate change." Unfortunately, it is more so the case that "framing climate change as a security issue may influence the perceptions of the actors in local and regional conflict and lead to militarized responses, and thus perhaps contribute to a self-fulfilling prophecy" (Gleditsch 2012, 7). With the erosion of civil society organizations and the economic safety net in many countries, as well as the concomitant preclusion of community-based entities that could provide alternatives to top-down securitized forms of mitigation, we often thus find ourselves in a situation where "we will send our military over, because we have no one else to send" (Matthew 2010, 48).

As we have seen throughout this volume, entrenched interests frequently construct such self-fulfilling scenarios, positing themselves as the only viable solution to problems they have caused. As best, these dominant forces are merely "treating the symptoms" (Matthew 2010, 38); at worst, they are actively fomenting drastic changes and massive degradation to further their interests in consolidating power and wealth. In the next chapter we will look more closely at how climatic shifts are contributing to a global race among elite sectors to acquire resources that were previously unattainable. For now, it is interesting to note that some are already touting environmental changes as potentially *preventing* conflicts, such as the article in *The Diplomat* written by a US Navy commander (VornDick 2012) somewhat ironically titled "Thanks Climate Change: Sea-Level Rise Could End South China Sea Spat." Embedded in this view is the notion that this conflict might be prevented simply because rising waters will overwhelm islands and render any conflicting claims to them moot. This is not the sort of "peace" that many would hope for in global affairs, and it flies in the face of numerous predictions of more difficult paths to concord (as noted in the article) if not increased conflict.

In fact, we already have enough information to conclude that militarism and warfare are actually significant drivers of climate change and environmental destabilization, thus existing in a vicious cycle of conflict and degradation in which neither pole brings peace. There are at least three primary characteristics of warfare that specifically bear upon climate change: (1) damage to the environment that serves to accelerate global warming (including the military's consumption of fossil fuels and its massive carbon footprint); (2) an enormous cost that takes resources away from mitigating climate change; and (3) the loss of "cultural space" to forge international agreements and cooperation (Vintila 2007). In this light, it becomes apparent that "war and the culture that sustains it are among the climate's greatest enemies" (Vintila 2007, 11), and ultimately that "militaries are a problem rather than a solution to environmental insecurity" (Barnett 2003, 13). The militarists have it right that national security and ecological conservation are inextricably linked, and likewise that the threats posed by climate change and environmental degradation are all too real. But what we need are non-militaristic responses to these challenges, not ones that serve to exacerbate the problem or perpetuate an inherently unsustainable system.

As noted above, a spate of literature has emerged that correlates the impacts of climate change and the presence of conflict, violence, and warfare. The analysis of these processes is nuanced, arguing that climate and conflict are "linked in a series of stages and only exceptionally present a direct cause-effect relationship" (Welzer 2012, 73). Among the factors in this attenuated causal chain are resource scarcity, environmental depletion, displacement, refugeeism, nationalism, border tensions, declining global wealth, and weakened social bonds (Lee 2009, 1–7). Parenti (2011, 7) has termed this confluence of factors "the catastrophic convergence," observing that these are not merely linear or simultaneous phenomena, but more so that they "compound and amplify each other, one expressing itself through another." Climate change is an accelerant of preexisting crises, what the Pentagon calls a "threat multiplier" for its capacity to exacerbate existing threats and thus feed back into even more rapid environmental alterations. Parenti explores numerous cases typifying this cycle, including the political situation surrounding the US-Mexico border as an illustration of the convergence of factors that drive the conflict-degradation loop—from massive droughts and neoliberal economics to refugeeism and border militarization. While such analyses cannot always trace a direct causal line, they indicate that "the danger of conflicts is never smaller as a result of climate change" (Welzer 2012, 76).

Such insights are plausible, with examples that seem to fit the paradigm becoming legion. At the same time, others have rejected the climate-conflict connection, arguing that it is merely an updated form of Malthusianism and that its empirical grounding is lacking. This opposing camp is defined by a "technological optimism" that sometimes includes advocacy of "weather modification" tactics such as cloud-seeding to mitigate the worst impacts of climate change (Lee 2009, 149, 156). [As James Lee (2009, 157) points out, however, weather modification is actually a "weapon of warfare," having been utilized for instance by the United States in the Vietnam War to disrupt enemy supply transports.] Resurrecting the long-standing Malthusians-versus-Cornucopians debate discussed in Chapter One, the latter camp finds the climate-conflict position to be a form of "environmental determinism" that "ignores human agency, ingenuity, the potential for technological innovation, and the vital role of political institutions" (Salehyan 2008, 317). The other side again responds that while the causality may be non-linear, "climate-related disasters ... increase the risk of violent civil conflict" (Nel and Righarts 2008, 162).

What are we to make of these competing claims? As with the resource issues considered in Chapter One, part of the peace ecologist's task is to resist easy dichotomies and instead explore potential "third ways" for deconstructing social and environmental problems, while also posing constructive alternatives. Throughout this volume, we have seen a number of these paired opposites: war/peace, scarcity/abundance, conflict/cooperation. It would be tempting to argue that peace, cooperation, and abundance inevitably coexist, and likewise that resource conflicts inexorably lead to forms of scarcity that can serve as a basis for warfare. Indeed, while examples of each chain can be found, it is also the case that abundance can yield conflict, whereas scarcity sometimes promotes cooperation. Peaceful cultures are not automatically sustainable, and better environmental practices do not necessarily cultivate peace. What we can say at this juncture is that the same set of variables that are surmised to spawn conflict (e.g., resources, the commons, disasters) can also be among the most profound drivers of peace. By accentuating the positive potentials at work, our ability to transcend the negative ones might be enhanced.

Shock Treatment

Even so, as is the case when confronting instances of conflict or injustice, we cannot simply skip ahead to the resolution or remediation phase without first fully articulating the nature of the problem. This has been another recurring theme in this work, namely that the quest to convert crises into opportunities—or at least to establish a constructive dialectic between them—requires a robust rendering of the former in order to develop equally vigorous manifestations of the latter. In the case of climate change and environmental degradation, the "problem" side of the ledger turns out to be less than spectacular when traced to its origins, residing squarely in the mundane "business as usual" of the globalized system of production and consumption that is steadily subsuming all phases of modern life. As we saw in Chapter Three, the co-optation of life's essentials into this global system makes us more vulnerable by replacing diversity with homogeneity, diminishing resiliency in favor of dependency, and supplanting sustainability through disposability. Here, then, is the proverbial "elephant in the room" of climate change: for the bulk of the planet's inhabitants, it is our daily living that has made us the enemies of the earth, and of ourselves in the process. This is all so utterly ordinary that we hardly notice it.

Hence, as Parenti (2011, 12) surmises, "The best way to address the effects of climate change is to tackle the political and economic crises that have rendered us so vulnerable to climate-induced chaos in the first place." The problem is that time is running (or perhaps has already run) out in terms of crossing certain environmental thresholds that may be irreversible. Equally disconcerting is that a global problem seemingly begs for a global solution—leading us back to the doorstep of the same globalized economic system that has brought us to the brink of collapse in the first place. "The metabolism of the world economy is fundamentally out of sync with that of nature," writes Parenti (2011, 225, 241), leaving us with a scenario in which "either capitalism solves the crisis, or it destroys civilization." In effect, we are caught between the Scylla of ecological collapse and the Charybdis of capitalist captivity. Even to those preferring the latter, including Cornucopian proponents of economic development as a purported pathway to peace, there remains the realization that "the same forces that are polluting our planet and altering the climate" are the ones that are driving the global economy (Gartzke 2012, 189).

"Disasters are not exceptional events," as Gregory Button (2010, 247) observes in *Disaster Culture*, and thus we must learn "from everyday disasters as well as major catastrophes." In this lexicon, disasters—from wars and famines to hurricanes and earthquakes—are always already "political events" involving the "control of information" about their true nature, oftentimes contingent upon "the production of uncertainty as an ideological tactic" (Button 2010, 16, 247). Button investigates in particular post-Katrina New Orleans as archetypal of the sociopolitical aspects of disaster production, from the preexisting everyday injustices in the region to the grossly negligent governmental response—followed in relatively short order by the calamitous Deepwater Horizon oil spill that was notable for its environmental devastation to an already-ravaged region, as well as for its display of unremitting corporate obfuscation and outright prevarication in an attempt to control the narrative. As shocking as these events were, they also possessed a routine quality in the sense that we almost have come to expect that corporations will dissemble in order to avert sanctions for their irresponsible behaviors, and likewise that mainstream media outlets will sensationalize isolated episodes of "looting" and the like while flagrantly ignoring widespread patterns of racialized violence and official malfeasance.

Thus do we find ourselves in a world that conveniently ignores the everyday suffering of multitudes of people at the hands of the very system that is responsible for rampant degradation, persistent conflict, and potentially apocalyptic climate shifts. An important environmental justice report highlighted many of the salient details of this situation:

> Climate change is not only an issue of the environment; it is also an issue of justice and human rights, one that dangerously intersects race and class. All over the world people of color, Indigenous Peoples and low-income communities bear disproportionate burdens from climate change itself, from ill-designed policies to prevent it, and from side effects of the energy systems that cause it. (Hoerner and Robinson 2008)

Climate change is quintessentially a socioecological issue, a function of runaway greenhouse gas emissions as much as it is of the endemic poverty and political inequality that underscore the "structural violence" (Galtung 1996) pervading the dominant order. Jon Barnett (2003, 14) thus appropriately discerns a form of "double vulnerability" in which people who are already negatively impacted by a system that produces widespread socioeconomic insecurity are rendered even more acutely insecure by the rapacity of climate change and environmental degradation. Making matters even worse, many of the elite-driven "solutions" to climate change seek to curb the growth potentials of developing nations in particular, potentially creating a scenario that would "trap them in both relative and absolute poverty forever" (Kane 2007, 537).

One of the most influential treatments of the normalization of disaster and the ways in which the military-industrial complex actually thrives on it was delivered by Naomi Klein in her 2007 book, *The Shock Doctrine: The Rise of Disaster Capitalism*. Klein (2007, 9–11) documents "the free market's dependence on the power of shock" and the ways in which "capitalism has always needed disasters to advance," citing numerous examples including Iraq and New Orleans as archetypal "bold experiments in crisis exploitation." Her painstaking research lays bare the intertwining of military might and crass commercialism, finding that in the context of both war (Iraq) and disaster (New Orleans), "no opportunity for profit was left untapped" (Klein 2007, 520). These US-oriented examples demonstrate the tendency of capitalism to exploit crises, but they are hardly alone in the annals of disaster profiteering. Following the devastating Asian tsunami in 2004, which killed a quarter million people and displaced ten times that amount, developers seized the opportunity presented by this ostensible "blank slate" left in the wake of the storm's destruction. "Backed up by the guns of local police and private security," writes Klein (2007, 508), "it was militarized gentrification, class war on the beach." The dominant paradigm of disaster exploitation is thus well established; the issue is what to do about it.

Mitigation, Adaptation, and Catastrophism

As ecological thresholds are being broached, and as the frequency and intensity of disasters increase, the differential impact of patterns of environmental degradation comes into sharper focus. Climate change is a global phenomenon whose effects play out most acutely in concrete locales, oftentimes disproportionately impacting those who have contributed the least to the problem or who are otherwise rendered vulnerable by the day-to-day operations of political and economic systems. Wherever one is located on the scale of power and privilege, there are environmental challenges to be addressed, even as we must recognize that "climate change certainly doesn't affect everybody equally" (Moore and Russell 2011, 11). Ethnic minorities, poor people, and the elderly, among other marginalized groups, "are likely to have fewer resources available to mitigate the risks of a major storm, before and after the event" (Basolo 2009, 111). At the level of communities and localities, the solution to the problems associated with climate change is "to reduce inequalities" in the social, economic, and political realms, while "increasing the capacity of vulnerable populations" to ensure their security (Basolo 2009, 111).

Yet this is a tall order, since to fully accomplish it we would find ourselves, in short order, calling into question many of the basic workings of society as it is presently configured. This is indeed a worthy pursuit, since it is these baseline operations of our political and economic systems that undergird the production of disasters at the micro and macro levels alike. In the next section we will explore the notion of community resilience more fully; here, the macroscopic challenges of environmental change are paramount as we trace the contours of the interlocking systems that drive the vicious cycle of conflict and degradation. At this scale, the primary options for navigating the vicissitudes of climate change are *mitigation* and *adaptation*—in essence, trying to stop it from happening in the first place, but learning to cope with it when it does. The coincidence of these strategies in relation to climate issues parallels that found in two of the larger global movements in recent decades, namely anti-war and anti-globalization. In these instances, massive mobilizations have sought to end warfare and corporate globalization, respectively; while obviously unsuccessful in terms of halting these processes altogether, these movements did hinder their progress to an extent and opened a space for exploring adaptations.

In the case of climate and environmental change, we are fast approaching a tipping point where full-scale mitigation may no longer be possible, as critical thresholds are crossed regarding atmospheric carbon, ocean chemistry, soil nutrient levels, biodiversity, and other related phenomena (Rockström et al. 2009). Indeed, even if we were to suspend all carbon emissions today (seemingly a political impossibility), we could still experience acute impacts of climate change due to what has already been released into the planetary system—the leading edge of which we are already realizing with more frequent and severe weather-related events. "There seems no way to reverse worldwide climate change in the short run," as David Barash and Charles Webel (2009, 404) observe; however, "it can be ameliorated, essentially buying time for future generations." By substantially decreasing the use of fossil fuels, strictly conserving resources, moving immediately to renewable forms of energy, and implementing major reforestation efforts, humankind might avert the potential runaway cataclysm we have been irresponsibly courting. Yet hardly anyone expects this to happen, given the failure of previous climate summits to make any meaningful progress on greenhouse gas emissions, coupled with the determined opposition of many elite interests and corporate entities. An escalating sense of urgency, as Klein (2013) discerns, has led some scientists to raise their voices, locating potential "hope" in the appearance of resistance movements including those involving "environmental direct action [and] resistance taken from outside the dominant culture, as in protests, blockades and sabotage by indigenous peoples, workers, anarchists and other activist groups." This is not akin to advocating such tactics, Klein notes, but more so to sound the alarm for exigent change.

Whereas "mitigation is about gasses," it has been surmised that "adaptation is about water"—which further implicates other essentials, since "climate change poses significant threats to global food security and peace due to changes in water supply and demand" (Hanjra and Qureshi 2010, 367, 371). Vandana Shiva (2002, 40) confirms the centrality of water to the monumental task of adaptation: "The impact of climate crisis on all forms of life is mediated through water in the form of floods, cyclones, heat waves, and droughts.... More than anything, the oil economy's environmental externalities, such as atmospheric pollution and climate change, will determine the future of water, and through water, the future of all life." Water is the *sine qua non* of existence, and it is the lifeblood of the planet's regulatory systems. Adapting to rapacious environmental change means coping with significant alterations in hydrological cycles, weather patterns, and food production capacities. Reflecting on these challenges, Parenti (2011, 10–11) discerns two related spheres of necessary engagement: "technical adaptation" (building seawalls around coastal cities, replenishing mangroves and everglades as protective barriers, and developing sustainable forms of agriculture), and "political adaptation" (transforming social relations toward greater equity, containing and resolving environmental conflicts, and redistributing wealth and power). If we fail to do this, the result might instead be "militarized adaptation"—meaning greater authoritarianism and even "climate fascism" (Parenti 2011, 11).

This insight counsels caution when considering what has become a nascent "third way" beyond mitigation or adaptation: the open courting of *collapse* as a means of transformation and reorientation. Considering the entrenched nature of the military-industrial complex, it is understandable that some advocates of peace and sustainability might embrace system wide failure as a potential impetus toward new forms of sociopolitical organization and environmental consciousness. However, as Klein (2007, 23) observes, notions of a "clean slate" brought on by cataclysm are actually more consistent with fundamentalist ideologies that are rooted in "a logic that leads ineluctably toward violence." Thus, while it may be tempting to see climate change as a global "wakeup call" or even a chance to start over and reorganize our societies in more positive and productive ways, the greater likelihood is that such crises will be capitalized on by powerful interests to further consolidate their power and control. We have already begun to see this, as Klein's "shock doctrine" has indicated, and there is little reason to expect that collapse will bring peace. Indeed, "stoking our cultural fear of some 'doomsday' in the future is not useful for building organizations, community, and mobilizing people to create a livable future; or for preventing the worst impacts of runaway climate change" (Moore and Russell 2011, 8).

In the collaborative book *Catastrophism*, Sasha Lilley (2012a, 5) recalls the illusory nature of the assumption on the part of some environmentalists that "If they are able to disseminate enough information about the dire state of the environment, the people will take action." This often instead has the effect of resulting in greater apathy, especially when the information presented suggests that certain outcomes are inevitable and that individuals are relatively powerless to do anything about it. On the other side of the coin are those environmentalists who likewise highlight the gravity of the situation, but opt for feel-good and largely ineffectual suggestions about replacing light bulbs or being more diligent about recycling (not that these are bad ideas, but they are not sufficient in themselves to forestall runaway climate change).

In both cases, there is a presumption that if things get worse, the better it will be for environmentalism—either through the "clean slate" of collapse or by motivating people to act in more responsible, conservationist ways. The problem, as we have seen, is that "capitalism has shown itself destructively adept at vaulting obstacles to accumulation, and creating opportunities out of the misery of others" (Lilley 2012b, 72). In the end, despite deepening crises, "it appears to be wishful thinking that 'industrial society' will simply break down" (Lilley 2012b, 72).

In his contribution to this provocative volume, Eddie Yuen (2012, 15) initially observes that the concept of ecological collapse is actually plausible, having been "verified by a consensus within the scientific community." By focusing primarily on acute crises or global cataclysms, however, advocates often take for granted "the grinding, quotidian catastrophe of capitalism"— thus failing to articulate a critical perspective that "links environmental crises to social inequality and the 'normal' functioning of the system" (Yuen 2012, 18, 32). This failure has two main effects on the prospects for meaningful change. First, as noted above, it gives cover to the advent of "military 'humanitarianism'" and encourages elites to "double down on the strategies of militarism and geopolitical realpolitik" that are already becoming the operative premise of "disaster relief" (Yuen 2012, 35). Second, when crises are detached from the ordinary operations of sociopolitical systems and instead rendered as extraordinary events, power is wrested from people and communities to remediate the effects through local, solidarity-based initiatives. In other words, what we require is a vision for coping with catastrophes that intervenes *before* they emerge, and that doesn't merely turn to those responsible for causing them to find solutions.

Phoenix from the Ashes

Fortunately, we have a plethora of precisely such exemplars to draw upon. Again, a recurring theme in the peace ecology paradigm is the capacity to move from crisis to opportunity—not in a crude or mercenary way, but in the sense of cultivating the resilience and adaptive capacity to cope with the seemingly never-ending array of challenges presented by the modern world. One of the potential conundrums with this strategy is that the more we develop the ability to adapt to crises, the more likely they are to occur since we have less energy to expend on mitigating or forestalling them in the first instance. When it comes to climate change in particular, there is a real debate about whether responses should seek to mitigate or adapt to the leading edge of the impacts we have already seen, such as droughts and floods, more frequent and intense storms, heat waves and wildfires, and rising sea levels. Oftentimes overlooked in this debate—which represents yet another misapplied dichotomy—is that many of the most profoundly adaptive strategies are reflective of practices that, if widely embraced, would also be mitigative. Looking at the post-disaster context in particular, we see that communities impacted by calamitous events often display incredible resilience typified by practices of solidarity and mutual aid, as well as demonstrating the ability of large numbers of people to live without consuming many of the creature comforts and corporate wares that are generally taken as indispensable.

The ground for such inspiring examples is paved by the realization that "times of crisis can bring out the best in people" (Lilley 2012b, 56). What we are seeking is not merely a reactive movement that cascades from one crisis to the next, nor one that simply waits "for capitalism to implode before offering solutions," but rather a set of proactive solutions that are "prefigurative and practical as well as visionary and participatory" (Yuen 2012, 42). At root, "such a movement must make a positive appeal to community and solidarity" (Yuen 2012, 42), providing people with a grand vision for a better world while at the same time meeting basic needs of "energy, water, housing, hope and dignity" (Matthew 2010, 49). An effective movement does not seek an unattainable clean slate from which to begin anew, nor does it advocate a "rearranging deck chairs on the Titanic" approach that does little more than sustain an unsustainable system. Instead, such a movement seeks to rebuild "from the rubble that is all around" (Klein 2007, 589), appearing as a phoenix from the ashes of both acute and ongoing disasters. These experiments are intensely practical, deeply rooted in local communities, appropriately focused on equitable processes as much as dramatic results, and daringly unafraid to confront authoritarianism with compassion and steadfastness alike. And they have manifested in nearly every disaster zone.

Klein (2007, 589) ends her daunting tome with a brief nod to the power of these "people's reconstruction efforts" that are aimed mainly at "building in resilience" to deal with both current and future crises. Picking up this thread, Rebecca Solnit's 2009 book *A Paradise Built in Hell* investigates (as per its subtitle) "the extraordinary communities that arise in disaster." Prior to this work, Solnit (2007, 72) had already looked at one such community, namely that of the longtime sustainability and social justice advocates in post-industrial Detroit, who rather than seeking to reestablish a relationship with industry sought instead to "create an economy entirely apart from the transnational webs of corporations and petroleum." Others have taken up this sensibility, observing that the alternative to perpetual crises and climate-induced disasters is to "radically re-shape the political landscape and build a more just and sustainable society," including the creation of an economic system that goes beyond mere "green consumerism" in favor of one that "addresses the longstanding suffering ordinary people face in their lives" (B. Smith 2010). In the wake of Superstorm Sandy, which devastated large swaths of the northeastern United States in the fall of 2012, activists (many from the Occupy movement that spiked the year before) advocated for a "shift from relief to resistance," working diligently to meet basic needs of food and water, to confront the efforts of disaster profiteers, and to develop "the community power that will eventually be the basis for a real recovery" (Marom 2012).

The key to developing resilient, resistant communities is to create "coupled systems of humans and nature" that possess "the ability to adapt to a changing environment," in the belief that "just as ecosystems undergo phase shifts ... so can neighborhoods, towns, and cities" (Gunderson 2010, 24). The extant studies of these processes, which can serve to simultaneously mitigate climate change while generating adaptive capacity, highlight the best practices of peace ecology. Rejecting the Hobbesian, Malthusian logic of the dominant system, Solnit (2009, 2, 8) finds that the "image of the selfish, panicky, or regressively savage human being in times of disaster has little truth to it," and concludes that instead "the prevalent human nature in disaster is resilient, resourceful, generous, empathetic, and brave." The communities that often develop in response to disasters, both of the natural and man-made variet-ies, embody a spirit of *emergence* in the face of an emergency while at the same time representing "another kind of power" that can supplant the failed structures of the prevailing order through "collaborative, cooperative, and local" processes (Solnit 2009, 10). Surveying a remarkable range of historical and contemporary disasters—from earthquakes in San Francisco (1906) and Mexico City (1985) to New York City after the events of 9/11 and post-Katrina New Orleans—Solnit discerns great potential for post-disaster communities to establish a new way of being in the world altogether:

> The existing system is built on fear of each other and of scarcity, and it has created more scarcity and more to be afraid of. It is mitigated every day by altruism, mutual aid, and solidarity, by the acts of individuals and organizations who are motivated by hope and by love rather than fear.... Disaster reveals what else the world could be like—reveals the strength of that hope, that generosity, and that solidarity.... A world could be built on that basis, and to do so would redress the long divides that produce everyday pain, poverty, and loneliness. (2009, 313)

I was part of grassroots relief efforts in New Orleans shortly after Hurricane Katrina, and saw firsthand this spirit of mutual aid as it served the dual purpose of resisting the impetus of "disaster capitalism" while modeling what hopeful, just communities could be like. Some years after that, I wrote a column for a local newspaper in Arizona posing the rhetorical question: "Why does it take a disaster for us to meet our neighbors?" When solidarity efforts appear to spontaneously arise in the wake of a catastrophe, it often catches us off guard, as if we expected either the Hobbesian narrative to reify or the powers that be to have all the answers. Yet in case after case, it is ordinary people who quickly mobilize to form resilient mutual aid communities. Why we are surprised by this tells us more about the society we have created than about human nature; to experience such moments of deep-seated solidarity and compassion reminds us of something far more basic than the news of the day or the political machinations in our midst. Disasters can serve as critical moments in which business as usual is suspended, centering our collective gaze on the inescapable reality that we are all individually vulnerable, collectively strong, and fundamentally interdependent with one another and the larger environment as well.

As it turns out, these attributes are indeed the norm rather than the exception. Looking at natural disasters around the world—including the 1985 Mexico City earthquake, the 2004 tsunami in Asia, and Hurricane Katrina in 2005—Anouk Ride and Diane Bretherton document widespread patterns of "community resilience" in every case they investigated. The hallmarks of these efforts include a focus not only on "bouncing back" but on "bouncing forward" so that weaknesses exposed by the disaster are addressed; a sense of "shared humanity" that manifests in "gifts of food, water, clothing, shelter, and helping each other rebuild"; and the perception of a "common threat" that encourages "peaceful relations between people" (Ride and Bretherton 2011, 6, 174, 191). These are not static utopian visions set in idyllic landscapes but rather complex human associations that continually evolve as conditions change; this is what makes these post-disaster communities so resilient, namely that they are adaptive, process-oriented, pragmatic, and visionary. Such displays of community resilience are found *everywhere*, constituting the "usual story" despite the media's tendency to report otherwise and the desire of authorities to centralize relief efforts through established, top-down "command and control" networks (Ride and Bretherton 2011, 171, 177). Deeper truths are revealed in these moments:

> Peace and natural disasters are linked at each stage of a community's response to the crisis. The response of a community to a natural disaster can become a "peace litmus test" to indicate the level of positive peace in a community, for it tells us how a community deals with crisis—whether peaceful cooperation between community members is evident, whether the community is inclusive or exclusive with regard to others in need, whether there are underlying disagreements that newly surface at a time of stress, and whether the community can adapt and learn from the experience. (Ride and Bretherton 2011, 10)

In 2007, the Worldwatch Institute published a report titled *Beyond Disasters: Creating Opportunities for Peace* (Renner and Chafe 2007). Again looking at earthquakes, hurricanes, and tsunamis, the report's authors discerned a "silver lining" in the potential for peace to develop through the recognition of shared hardships, the experience of common needs, and the disruption of the usual political landscape (Renner and Chafe 2007, 17). "Disasters have the potential to unite people from opposing sides around a common goal," serving as a possible "door-opener" that allows even adversarial parties "to meet and build the trust necessary to discuss grievances and political issues" (Renner and Chafe 2007, 18). These prospects mirror those found in the "environmental peacemaking" framework, which will be discussed at length in the following chapters—with the basic premise being that shared environmental challenges (including prior degradation that often exacerbates a disaster, and restoration efforts afterward) can spur wider forms of cooperation and enhance the potential for peace across a range of actors and conditions. In the context of disasters there is often a confluence of factors at work—including preexisting sociopolitical inequalities and environmental degradation as well as the overarching processes of global climate change—that can serve to link critical issues together and potentially yield a "peace" that is not piecemeal.

Meeting the Challenge

What we can take from all of this is threefold. First, without courting or fetishizing catastrophes, there are undoubtedly profound lessons to be learned from the resilient communities that rise up to meet the acute challenges found everywhere. Second, these mobilizations may be imperfect and are oftentimes transient, but they provide a template for envisioning strategies that are both mitigative and adaptive in the face of global disasters that are increasing in their frequency and severity. Third, by highlighting these exemplars we come to appreciate more deeply how every crisis is also an opportunity, representing a fork in the road that compels us to choose whether conflict or cooperation will ensue. Ultimately, as the next chapter articulates, we are squarely presented with this critical challenge: to live together in peace and within the planet's capacities.

Chapter Six
Resource Conflicts, or Sustainable Collaborations?

Conflicts over resources have persisted for centuries, perhaps even millennia, and by some accounts they are reaching a fever pitch in the present era of globalization. Whereas in the Cold War period most of the competition for resources was limited to a small number of global hegemons, today we are seeing not only those nations but a host of up-and-coming powers scouring the world for access to and control of resources including oil, gas, water, arable land (and thus the capacity to produce food), timber, gems, metals, and rare-earth minerals. Many of these items are considered essential resources for human survival, although it is debatable whether any beyond food, water, and perhaps energy are truly indispensable. Still, perceived value and connectivity to modern conveniences are in themselves enough of an impetus to spur many nations and private enterprises to vie for control of resources. Such a global contest is now pushing into every nook and cranny of the planet—from the arctic regions being steadily unearthed by ice melt due to climate change, to the equatorial regions that hold much of the world's remaining biodiversity. Scholar Michael Klare (2012a) has termed this "the race for what's left"—and increasingly it appears to be shaping up as race with no winners and a lost planet.

In Chapter One we looked at both the scarcity and abundance of natural resources as critical factors in defining the pitfalls and possibilities inherent in these patterns of acquisition and control. In the subsequent chapters we investigated specific aspects of these issues, focusing on basic materials and alternative socioeconomic arrangements as they have been applied by various communities. Here, we will enlarge the inquiry to consider the nature of the resources themselves, the types of conflicts and regimes of control that exist around them, and some of the key examples of these phenomena that are likely to dominate the discourse in the years ahead. We will also explore potential solutions to the problem of "resource wars," most significantly the ways in which resource scarcity can actually be a springboard toward peace, as well as the manner in which environmental cooperation can spark broader peace initiatives between even hostile parties. Ultimately, we will consider how the collective war humankind appears to be waging against the earth itself can be turned into a collaborative framework consistent with the tenets of peace ecology as we have been tracing their development throughout this volume.

The dominant paradigm often represents a feedback loop in which perceived resource degradation (or the value associated with abundance) leads to conflict and warfare, which further depletes available resources and yields more conflict, and so on. This vicious cycle is exacerbated by the inherently destructive impact of warfare on the environment, as well as the ways in which conflicts around the globe may be initiated or prolonged by access to resources. Hence, one of the peace ecologist's tasks is to develop alternatives to help break this cycle, by highlighting examples of cooperative resource management and collaborative efforts to sustain human communities and natural systems alike. Such a framework includes within its ambit various local and regional systems of resource sharing across the globe, especially those that work simultaneously to mitigate environmental degradation and violent conflict. The illustrations and examples considered here suggest the viability of a potential shift from the political economy of conflict to a peaceful ecology of collaboration. But in order to envision workable solutions to such a protracted problem, we must first deepen our understanding of what has gone wrong.

The War for More

The relationship between conflict and the environment has been well explored in the literature, and it is widely accepted that ecological factors such as resource acquisition, droughts and other forms of scarcity, and the ravages of climate change are potentially connected with the appearance of violence if not outright war. Indeed, it is generally presumed by many scholars and policymakers alike that the world will be wracked by competition and conflict over dwindling resources, increasingly intensified by the environmental challenges in our midst. The resultant *resource wars*, as Klare (2002, 213) presciently discerned at the dawn of the millennium, are likely to be "fought over the possession and control of vital economic goods—especially resources needed for the functioning of modern industrial societies. . . . Resource wars will become, in the years ahead, the most distinctive feature of the global security environment." Despite the recent surge in interest, the concept of environmentally induced wars is not new; for instance, speculations about the fate of early desert dwellers in the southwestern United States have long included such notions, including that conflict was triggered by drought as well as the isolationism brought on by regional environmental stresses after a period of rapid growth. Historical accounts and future projections alike suggest that resource wars will remain a significant challenge.

In fact, the issue is even more pressing than that: *resource control* is becoming a dominant impetus of the military-industrial complex, with US foreign policy documents explicitly citing this as a primary strategic battleground in the coming decades. In its 2008 Army Modernization Strategy document, the US military specifically foretold a global near-future of "perpetual warfare," "persistent conflict," and "resource competition" over items including "food, water, and energy" (Clonan 2008). We are today seeing that worldview harden through the conflation of "national security" with "energy security" (Sanders 2009, 33), among other factors, even as the operational validity and purported inevitability of the resource conflict paradigm is being critically reassessed by scholars and researchers from a broad array of disciplines and perspectives (e.g., Dinar, ed. 2011). While there is a great need for the articulation of alternative models of resource allocation that do not necessitate militarism and despoliation, it appears that at least in the near future the field is likely to remain dominated by the conflict-oriented perspective. As Klare (2002, 9, 14) has observed, "while the military can do little to promote trade or enhance financial stability, it *can* play a key role in protecting resource supplies. . . . For almost every country in the world, the pursuit or protection of essential materials has become a paramount feature in national security planning." Ostensibly confirming this sentiment, President Barack Obama boldly asserted before the United Nations in September 2013, with regard to US policies vis-à-vis the Middle East:

> The United States of America is prepared to use all elements of our power, including military force, to secure our core interests in the region. We will ensure the free flow of energy from the region to the world. Although America is steadily reducing our own dependence on imported oil, the world still depends on the region's energy supply and a severe disruption could destabilize the entire global economy. (Washington Post Staff 2013)

Despite its predictive capacities and influential bearing, Klare's analysis is also noteworthy for its pessimistic "realism" and its penchant for validating the scarcity-conflict paradigm that, as we have seen and will explore more below, is only part of the equation. Nonetheless, there have been compelling accounts in recent years that support the resource wars thesis, including Geoff Hiscock's *Earth Wars* and its main argument that resource conflict flashpoints are everywhere due to increasing demands and dwindling supplies, triggered in large measure by the rise of numerous consumer nations—including most notably China and India, but also up-and-comers like Indonesia, Brazil, and Mexico—on the global stage. "That is why," Hiscock (2012, 2) writes, "the great battle for control of the world's resources is well and truly underway." For his part, Klare has confirmed and updated his genre-defining thesis, arguing that both governmental and corporate actors (oftentimes in concert) recognize that existing reserves of the planet's raw materials are being rapidly depleted, and thus have "embarked on an extended, calculated drive to gain control over the world's remaining preserves of vital natural resources"—and most disturbingly, these entities are willing "to put in place whatever measures are needed in the coming decades" to expand and secure their resource bases (2012a, 12–15).

There are other salient factors at work here as well, including that "recurring conflict over resources will also squander vast quantities of critical materials—especially oil—and cause significant damage to key sources of supply" (Klare 2002, 222–223), further exacerbating the problem and contributing to even more conflict. This point has been echoed by others noting that "wars fought to retain precious environmental resources would probably destroy them in the process" (e.g., Lanier-Graham 1993, 132). Oil well fires, gas flares, sabotage of pipelines, leakages, and excessive military consumption of fuels and other resources are all part of a pattern in which resource wars start to look more like wars *on* resources than *for* them. All too often, a conflict will be waged for control of some territory and/or its riches, only to find the landscape denuded in the process and the full value of the resources accordingly squandered. The old expression reflecting upon "the spoils of war" contains an unfortunate linguistic truism: to the victor literally go the *spoils*. Conquest may prop up certain interests, but the net gain in terms of overall wealth creation can be minimal—perhaps even a net loss—when all inputs are tallied.

Oil in particular represents a critical touchstone for global conflict. Indeed, are there any two concepts in the realm of contemporary geopolitics more closely associated than oil and warfare? As the primary lubricant of the global economy, oil earns special status as a *sine qua non* of our profligate modern lifestyles and simultaneously as an overt security interest that triggers military mobilizations. We know about Iraq, of course, but the world is brimming with potential sites of future conflict over black gold, from the Arctic to Western Africa and across the Caribbean shelf. It might be said that wherever there is oil there is war, or at least the seeds of conflict over this singular resource; as Michael Watts (2004, 273) has opined, "where oil reigns supreme the military is sure to follow." For example, in the early 2000s it was argued in some quarters that West African oil (in particular from the Niger Delta) should be a priority for US national security, citing factors including potential terrorism there as reasons for heightened interest (Watts 2004, 274). A decade later, it was announced that there would be "a growing American [military] presence in west Africa," including stationing troops in Niger and establishing a base there for unmanned aerial drones (Williams 2013). The new millennium has shown that many nations will do almost anything in their power to control as much of the world's remaining oil supplies as possible—either through direct military interventions, by escalating its enterprises in sensitive environmental areas, or simply by legislative fiat as a matter of national security. There is nothing light or sweet about any of this; it is almost wholly crude.

The tally of central oil hot spots is growing with each passing day, as new technologies of discovery and extraction map the farthest reaches of the earth, the depths of the ocean floors, and even the inner realms of mountains and rocks. Powerful multinational interests seem determined to extract every last drop of refinable petroleum from the planet before considering the vigorous pursuit of adequate substitutes. In truth, oil will be difficult to replace straightforwardly, requiring alterations in basic infrastructure from pipelines to engines. And yet, the best estimates of credible science indicate that it would be catastrophic for human life on earth to burn more than about a quarter of the known petroleum reserves, as the talismanic carbon threshold of "350 parts per million" in the atmosphere (e.g., Rockström et al. 2009) would cause irreversible (and potentially runaway) climatic shifts. Such doomsday scenarios have been moving from the realms of speculative fiction and activist alarmism to the fore of popular consciousness—but the oil wars still rage and the drills keep pressing. This state of affairs prompted Klare (2012b) to issue a dire warning that "key state actors will be more likely to employ force" to control remaining oil and gas reserves, representing "the conviction of ruling elites around the world" that such efforts are essential to prop up their "wealth, power, and prestige."

Specific conflict zones include Sudan (north/south split between oil producers and pipeline routes), the South China Sea (numerous countries making claims to untapped deposits), the Falkland Islands (Argentina and Britain, previous warring nations in the 1980s, vying for massive deposits), and Iran (control of the Strait of Hormuz through which a third of the world's tradable oil passes daily) (Klare 2012b). In the case of the latter, the United States is continually engaged in multiple forms of saber rattling, including building up military forces in the Persian Gulf. Aside from acute hot spots, there are continual conflict situations, such as in Nigeria, where people have seen their ecosystems and livelihoods destroyed by decades of oil extraction—including spills, flares, and water contamination—resulting in widespread political dislocation and human deprivation as a result of the clamor for resource control (Babatunde 2010). In North America, a pitched political contest has been engaged by activists over the massive Keystone XL pipeline that is slated to bring oil from Canada's "tar sands" fields—the extraction of which is difficult and dirty—to refineries in Texas. While the United States and Canada enjoy generally peaceful relations, this example indicates that conflicts over oil are not merely between nations, but (as in the Niger Delta) sometimes look more like low-level wars waged on people and habitats alike.

Two cases in particular merit further attention for their uniquely integrative aspects as illustrations of the complexity of the problem. The first is Afghanistan, notable of course for the decade-plus-long US occupation of the country, constituting the longest continuous war in US history. As Klare (2012a, 138–139) has observed, "Afghanistan has long been known to harbor significant reserves of valuable minerals ... estimated to be worth well more than $1 trillion." In 2010 the Pentagon confirmed these estimates, noting in particular the potential presence of huge veins of gold, iron, copper, lead, and zinc, as well as significant amounts of rare-earth minerals that are used in the production of myriad digital devices and computer systems—prompting the conclusion that Afghanistan could become "the Saudi Arabia of lithium" (Risen 2010). (Lithium is a lightweight element used in many rechargeable battery systems.) Apart from the difficulties with mining these resources in a war-torn country, there is the larger issue of how the war in Afghanistan has utterly decimated the environment and people there: it is estimated that over three-quarters of the population live without adequate water and sanitation, and there has been a concomitant rise in pollution and deforestation while biodiversity is diminishing (Vidal 2010).

The other revealing case is the arctic region, which was long considered a frozen wasteland but "is now believed to harbor vast deposits of oil, natural gas, and valuable minerals—resources that will become increasingly accessible as global warming melts the polar ice cap" (Klare 2012a, 2). Hence, problematically, it is the larger frame of climate change (itself a driver of potential conflict, as detailed in Chapter Five) that makes possible greater exploitation of arctic resources, and unsurprisingly this has yielded a new locus of geopolitical conflict in the process. The Arctic has drawn the interest of the world's biggest energy companies and may contain the largest untapped reserves of oil and gas on the planet, prompting territorial claims by nations including Russia, the United States, Canada, Norway, Denmark, and Greenland. In 2007 Russia planted a titanium flag at the North Pole to indicate its claim, but this has not resolved the issue by any means (Hiscock 2012, 33). In fact the opposite has been the case, with tensions likely to continue rising as the full potential valuation of the Arctic's resource reserves become clearer. This prompted Russian Prime Minister Vladimir Putin to call for the Arctic to remain a "zone of peace and cooperation" (de Carbonnel 2010)—even as it is readily apparent that this flies in the face of the dominant order in which every player "will do whatever it can to advance its own position, while striving without mercy to eliminate or subdue all the others" (Klare 2012a, 215).

Without overstating the point, since at least the advent of industrialization it appears that humanity has made a Faustian bargain that renders us the enemies of the earth in order to survive, as the oil wars indicate. Notions of complementarity and sustainability have been supplanted by consumption and separation instead, constituting "a product of artificial divisions within humanity, alienating us from the material-natural conditions of our existence and from succeeding generations" (Foster, Clark, and York 2010, 7). The cruel joke is that our willingness to continually flout nature yields a perpetual state of scarcity and requires a regular doubling-down on the very same logic that made things scarce in the first place. Thus, in order to extend the life of the petroleum economy and provide the massive energy inputs that we rely upon, we have to drill deeper and squeeze harder to procure the substance at ever-increasing financial and environmental costs in the process (to wit, the devastating Deepwater Horizon oil spill in the Gulf of Mexico in 2010). This literal sense of "diminishing returns" is compounded by the attendant toll exacted on our collective health from fossil fuels, as well as the concomitant stratification of wealth and power that subverts the potential of democracy. Massive spills and other calamities are part and parcel of this normalization of a warlike attitude toward nature (and thus ourselves), and are blithely considered little more than business as usual by global elites.

As Isaac Asimov once said, "It is not only the living who are killed in war." Cherished ideals, future generations, hopefulness, the earth itself—all are among war's many casualties. Grasping the self-fulfilling nature of resource wars may be the first real step toward peace, both among ourselves and with the environment. Yet while oil may be special for its role in the global economy, it is certainly not alone in triggering conflict. Thinking more deeply about the nature of resources and various criteria for their use and control is necessary for a fuller accounting of the scope of the problem, as well as for imagining and implementing equally robust solutions.

Control, Dependency, and Resource Typologies

Regimes of control tend to inculcate patterns of dependency; this is particularly the case when control devolves upon essential items for which open-access substitutes are not readily available. In most developed (and developing) societies, the vast majority of people are no longer able to procure basic items such as food and water for themselves or their communities, without reliance upon powerful interests for energy inputs, transportation routes, marketplaces, and computerized systems of accounting. This generates high levels of vulnerability among the populace, as the condition of their existence requires either tacit complicity with or begrudging acceptance of this state of affairs. Control of essential and valuable materials, in this light, is not merely a global competition among national and corporate elites; it is more about the manner in which the union of these elite interests imposes its will on the remainder of the population by forcing the masses, in essence, to pay fealty to their overlords for the privilege of survival. This neo-feudal globalized system of resource control is not a matter of conjecture but is rapidly materializing with the "race for what's left"—and it is reinforced through numerous methods of subsidization that require the public to foot the bill for their own subjugation.

Subsidies to extractive industries (drawn from public funds in most instances) are legion: road construction in remote areas; licenses for rights of access granted at little or no cost; tax credits and abatements; transportation and telecommunications infrastructure; military and governmental contracts for raw materials and finished products; exemption from public safety and environmental laws; lobbyist access to policymakers; lax regulation of industrial processes and labor practices; lack of accountability for corporate officers; and the use of military forces in order to secure access to and markets for resources. In the case of the latter, exemplified by the US invasion of Iraq and the myriad no-bid contracts secured by commercial interests, the cost to taxpayers has been exorbitant, with the *Wall Street Journal* estimating the final tally at $4 trillion (Hinton 2011). The argument that resource control is essential to national security rings hollow in light of record corporate profits coupled with depressed home-front economies, and is at best paradoxical since the more that resources are controlled by elite interests the less secure the people are in their capacities to provide for themselves and their communities. In the end, we come to see in short order that no one can be secure unless everyone enjoys a sense of security.

Not all resources are created equally, of course. The accumulated insights from the literature suggest that a number of typological factors are relevant in determining the conditions under which a given resource is likely to yield patterns of control and conflict of the sort we have been investigating. In each category there is a range, but with discernible poles as well. For instance, the primary factor for any resource is its *necessity*, ranging from absolutely essential (food, water) to luxury consumption (diamonds, rare-earth elements); timber and metals would fall somewhere in the middle leaning toward one side or another depending on the context. Related to necessity is the *renewability* of a given resource, with those able to regenerate quickly (soils, freshwater) contrasted with those (oil, gas) that are essentially viable only on a one-time basis. This further suggests a *temporality* factor for resources, ranging from those with short or long spans of durability, which often correlates with a sense of *usability* in terms of the relative ease of turning the raw material into something fit for human consumption. Food, of course, is quite easy to convert and is obviously a long-term resource; uranium, on the other hand, is extremely difficult to transform into energy and once used is not going to be quickly replenished.

There are additional typological factors that figure specifically into the impetus of a given resource to trigger potential conflicts, violence, or outright warfare. Among these are *lootability* (relative ease of being controlled and transported, either by elite interests or insurgent entities), *locality* (compliant versus hostile terrains, such as open prairies versus polar regions), *concentration* (whether the resource exists diffusely or is focused at a particular point), *marketability* (the economic potential, either in raw form or finished products), and *scalability* (highly situated unique resources versus those existing globally). Other items to consider in this calculus include the political system in place where the resource is located, the ideologies and mythologies of the people living there, the legal and institutional frameworks in existence, the military capacity of those staking a claim to the resource, the personal attributes of the key actors including authority figures, and the structural conditions of the given society. The voluminous literature on these issues yields a complex picture in which predicting when conflict will ensue over a particular resource in a particular place is problematic at best. Indeed, such attempts at linearity and causality may even be superfluous, since it is the accumulated mindset of competition among ourselves and our collective exploitation of the earth that tells the tale.

This sophisticated set of processes is part and parcel of capitalism—the ultimate extractive industry, after all—and contributes to what Tina Evans (2012) describes as a condition of "enforced dependency" to indicate both the commercial and militaristic aspects of the problem. The value ascribed to the resources we have come to be dependent upon is not inherent in the items themselves, but in the social constructions of desire, need, and greed attendant to them (Le Billon 2001, 563). We may cloud these values by thinking in terms of "consumer goods," but they are in large measure undeniably *bad*, for people and the environment alike—leading to the emergent realization that the global economy itself can be viewed as a major contributor to violent conflict (cf. Smith and Verdeja, eds. 2013). The innocent, mundane purchases we make are akin to faintly ticking time bombs, spin-offs of the same forces that produce military hardware, embedded with the nonrenewable resources that drive global conflict and climate change, taxing our health into skyrocketing maintenance costs, and in the process rendering us utterly dependent on and essentially complicit with the forces of destruction. Insidiously, wherever such regimes of control exist, so too does a stratification of wealth and power (Le Billon 2001, 567)—whether it is local elites decimating their own populations in resource-rich locales, elected officials in consumer-oriented nations undermining democracy through patronage, transnational corporate interests enjoying profits in the face of financial austerity, or well-armed nations plying open access to weaker ones.

These are profound questions of justice, and in a world where they are rarely considered in the public dialogue the results are potentially disastrous. From gross inequity often arises conflict; from deprivation and desperation can spring violence and even terrorism; from powerlessness and habituation can come apathy to the violence being inflicted on others. In this manner, we come to see resource control as more than merely a geopolitical phenomenon that pits nation against nation or corporation against corporation; it is the elite global interests taken as a whole that are exerting control over the planet and people alike, creating a system of profound dependency and vulnerability that is increasingly immune to any accountability. It would be an oversimplification to posit this as simply "elites versus the masses" since there are certainly gradations within this spectrum in terms of socioeconomics, but at the level of global resource acquisition and control, the poles on this continuum tend to harden more in terms of who actually has the capacity and infrastructure to access, extract, and securitize basic resources. Even in the face of public demand for greater equalization, profit margins often mold political will.

This is a grim accounting but is one that arises from a fair reading of the situation, as discerned by many careful scholars and dedicated activists alike. The central question, as always, and in particular for the promotion of peace ecology as a viable alternative, is what is to be done about it? In the preceding chapters we have already seen how people and communities are moving toward reclaiming common pool systems and relative autonomy regarding basic resources, doing so even (or especially) in the face of acute disasters. These constitute powerful innovations that run counter to the dominant control-conflict paradigm, and their presence provides a solid grounding for a renewed sense of optimism in a time of mounting crises. Moving beyond local manifestations of such alternatives is a challenging task in light of the geopolitics of resource control and the global implications of climate change, depletion, militarism, and the like. In the balance of this chapter, we will explore the macroscopic potential for resource issues and environmental challenges to promote more cooperative, egalitarian, and peaceful outcomes. The aim is to transcend resource conflict in favor of collaborative models.

Rethinking Conflict, Sustaining Peace

Despite the potency of the resource conflict perspective, a competing narrative has begun to emerge that looks more deeply at the positive potentials embedded in the peace-environment nexus. With the connectivity having been validated through the conflict-degradation lens, we can surmise that an equally potent set of outcomes might be fostered by highlighting the peace prospects of environmentalism, and likewise the environmental benefits of peaceful relations among peoples and nations. Indeed, this is a primary purpose of peace ecology, to analyze concepts including resource sharing, peace cooperatives, and "just sustainabilities" (Agyeman et al. 2003a) that link social and ecological factors together in a manner that emphasizes their mutually reinforcing potential for peace. As we come to understand the interrelated nature of social and environmental issues, we thus also come to recognize that "no country can achieve sustainability alone," since environmental issues are inherently global in nature (Rees and Westra, 2003, 119); in a rapidly globalizing system, "the increased interconnection of the biophysical world" is becoming increasingly evident, and thus "requires that adaptation to challenges occur at multiple levels" (Dolšak et al. 2003, 338).

This sense of deep-seated interrelatedness is central to peace ecology, with the ultimate aim being the cultivation of a perspective that unites the human-human and human-environment interfaces in a substantive manner. It would be facile to assume that some magical process will emerge that delivers peace on our collective doorstep; such a transition will be possible only through tangible actions, hard work, open-mindedness, and above all a willingness to change. It is tempting to conclude that such a transition could be triggered by a crisis or even the collapse of existing structures, but as the previous chapter has indicated this is a dubious prospect. More to the point is that we have the capacity—informed by ongoing empirical research and shifting sensibilities alike—to purposefully point our collective enterprise in another direction. Reorienting our societies away from perpetual conflict, environmental exploitation, and gross inequalities is a matter of will; moving to a paradigm of sustainability is something that we can—and must—choose, irrespective of what powerful interests are seeking to impose upon us.

Peace ecology calls upon us to reclaim these powers of "collective auton-omy" and to establish peace itself as the primary commodity that is most in need of being sustained. We can declare peace on a planetary scale—with each other and the earth, in the present and for the future—by minimiz-ing our reliance upon conflict-laden materials, equalizing the distribution of resources and opportunities, democratizing political arrangements from the local to international scales, restoring life's essentials to their status as the common repository of humankind as a whole, and reestablishing our place within the larger environment that sustains our existence. Again, this isn't magic or wishful thinking—it is what we must do in order to survive the ravages of this era that we have visited upon ourselves and the habitat. It is not a matter of retrogressive longing for a pristine age or the desire for a transcendent future of evolved humans; we will remain complex, conflictual beings with a penchant for exploration and innovation. This is as it should be, and as it turns out we do not have to make a choice between competition and cooperation, or between conflict and peace. These values are intercon-nected, and in a healthy system it is the tension between them that often adduces our better instincts and capacities.

One caveat to consider in all of this positivity is the tendency to fall back on top-down solutions, since it is often presumed that the problems were created in such a pyramidal manner. For instance, many of the leading articu-lations emphasize the need for corporate social responsibility, better domestic governance, international legal instruments, voluntary commitments by commercial interests, enforcement and sanctions, partnerships between the public and private sectors, developing "green" technologies and environmen-tally friendly industrial (and military) practices, and in general deploying an entrepreneurial spirit (Le Billon 2005, 10, 72, 82; Klare 2012a, 227–234). Still, even in these formulations, it is recognized that such efforts (necessary as they may be, even if perhaps insufficient) can be limited by the role that corporations often play in exacerbating inequalities, undermining democratic governance, impinging upon human rights, and hindering peace processes (Le Billon 2005, 70). While it may be true that it will take the efforts of all constituencies to right the ship in time, we should also be mindful of Audre Lorde's famous and oft-quoted insight that "the master's tools will never dismantle the master's house."

However, by asserting (as we have done here) that "the people" are also complicit with destructive forces and not merely passive bystanders, a space is opened up to consider not only our culpability but our capacity to implement viable solutions as well. It is, in short, a nod to our largely untapped power to manifest alternatives—since the forces of exploitation are reliant upon our participation, and thus are beholden to us more than we are to them. The task, then, is to reorient our politics and practices toward the needs of actual people, their communities, and the ongoing viability of the resources that sustain them. As fortune would have it, a multitude of inspiring examples of peace ecology in action indicate that we already know how to do this.

Environmental Cooperation and Collaboration

In the new millennium, a plethora of case studies and analyses have emerged around the broad concept of *environmental cooperation*, constituting an emerging body of knowledge and experience about the potential for the environment to serve as an impetus toward peace, and for peace to become a basis for preserving and sustaining the environment. These works suggest that there are a number of interrelated bases for thinking about cooperative and collaborative efforts regarding environmental issues, with the chief categories being those methods that apply to conflicts *about* the environment (e.g., resource wars) and conflicts about other issues that might be resolved *through* the environment (e.g., border disputes). Examples of the former generally fall under the heading of *environmental dispute resolution*, while the latter are sometimes referred to as aspects of *environmental peacemaking* or *environmental peacebuilding*. While the line between these categories can be blurry (for instance, environmental peacemaking could apply in both the *about* and *through* contexts), the lesson to be derived from them is clear: environmental issues need not be sources of conflict, but can instead be potent bases for peace.

The first systematic articulation of environmental peacemaking was developed in Ken Conca and Geoffrey Dabelko's influential 2002 book by that name, where a serious attempt was made to adduce precisely how environmental cooperation can help forestall conflict and preserve peace. Rather than relying upon anecdotal evidence or lofty desires, the argument proceeded from a call for concrete interventions, seeking to avoid well-meaning generalizations by articulating two necessary elements for environmental peacemaking to have traction: (1) "it must create minimum levels of trust, transparency, and cooperative gain among governments that are strongly influenced by a zero-sum logic of national security," and (2) "it must lay the foundation for transforming the national-security state itself, which is too often marked by dysfunctional institutions and practices that become further obstacles to peaceful coexistence and cooperation" (2002, 10–11). The operative principle is that an environmental crisis or conflict can be transformed into an opportunity for peace when it can be demonstrated that there is more to be gained by cooperating than competing, and when the essence of peaceful cooperation transcends the interests and aims of nation-states that are generally focused on security as a function of resource control. This work includes examples of collaborative environmentalism in the Baltic region, South Asia, the Aral Sea Basin, Southern Africa, the Caspian Sea area, and the US-Mexico border (which we will explore further in the next chapter). One of the quintessential examples cited is the cooperative relationship between India and Pakistan concerning the shared Indus River basin, even as these nations have been on the verge of war (Swain 2002, 61–62).

An important caveat from this line of inquiry is that we cannot rely upon generalized suggestions that environmental cooperation somehow yields peace in general. Rather, the authors (and subsequent analyses in the field) have attempted "to pinpoint the cooperative triggers of peace that shared environmental problems might make available" (Conca and Dabelko 2002, 5). Among these "cooperative triggers" are concepts including trust-building, transparency, reciprocity, mutual benefits, shared essential resources, habituation to cooperation, open lines of communication, and long-range thinking among the actors involved. Taking these factors together, the central questions become "whether environmental cooperation can generate movement along the peace continuum, rendering violent conflict less likely or less imaginable," and "whether environmental cooperation can be an effective general catalyst for reducing tensions, broadening cooperation, fostering demilitarization, and promoting peace" (Conca and Dabelko 2002, 9). At present, while the early returns are promising, more research remains to be undertaken in order to fully understand how and why environmental cooperation can yield peace.

In his seminal work on peace parks, Saleem Ali (2007, 3) likewise emphasized the positive sense of peace ecology by exploring "how environmental issues can play a role in cooperation—regardless of whether they are part of the original conflict." Examining a range of international conservation efforts, Ali (2007, 6) posited that "positive exchanges and trust-building gestures are a consequence of realizing common environmental threats," and that "a focus on common environmental harms (or aversions) is psychologically more successful in leading to cooperative outcomes than focusing on common interests (which may lead to competitive behavior)." This work sought to bring together strands of environmentalism, conflict resolution, psychology, and resource management in a manner that anticipated what peace ecology continues to work toward. While peace parks and similar conservationist initiatives are not without their critiques (including that they can displace indigenous people and subsistence users of biodiverse areas), a growing list of transboundary conservation efforts is being compiled by organizations such as the Peace Parks Foundation (www.peaceparks.org), which is seeking to establish a network of protected areas linking ecosystems across international borders.

Drawing together environmental issues and conflict analysis, Richard Matthew and Ted Gaulin (2002, 39) observed (in the aftermath of the events of 9/11) that "the environment even appears to be relevant to the recent terrorist attacks on the United States, as research . . . has shown that in Pakistan environmental degradation is a significant source of political instability." Seeking methods for bridging environmentalism and peacemaking, the authors concluded that

> it is widely accepted in the environmental community that conservation measures and programs geared towards sustainable development may reduce the likelihood of violence and help preserve conditions of peace. For example, protecting the environment can eliminate a growing cause (scarcity) of social tension and dissatisfaction. It can relieve pressure on other conflict-inducing social variables such as poverty and population

flows. It can serve as a topic that can bring diverse parties into the same room for discussion and confidence-building. (2002, 36)

These insights highlight the ways in which real-world conflicts can be driven by resource issues, as well as how environmental preservation efforts can encourage parties to surmount such outcomes.

As these treatments indicate, the unique interdependence of humankind on the environment can yield advantages for all participants through the cooperative management of natural resources. This potential for environmental conflicts to create opportunities for peace is enhanced by the fact that environmental issues do not abide national borders, and often require long-range planning with the active participation of deeply rooted communities as well as civil society organizations. The shared management of resources both among and within nations can be seen as a crucial aspect of peacebuilding that has often been omitted from the analysis of how to confront our present crises—even as it is now entering the dialogue with greater rigor (e.g., with the nexus of researchers and policymakers found at www .environmentalpeacebuilding.org). In short, environmental issues transcend humankind's narrow divisions and connect us back to the underlying reality of a shared existence in a finite, fragile, interlinked world. Broadening the conversation in ways that will be explored further in Chapter Eight, we can consider frames of analysis including the *ecological* ("earth interconnects"), the *ethical* ("earth equalizes"), the *economic* ("earth sustains"), and the *spiritual* ("earth heals"). Summarizing the potential inherent in these frames, Alexander Carius has observed:

As a mechanism for peace, the environment has some useful, perhaps even unique qualities that are well suited for peacebuilding and conflict resolution. Environmental problems ignore political borders. They require a long-term perspective, encourage participation by local and non-governmental organizations, help build administrative, economic and social capacities for action and facilitate the creation of commonalities that transcend the polarization caused by economic relations.... As environmental cooperation develops and societal and political stakeholders are systematically integrated in negotiation processes to protect natural goods, a simultaneous thrust is given to building trust, initiating cooperative action and encouraging the creation of a common regional identity emerging from sharing resources. It also helps establish mutually recognized rights and expectations. (2006, 63)

One of the more intriguing implications of this line of thought is that environmental issues simultaneously evoke qualities of both *dependence* and *interdependence*. As to the former, it is incontrovertible that human beings are dependent upon environmental resources to survive; this basic fact, as we have seen, can trigger competition and conflict if viewed in Malthusian terms. When we introduce the latter notion of interdependency, however, the mutualistic nature of our relationship to the environment and to one another through the environment is highlighted, opening up the prospect of moving from conflict to cooperation. From the example of India and Pakistan noted above, we come to see that it is possible for even hostile parties to develop a sense of concomitant mutual obligations and interests when it comes to negotiating over scarce, essential resources—not by force or wishful thinking, but because conjoined reliance on the environment can often yield an easier path to cooperation than political, economic, or cultural apparatuses. And this in turn can "spill over to help the countries in the region build the mutual trust necessary to address other traditional issues of dispute" (Swain 2002, 81). This central question of "spillover effects" lies at the heart of the environmental cooperation paradigm, and while empirical inquiry is still in its relatively early stages, there is no downside to pursuing a world in which environmental issues "create opportunities to build peace, lessen ecological insecurity, and break out of the zero-sum logic that so often dominates interstate relations" (Conca and Dabelko 2002, 17).

This constitutes a basis for *collaboration*, which we may take as "the collective integration of interests throughout decision-making processes" (Tanner et al. 2007, 196). Collaborative decisional models are based on respect, communication, and mutually beneficial outcomes, and are aligned with environmental peacebuilding as proactive methods for preventing conflicts. In moving from soft notions of environmental cooperation as merely a "good idea" toward more grounded processes and applications, it is crucial to consider that all of the keystone issues—from scarcity and abundance to conflict and cooperation—are the product of human decisions. People living in proximity to one another, and to the materials that sustain them, are faced with myriad choices about how to negotiate with their neighbors and navigate their terrains in ways that are conducive to positive outcomes. For instance, one of the more successful peace parks was forged out of an armed conflict between Ecuador and Peru; the resultant peace treaty signed in 1995 specifically cited "conservation measures" as part of the overall resolution of the larger conflict (Ali 2007, 9). In 1998, the Cordillera del Condor Peace Transborder Reserve was established in a section of rainforest on the border (Clayton 2004): "Where for decades the two nations had fired periodic artillery barrages at each other along this disputed section of border land, the two now co-manage a park." As Ali (2007, 15) has argued, it is thus possible to envision a robust framework in which "collective environmental protection [serves] as a means of conflict resolution"; one of the ways of manifesting this is to recognize that conflict can actually be beneficial by encouraging "new thinking and innovative problem solving" when the right conditions and mechanisms are present (Matthew, Brklacich, and McDonald 2004, 6).

An intriguing rubric for engaging these issues is sometimes referred to as *environmental dispute resolution* (EDR). Championed by figures including James Caplan, EDR begins with the premise that the greatest ecological threat facing humankind is not degradation or destabilization, but rather "the intractability of our environmental disputes and our collective lack of *will* and *skill* to resolve them" (Caplan 2010a, 7; emphases in original). EDR acknowledges that humans will often compete over the environment and its resources, but envisions equally robust opportunities for peacemaking at both the human-human and human-environment interfaces: "Environmental peace means creating harmony between people and nature and among the people who live with nature" (Caplan 2010a, 25). The practice of EDR draws upon methodologies of conflict resolution, mediation, and facilitation from both Western models of justice and indigenous systems that "often deal with disputants holistically, engaging conflicts fully as [extensions of] people and within the context of their culture and community" (Caplan 2010b, 94). In this sense, EDR is scalable from interpersonal to international disputes, with an emphasis placed upon designing human dispute resolution systems that "emulate natural systems" and that are equally "complex, cooperative,

[and] adaptable" (Caplan 2010a, 151). Human nature may not fundamentally change (i.e., competition and conflict will persist), but human systems can evolve.

As we have seen, natural resources in particular tend to trigger basic instincts toward either conflict or cooperation, due not only to the mutual reliance upon them but also to their "symbolic dimensions" as representative of certain ways of life, ideologies, heritages, histories, mythologies, and even spiritual beliefs (Buckles and Rusnak 2000, 4). Unfortunately, often the same elite interests that wage conflicts over resources also position themselves as the arbiters of conflicts, denying local and regional communities the opportunity to engage in meaningful dialogue over these central issues. When local resource users are able to participate in these efforts, the resultant peace achieved through environmental conservation efforts is likely to be far more durable—as in the case of the Cahuita National Park in Costa Rica, which moved from a top-down model of administration to one that included subsistence users as stakeholders in determining the nature and scope of the project. The collaborative model utilized in this instance, while far from perfect, still contained many of the hallmarks of successful collaboration regarding environmental issues—namely the willingness of actors from a wide range of perspectives to work together; the establishment of trust among stakeholders; broader conceptions of the range of issues involved; and strong community ties to (and even control of) the project (Weitzner and Fonseca Borrás 2000, 140).

Nonetheless, as befits the inherent complexity and dichotomous nature of these issues, other treatments of environmental peacemaking have noted the "failure of 'people-to-people' initiatives" as being more "feel-good" than tangible, arguing instead for more organizational engagement combined with educational efforts as a pathway to success (Zohar, Schoenfeld, and Alleson 2010, 2). In the acute case of the Israeli-Palestinian conflict, the longer-term capacity of educational organizations to engineer authentic "immersion experiences" and to help "forge relationships built on trust" has yielded positive benefits toward overcoming dominant security apparatuses in favor of "an emergent narrative of regional identity based on a common ecology" (Zohar, Schoenfeld, and Alleson 2010, 6). An earlier study of environmental entities bridging Israel and Palestine (Chaitin et al. 2002) found that, while differences in motivations and viewpoints were evident, nongovernmental organizations in the region had some measurable success in cooperatively managing issues including water, pollution, and health; ultiwmately, the disparities in relative power and voice between the respective parties altered their perceptions of the success of these efforts. In exploring the impacts of resource scarcity on small island states (including the quintessential historical example of Easter Island), Matthew and Gaulin (2001) similarly concluded that regional coordination is critical for successful environmental collaboration, coupled with economic exchange and the democratization of decision-making procedures.

In light of the varied examples cited here, it becomes apparent that mechanisms of environmental peacemaking and the like are potentially viable at all scales (local, regional, national, global) and likewise throughout "the entire conflict cycle, from prevention, mitigation, and management to post-conflict peacebuilding" (Parker, Feil, and Kramer 2004, 2). As such, the utility and import of collaborative, cooperative approaches to environmental issues cannot be overstated. As the United Nations Environment Programme (UNEP 2009) has asserted, "integrating [the] environment and natural resources into peacebuilding is no longer an option—it is a security imperative." Indeed, the gravest challenges confronting humankind—including environmental degradation, climate destabilization, maldistribution of resources, and endemic conflict—are directly tied to the principles and practices embedded in the peace ecology paradigm. While the environment-conflict perspective is by now widely recognized, the precise processes for moving to an environment-collaboration framework are less evident, and thus are in need of both policy-oriented development and visionary articulation in order to become a viable alternative to the dominant conflict-laden worldview. As the analysis presented here suggests, there is great promise in the peacemaking perspective on environmental issues, and perhaps nowhere is this more evident than around the most essential natural resource in our midst: *water*.

Spillover Effects

Consistent with the aforementioned notion of environmental efforts "spilling over" into other realms as a pathway toward peace, let us consider (by way of conclusion to this chapter) a topic that will provide the impetus for the discussion in the ensuing chapter. There is an extensive body of literature exploring examples of water sharing across cultural, political, and national boundaries, even under conditions of scarcity that might otherwise seem rife with the potential for conflict. As we saw in Chapter Two with the acequia system, such models exist locally and regionally around the world as well, and indeed many systems of water cooperation are to be found at those levels. There has been a great deal of speculation about why water scarcity, more so than with any other resource, tends to engender cooperation rather than conflict. Some have suggested that water's unique qualities—including its primordial nature and its metaphysical significance—can contribute to more collaborative outcomes. Others take a rationalistic view, arguing that parties sharing water systems often make cost-benefit calculations and conclude that there is more to be gained than lost by cooperating. Either way, the concept of water sharing is a powerful rubric for inquiring as to the nature of peace-building efforts across borders. This is the subject of the next chapter, which begins with reflections on water as a basis for global peace.

＊

CHAPTER SEVEN
TRANSBORDER PEACE ECOLOGY

In this chapter we will further broaden the discussion about the robust connections between ecology and peace by examining conflict resolution efforts
and instances of resource collaboration that function across national borders.
A central notion developed in these examples is that cooperative, cross-border
peace initiatives oftentimes include an environmental component through
which people can work to resolve conflicts, build trust, and sustain the ecological bases of their lives. Among other conflict-ridden "hot spots" around
the world, the US-Mexico border region in particular contains within its
parameters a number of potential transborder environmental initiatives and
peacebuilding opportunities that illustrate the potential inherent in peace
ecology to address some of the planet's most intractable conflicts by promoting international environmental cooperation. The aim will be to elucidate
the patterns and processes that show the greatest promise for mitigating
global conflict, including the ways in which shared resources (and waters in
particular) can serve as a powerful basis for transborder peacemaking.

The Colorado River is one of the most contentious sources of surface
water in the west. Originating from glacial melt in the heart of the Rocky
Mountains, and charting a course through one of the most arid—and visually
stunning—regions of North America, the river reaches its terminus at a delta
in northern Mexico before emptying its waters into the Gulf of California.

Unfortunately, due to the water politics of the region (which includes Las Vegas, Phoenix, and Southern California as major players), nearly every drop of the Colorado is spoken for (Lohan 2009), and since 1960 it has rarely reached the delta on the Mexican side of the border. This has created desert-like conditions in an area that historically had been known for its fertile soils and lush landscapes; the lack of water—both as to quantity and quality—flowing to the Mexican side contravenes a 1944 treaty between the two nations. In late 2012, a promising new agreement was signed between the United States and Mexico to preserve the flow of the river and allocate its waters bi-nationally in a more equitable manner. Observing that this new agreement would go a long way toward ending "water wars" in the region, US Interior Secretary Ken Salazar noted that sharing the Colorado River "makes us one people" (Lovett 2012). (History often tells another story, as with the security-driven concerns that led to the creation of the aptly named "All-American Canal" to bring Colorado River water to Southern California.) Notably, the new agreement expires in 2017, indicating the potential for the river waters to remain in dispute.

The fate of the Colorado is one of many sites of direct environmental contact between the United States and Mexico, with the critical flashpoints often devolving upon shared water resources along the nearly 2000-mile border that cuts a swath across the vast deserts of the American Southwest. From the Tijuana River and its extensive watershed near the Pacific coast, to the Rio Grande that marks nearly a thousand miles of the international border with Texas, the history of US-Mexico environmental management is bound up with water issues, among other factors such as pollution, wastes, and the impacts of human migration. Indeed, as María Rosa García-Acevedo (2001, 57) has observed, "Images of water continually float to the surface of popular discourse" regarding the border—including invocations such as the "waves or tides of illegal immigrants [that] are said to be streaming or flooding across the leaky, porous US-Mexico border." The pervasive allusions to water, coupled with the inescapable reality of having to share it, parallels the global situation in which hundreds of shared river basins link nations together—including in locales where antipathies persist—and constitutes one of the primary loci of international relations as a body of knowledge and a set of working practices for analyzing matters of war and peace.

Throughout the course of this volume, we have been considering how it might be possible to move from a world marked by resource conflict and environmental degradation toward one in which the dominant motifs are collaboration and sustainability. In order to accomplish this transformation, the tenets of peace ecology will necessarily be called upon to apply across national borders. Highlighting examples from around the world, and focusing in particular on the US-Mexico border, this chapter will extend the discussion beyond the local, national, and regional frames that have largely been considered up to this point (for instance, as with the acequia system detailed in Chapter Two). Given its centrality as the basis for all life and the most essential natural resource, water in particular provides an initial basis for exploring these issues concretely, especially in light of its relative scarcity in arid regions such as along the interface between the United States and Mexico. As the analysis proceeds, we will explore more fully how transborder environmental and peacebuilding efforts can take hold, and how the two paths converge through peace ecology—with water issues serving as the point of departure.

Reflections on Water

Mark Twain once purportedly said that "whiskey's for drinking—water's for fighting." While the evidence for attributing this to Twain is shaky at best, the quote is nonetheless frequently invoked as a foregone conclusion: people will fight over water because it is scarce, essential, and invaluable for the growth and development of human societies. In reality, "water wars" are exceedingly rare, with the overwhelming majority of the world's 263 shared river basins being subject to treaties, agreements, and other mechanisms for allocating their flow. Still, there is a deeper concern reflected in Twain's apocryphal quote, namely that while water wars between nations may be rare, modern water utilization on the whole often reflects a collective war that humankind is waging on the environment. All too often, what are coded as "shared waters" and "peaceful resolutions" to human-human conflicts still involve deep incursions against the natural flow of surface waters, including channelizing rivers to fix national boundaries, altering the saline and sediment levels, and damming rivers for hydroelectric plants. Such outcomes are part of a larger orientation that comes to equate peace with control—especially control of nature.

As human cultures expand, water is emerging as the central resource in local and global politics alike. Pressures to privatize and commodify water are continually being brought to bear, often under the guise of development schemes that are portrayed as linking growth with security. To ensure that water flows even in places where it is highly problematic—from Abu Dhabi to Phoenix—massive delivery infrastructures are contemplated, including energy-intensive desalination plants and circuitous concrete canals transporting water hundreds of miles across deserts. Science fiction scenarios abound, as plans are conceived to capture clouds, drag icebergs, and create mountains and lakes for delivering water supplies to thirsty nations. One of the first high-tech regional water projects, which would serve as a template for similar projects worldwide, was the Tennessee Valley Authority (TVA) developed in the 1930s, composed of a series of elaborate dams and hydropower generating stations. When World War II broke out, the project was reoriented toward wartime production, doubling its power generation and producing a majority of the phosphorous used by the US military for bullets, bombs, and chemical weapons, as well as aluminum for aircraft. The "most significant contribution to the war" was created at a TVA-powered laboratory: the fissionable uranium-235 that was used to fuel the Manhattan Project that developed the world's first nuclear weapon (Ward 2003, 85).

The TVA example is stark for its specific militarism, yet it reveals something deeper about how we tend to view water. Oftentimes the choice for transnational actors appears to be one of engaging in either water wars or joint development projects—in essence, either militarism or capitalism, a World War or the World Bank. If we are inclined to associate the latter with peace, then it obviously becomes preferable to the alternative, and yet deeper questions about the meaning of water remain unresolved. Water is inherently fluid, unpredictable, prone to extremes of either floods or droughts, both transient and *in situ*, primeval in its simplicity and purity (cf. Postel 2010). Water reshapes images beneath its surface and accurately reflects those above it; it is "an active agent, changing all it touches … creating new courses and possibilities yet to be appreciated by humans" (Blatter, Ingram, and

Doughman 2001, 3). As we co-evolve with all of the essential resources in our midst, we must also apprehend "the limitations of instrumental rationality in capturing the meanings of water and shortcomings of modern science in improving our understanding of its treatment in society" (Blatter, Ingram, and Doughman 2001, 3).

Increasingly, we come to recognize that no peace between nations is possible without reconciling underlying water issues. It has been surmised that the failure to attain peace in the Middle East between Israel and its Arabic neighbors has been due in part to the concomitant failure to achieve a mutually cognizable agreement over the Jordan River and underground aquifers in the region, yielding a climate of "mistrust, fears of dependency, and perceived threats to national sovereignty" (Blatter, Ingram, and Levesque 2001, 38; cf. Klare 2002, 161–173). In the case of India and Pakistan, where border clashes and warlike tensions have persisted for decades, a treaty governing the Indus River basin was signed in 1960, following a World Bank proposal to divide the waters between the two countries. While the agreement may have helped forestall violent interstate conflict, it also led to "an all-out effort to build a monumental array of dams and canals"—leading one of the Pakistani (formerly Indian) engineers on the project to observe: "This was like a war. These were huge works.... Everybody was after us. They said we had sold the rivers, that we were traitors to our country" (Ward 2003, 93).

What we learn from these examples is that water is more than a mere resource, and that both fighting over it and dividing its spoils are equally problematic resolutions to emerging global water issues. As we have seen throughout this volume, both the hardware and software of conflict must be addressed, requiring a simultaneous emphasis on peacemaking at both the human-human and human-environment interfaces. As Vandana Shiva (2002, 66–67) documents, efforts to privatize water and dam rivers often result in the displacement of peoples and the despoliation of the environment—as well as an ensuing "centralization of power over water" that conjures a double meaning for the concept of "hydropower." While it may be the case that "the world is more conscious than ever of the unbreakable nexus between water and life" (Hiscock 2012, 58), this realization—coupled with depletion of freshwater sources and a rising contingent of global competitors for resources, as described in Chapter Six—has led many to speculate that the wars of the twenty-first century will be fought primarily over water, not oil or other valuable resources (Homer-Dixon 1999, 139; Klare 2002, 19; Shiva 2002, ix; Lohan 2009). On the other hand, more promisingly, a spate of literature has emerged in recent years suggesting that water can be a powerful basis for transborder cooperation, collaboration, conservation—and peace.

The Environment Knows No Borders

There are myriad lessons to be gleaned from the field of hydro-politics, which we may take as the "systematic study of conflict and cooperation between states over water resources that transcend international borders" (Elhance, quoted in Dinar 2009, 111). Chief among these lessons are that water highlights our innate interdependence with one another and the environment alike, and likewise that water directly connects the economic and ecological spheres of human life. As with other environmental components, "water bodies respect no political borders" (Dinar 2009, 111), thus engendering a wider perspective that is particularly useful in light of global scarcity and the essential nature of the resource. While studies of water in relation to violent conflict have reached varied conclusions (e.g., Gleditsch et al. 2006; Lecoutere, D'Exelle, and Van Campenhout 2010), there is an emerging consensus that scarcity in the context of renewability coupled with the "critical need" for water can provide the impetus for cooperation—yielding "peaceful and successful conflict management schemes" even among "states with recent militarized conflicts" (Dinar, Dinar, and Kurukulasuriya 2011, 810, 830). As a general matter, it has been observed that shared water resources appear to be "the most likely candidate for successful environmental peacemaking programs" (Parker, Feil, and Kramer 2004, 10). There is even a major Transboundary Freshwater Dispute Database (www.transboundarywaters .orst.edu) that is "intended for use in aiding the process of water conflict prevention and resolution."

If we take to heart the premise that scarcity and essentiality can promote cooperation, then the prospects for water to spur transborder peace initiatives are indeed promising. Nearly half of the earth's land mass abuts river basins shared by more than one nation, and more than three-quarters of the available freshwater flows through an international river basin—reminding us in stark geographical terms that "a river is without a nationality" (Ward 2003, 188). It is becoming increasingly clear that lasting peace is possible, from the Middle East to the American Southwest, "only if water is taken into account" (Ward 2003, 195). Highlighting these themes, the United Nations declared 2013 as the "International Year of Water Cooperation" and the years from 2005–2015 as the "Water for Life Decade"—optimistically citing the operative notion that "history has often shown that the vital nature of freshwater is a powerful incentive for cooperation and dialogue, compelling stakeholders to reconcile even the most divergent views. Water more often unites than divides people and societies" (UNDESA n.d.). In order to reach this ambitious horizon, we must strive to "build bridges between various meanings and understandings" and to enhance "the legitimacy of noninstrumental uses of water" (Blatter, Ingram, and Levesque 2001, 52). In short, we must recognize water as boundless—as *life*.

If we are thus seeking the robust *peace* contemplated by the peace ecology perspective, then we will need to do more than sign treaties that allocate every drop of water among competing users. Control and peace are often dichotomous, at least in the context of transnational security issues and a complex geopolitical landscape where looming resource wars and ongoing processes of economic colonization continue to dominate the discourse. Physical borders between nations are increasingly militarized in the post-9/11 era, even as the barriers to so-called free trade and footloose capital are simultaneously relaxed. This has the effect of diminishing the potential for genuine exchange among peoples and communities on opposite sides of national borders, interrupting the natural processes of ecosystems that do not abide the largely artificial lines on maps. It also serves to exacerbate tensions among nations, leading to the creation of permanent war economies whose explicit "national security" focus is the procurement and control of dwindling resources—down to even the essentials of food, water, and energy. The zero-sum logic of scarcity and competition is palpable, and has become a central norm of international relations, even as its workings are becoming little more than a self-fulfilling downward spiral in which vast resources are expended in the attempt to secure more of them.

In addition to reflecting an inherently unsustainable logic, such processes further reify a number of dualisms that reside at the core of the Western paradigm that has held sway throughout the industrial age. Resource wars and patterns of economic colonization are often initiated by the nations of the Global North vis-à-vis those of the Global South, yielding a two-tiered world of privileged consumers at the top and vulnerable producers on the bottom. The false scarcity created by such a system is reinforced by a mindset in which human cultures are seen as separate from nature, and where traditional societies that exist closer to nature are viewed (in Social Darwinist terms) as inferior to modern societies in their sociopolitical, economic, and moral development. These dichotomies (North/South, Nature/Culture, Traditional/Modern) are historically untenable, ecologically destructive, and self-refuting even when taken at face value. But even more problematically, these dualisms often provide the ideological software that serves to perpetuate an unsustainable world in which people are alienated from one another and are dislocated from the essential workings of the environment all at once.

In this light, any exploration of processes confronting these eventualities is potentially revolutionary in its full dimensions. The set of interrelated themes brought together under the rubric of peace ecology remain grounded in the notion that the crises of scarcity and conflict are also opportunities for mutually beneficial engagement born of necessity yet aimed at longer-term sustainability. The cultivation of a sense of shared destiny and mutual necessity can bring even ardent transnational adversaries to the negotiating table, since, as Alexander Carius (2006, 11) reminds us, "Environmental problems ignore political borders." This emerging holistic perspective suggests that peoples and nations have the potential to find ways of managing ecological concerns that not only work to avoid conflicts but can also serve to promote peaceful relations among human communities and with the environment itself. Again, this is reflective of the basic understanding that "ecosystems [do] not recognize national borders" (Kemkar 2006, 4), and that environmental matters in general obey a logic that transcends the demarcation of fixed boundaries. In this manner, we come to see that ecological issues possess an inherent impetus to call our attention "beyond the borders of the state" (Ramutsindela 2007a, 36), and that it is precisely the "increased globalization of environmental problems [that] has made it even more important for nations to act collectively" (López 2009, 292) in the pursuit of cooperative, efficacious, and peaceful resolutions to contemporary crises.

From Militarized Borders to Sustainable Peace

As noted in the previous chapter, a foundational work in this vein is Ken Conca and Geoffrey Dabelko's 2002 edited volume *Environmental Peacemaking*, in which the operative principle is that an environmental crisis or conflict can be transformed into an opportunity for peace when it can be demonstrated that (i) there is more to be gained by cooperating than by competing and (ii) when the essence of peaceful cooperation transcends the interests and aims of nation-states that tend to emphasize a version of security that inhibits cooperation. Such outcomes are intimately connected with the capacity of people to attain healthy, productive, and equitable livelihoods, since "the advance of sustainable human development is a significant element in successful conflict resolution between neighboring countries" (Paz 2007, 329), with due regard for the premise that "ecological sustainability and economic development go hand in hand, that each is prerequisite for the other" (Rees and Westra 2003, 100). *Sustainable development* is one of those malleable phrases that can be adopted by a range of actors and imbued with a host of meanings (not all of them peace-oriented), but the basic point of equitable living is noteworthy.

These trends toward resource collaboration, conflict transformation, and sustainable relations have been on the rise in recent years at various hot spot locations around the world, including disputed territories between Peru and Ecuador and along the China-Vietnam border (Clayton 2004). The basic recognition of the irreplaceable need for water (as noted above) and other basic resources, such as arable lands and timber, has yielded a situation in which environmental scarcity "offers the potential to bring about regional cooperation—even on very inhospitable terrain" (Swain 2002, 62; cf. Weinthal et al. 2005; Rowland 2005; Turton, Patrick, and Julien 2006). An assessment of the dire situation in Darfur highlights the underlying environmental issues at play there, including persistent drought and ensuing land-based changes in the relationships between farmers and pastoralists, concluding that conflict transformation and the cessation of hostilities in the region will not be possible "without addressing the issues of livelihoods, long-term development needs and the use and management of natural resources" (Castro 2010, 350). In these instances, we can see that the potential for militarism and peacemaking are equally palpable; transborder peace ecology suggests that it is possible to move from the former to the latter, if human-human and human-environment relations are reconciled.

The Brazilian Landless Workers Movement (Movimento dos Trabalhadores Rurais Sem Terra, or simply MST) offers another compelling example. The MST utilizes a model of cooperative agriculture to address issues of food production and environmental conservation, as well as to incubate "political and social activities designed to foster more equitable social relations" (Wittman 2007, 121). While the MST itself is not expressly transnational in scope, it is a key component of larger efforts, such as Peoples' Global Action, that work to link similar initiatives around the world. These synergistic efforts yield a framework in which "grassroots agrarian reform and associated visions of alternative co-operativism seek land not only as a productive resource, but as space for the installation of new democratic social relations" (Wittman 2007, 142). Likewise, an exploration of cooperative agricultural initiatives on both sides of the Israel-Gaza border emphasizes the work of transnational organizations that facilitate the sharing of knowledge, employment opportunities, and food production techniques, ultimately serving to foster the development of "mutually reinforcing relationships that are the basis of a sustainable peace process" (Goldman 2007, 338–339). In addition to river waters, India and Pakistan have also been embroiled in a transborder controversy over the Siachen Glacier, yielding grave impacts as a result of substantial military resources being directed at this "unique, fragile ecosystem" (Kemkar 2006, 15); advocates for demilitarization of this sensitive bioregion highlight the potential for a *transboundary protected area* to promote "collaborative management" that could help cultivate "mutual confidence" between the parties as they seek wider bilateral, peaceful relations (Kemkar 2006, 30).

Peace parks are transborder conservation zones that generally exist along contentious borders between nations that have endured conflict in the past but are working to create protected areas together; while they can exist within a particular nation (often as a commemorative park), "the international boundary dominates conceptions of and practices around peace parks" (Ramutsindela 2007a, 32). Examining international conservation efforts around the world, Ali (2007) has observed that positive exchanges and trust-building gestures are a consequence of managing shared environmental threats, and that a focus on common environmental harms can be very successful in leading to cooperative outcomes. As a general matter, the more that environmental issues are cooperatively regulated among nations, "the more permeable state boundaries become for transnational activities" in a wider sense that can serve to promote the prospects for peacebuilding (López 2009, 292). Peace parks are often premised on the assertion that "peace can be achieved through engaging states at the supranational level," in particular when confronted with a "common environmental threat" that can encourage cooperation even among acrimonious parties (Ramutsindela 2007a, 38). Indeed, it is the case that "the language of peace and co-operation is common among cross-border conservation projects of all sorts" (Ramutsindela 2007a, 40), reinforcing the foundational premise of environmental peacemaking.

The centuries-old conflict between Iraq and Iran provides a poignant illustration. The al Ahwar marshes that straddle the border between these nations are part of the Mesopotamian region that marks what is often taken as the birthplace of modern civilization. The impact of warfare has compromised the vitality of these critical marshlands, leading some in the region to advocate for the creation of a peace park on the premise that such a project "could potentially result in coordination and co-management of this globally significant area, and future establishment of a demilitarized zone between the countries" (Stevens 2007, 324). Despite the seemingly intractable nature of the political conflict, "restoration projects in the marshlands have continued" and there is "a visceral respect for conservation" among the diverse communities in the region, which ultimately "could provide a means of building trust and a cooperative nexus" between Iran and Iraq (Stevens 2007, 328). Again we see the potential for shared environmental concerns to transcend political conflicts, and thus to serve as a basis for cultivating mutual trust and building confidence between actors as a basis for broader peacebuilding initiatives. Joint conservation efforts between the United States and Cuba further illuminate the point:

> Cuban and American scientists have joined forces in an effort to protect baby sea turtles and endangered sharks. They're studying Caribbean weather patterns that fuel the hurricanes that have devastated the Southeastern United States. In the process, they're chipping away at a half-century of government feuding, helping to bring the nations together for talks on vital matters, such as what to do in case of an oil spill. The two countries are so geographically close, and the environmental concerns so similar, that scientists say it's crucial to combine forces.... Scientists and scholars have helped break through political barriers before. An environmental agreement reached with the Soviet Union in the 1970s is often credited with easing Cold War tensions. (Ordonez 2012)

Perhaps the quintessential example of the potential to turn the degradation-conflict cycle into one of collaboration and sustainability is the Demilitarized Zone (DMZ) between North and South Korea, which has become a massive wildlife and bird sanctuary since the end of the Korean War in 1953. Having remained relatively untrammeled by human activities, the DMZ is a rich habitat made up of marshes and grasslands, inhabited by rare and endangered species including the Asiatic black bear, leopards, lynx, and a significant portion of the world's population of red-crowned cranes (Machlis and Hanson 2008, 732). This case illustrates concretely that demilitarization can lead to species diversification and a thriving ecosystem, and that formerly warring nations can develop an equivalent interest in cooperating to maintain the integrity of unique regions and simultaneously to cultivate mutually beneficial relationships in the process. "The preservation of the DMZ ecosystems promises to provide an unusual opportunity for the two Koreas to work together toward common goals and economic and environmental securities. Such a strategy therefore could become an attractive vehicle for conflict resolution concerning North Korea's nuclear threat and for changing the political environment over the Korean issues toward a more flexible and optimistic future" (Kim 2007, 256–257).

There are a plethora of similar examples from around the globe, such as the work of 2004 Nobel Peace Prize winner Wangari Maathai and the Green Belt Project in East Africa, which links women's rights, economic self-sufficiency, resource conflict resolution, and environmental restoration (cf. Ramutsindela 2007a, 42). This project highlights the nexus between the ways that we manage our habitats and how we govern ourselves, and the interconnections between environmental sustainability and sociopolitical systems. The concomitant benefits of simultaneously undertaking peacebuilding and conservation efforts can serve to "encourage transboundary collaboration [and] promote exchanges of experience and information" (Kemkar 2006, 33). In this manner, a "community of interests" can be fostered, "making states richer in shared knowledge" and, in the end, "promoting development, peace, and human security" (López 2009, 300–302). While transnational efforts are not without their difficulties, both pragmatically and philosophically speaking, such initiatives in general possess the potential to "provide the basis for institutionalizing transborder cooperation across an even broader range of political activity" (Scott 1989, 155). Shared environmental issues between nations serve to remind us that "long-term and comprehensive sustainability is a prerequisite for a lasting peace" (Carius 2007, 62).

Transnational borders in general are often seen as areas of danger and opportunity alike. "The borderlands have a peculiar appeal to proponents of peace parks because the demarcation of state borders have often led to disputes, most of which erupted into bloody wars. It is therefore logical to assume that borders as sites of conflict can be brought under new cross-border regimes, with ecoregions acting as a catalyst for peace" (Ramutsindela 2007b, 70). By focusing collaboration and conservation efforts on transnational borders, the aim is to achieve a "change of scale from the national to the supranational" (Ramutsindela 2007b, 70)—a move of particular importance with regard to the global scope of environmental issues and the pervasive nature of global conflict. Since issues of degradation and injustice cross borders, so too must the workable solutions being created. A caveat to consider in such ambitious formulations, however, is that "disputes over borders have their own peculiar histories that cannot be subjected to general and common solutions" (Ramutsindela 2007a, 33). Nonetheless, despite this proviso, the general lessons learned from transborder engagement provide a framework for analyzing a particular conflict zone and its potential for peacebuilding, both among humans and with the environment.

Conflicts at the US-Mexico Interface

Before proceeding with this working case study, let us review the lessons discerned from the literature and examples around the world. First, environmental issues can provide a robust basis for cooperation, even in times of scarcity and even among hostile parties. The history of water relations in particular demonstrates that the prevailing international norm is one based on shared river basins, mutual interdependence, and multilateral negotiations. Second, environmental issues do not remain confined within borders, thus transcending parochial interests and arguing for common engagement. At a macroscopic level, we are all dependent upon the same global ecosystem, and it is becoming increasingly apparent that what affects one part of that system affects all of its components and inhabitants. Third, borders between nations can be important sites for peacebuilding, even as they also present points of potential conflict. The interface between entities provides an opportunity for exchange and collaboration, at times reformulating preexisting power relations in light of upstream/downstream positions and shared ecological concerns. Taken together, these lessons suggest that peace is more likely to be crafted out of tension rather than placidity, and that environmental issues can reinforce our common humanity.

The US-Mexico border presents many obvious points of conflict, ranging from the interpersonal and societal to the ideological and environmental. While "the border" as a general construct is widely considered a contentious political issue, as well as a place of violence and danger, there are also a number of efforts being undertaken to help transform border problems into opportunities for peacebuilding and cross-cultural comity. Individuals and organizations on both sides of this conflictual border are working in myriad ways and from multiple perspectives to ameliorate conflict and violence in the region, opening up opportunities for more positive concourse among peoples and nations alike. In particular, these actors strive to promote peaceful alternatives to border fractiousness in spheres including human rights, economics, health care, education, and the environment. Conservation efforts and resource management programs in particular possess great potential to improve the ecology of the region as well as the tenuous political scenario by fostering a climate of reciprocity, confidence, and shared interests.

In the case of the 1951-mile US-Mexico border, the significance of demonstrating peacebuilding and sustainability opportunities in a region rife with ostensible conflict and despoliation can have wide-ranging impacts on other locales facing issues of violence, mass migration, refugeeism, drugs, and a militarized version of "security" that includes steel walls, armed guard units, and unmanned aerial drones. The United States, in addition to stigmatizing undocumented immigrants, has funneled billions of dollars and substantial armaments in waging a failed "war on drugs" that has sparked extreme violence across Mexico (Regan 2013). In the face of this turbulent landscape, nonviolent movements (such as the Caravan for Peace with Justice and Dignity) have sprung up in the region, aiming to remedy the root causes of crime and violence by improving the lives of people through greater self-sufficiency, bearing witness, and putting a human face on the suffering (Regan 2013). Viewing these issues through a prism of peacemaking and conflict transformation, it becomes clear that the project of building peace in a conflict zone is intertwined with the process of comprehending the subtleties of the production of violence, as well as articulating how that violence is constructed and applied. In other words, there are many levels of conflict and violence, ranging from overt forms that are physically deployed to the more subtle forms that work at the level of psyche, ideology, and identity construction. Working to ameliorate conflictual borders requires an exploration of sociocultural factors including fear, divisiveness, and environmental sacrifice in the name of security that impacts the potential for peace in the minds of the people who reside in border communities.

The history of US-Mexico relations is a troubled one in many respects, dating to the Mexican-American War in the 1840s—and including more recent phenomena such as the passage of the North American Free Trade Agreement (NAFTA) in 1994 (allowing more unimpeded movement of goods, capital, and corporate enterprises) followed shortly thereafter by Operation Gatekeeper in 1996 (securing the border against unregulated human movements and driving would-be crossers into more treacherous, and ultimately deadly, landscapes). On the other hand, the United States and Mexico have been long-standing trading partners, and there is a high degree of cultural cross-pollination across the borderlands—from intermixed families and deeply rooted economic interrelations to wildlife corridors and fragile desert ecosystems. The border between the United States and Mexico transects diverse terrains and habitats, and includes numerous resource bases (including water) that are essential to both parties. This positive/negative duality matches that found in other transborder contexts, particularly those in which there is a military differential between nations and/or where economic and security matters trump other concerns.

Of particular significance in this regard is the dramatic interposition of a border wall (covering about a third of the total 1951 miles, non-contiguously), ostensibly intended to deter human migration, but with many negative additional consequences. At the macroscopic level, it often appears to be the case that the United States is "conducting cruel and inhumane dealings with the citizens of Mexico," and indeed "a powerful symbolic reminder of these improper dealings is the border wall" (Magee 2011). A cogent summary of the impacts of the US-Mexico border wall articulates the key issues:

> This reckless project has meant dire consequences for vast expanses of pristine wild lands, including wildlife refuges, wilderness areas, and national forest lands, among others. Several species of wildlife have been observed and photographed stranded by the border wall, suggesting that many threatened and endangered species are suffering the same fate. The border wall has also had devastating consequences for communities along the border. In Nogales, Sonora, the wall contributed to severe flooding that buried downtown homes and businesses underneath six feet of water, drowning two people and costing millions of dollars in damages. Condemnation proceedings against border municipalities and landowners in Texas led to a wall that blocks people and animals from access to the Rio Grande River. The greatest human toll of the wall is the thousands of migrants that have lost their lives as the border wall funnels them deeper and deeper into harsh and remote terrain. (Sierra Club n.d.)

Despite concerns over the ecological impacts in particular of the border wall, the US Department of Homeland Security has exempted itself from environmental laws and regulations, including the Clean Air and Clean Water Acts and the Endangered Species Act, in constructing the barrier (No Border Wall n.d.; Sierra Club n.d.; Lasky, Jetz, and Keitt 2011, 12; Magee 2011).

Data collected by conservation groups in the region paint a compelling and unequivocal picture in which "barriers on the US-Mexico border are disturbing ecosystems and endangering animal species," including the Coues' rice rat, the jaguarundi (a small feline), the California red-legged toad, ocelots, jaguars, bighorn sheep, pronghorn, quail, the desert tortoise, and black bears, among other species (Cruz 2011; No Border Wall n.d.; Flesch et al. 2009). A 2006 symposium that brought together park managers, biologists, and conservation groups concluded that the border wall "will fragment the Sonoran Desert ecosystem, damage the desert's plant and animal communities, and prevent the free movement of wildlife between the United States and Mexico" (Cohn 2007, 96). The Tijuana River estuary, home to at least seven endangered species, has seen 90 percent of its habitat "rapidly destroyed by pollutants and filled in with sediments from the wall's construction" (Magee 2011). A 2009 quantitative study concluded that the security infrastructure on the US-Mexico border potentially represents a threat to transboundary landscape connectivity that may be "essential for persistence" as to numerous species (Flesch et al. 2009, 2)—yielding a potential "rapid loss of genetic diversity" in animal populations and "an increased risk of extinction" for many species (Lasky, Jetz, and Keitt 2011, 2). These concerns were aptly reflected in an article published by the Worldwatch Institute:

> The U.S.-Mexican border region has the highest rate of species endangerment in the United States.... Well aware that the most important principle of biodiversity conservation is the need to protect the largest possible intact landscapes, we focused on identifying ways in which protections could be established that, in effect, crossed the border—regardless where the fences or guards might stand—to encompass whole ecosystems. Establishing effective cross-border policies is not easy.... Designed to stop humans from freely crossing, borders also stop other species.... While borders make environmental protection more

difficult in many respects, they can also provide unique opportunities for conservation—provided that the neighboring nations are amenable to cooperation. One such form of cooperation is through the designation of parks along borders as "peace parks." [These efforts illustrate] the ability of environmental concerns to serve as a sign that the link between biodiversity and security can be turned around so that it is not seen as an impediment or cost of security but as augmenting security. (Van Schoik 2004)

It is worth recalling here that all of these issues (i.e., politics, economics, security, conservation) occur in the context of an increasingly militarized landscape, bringing the urgency of establishing a nexus of ecological and sociopolitical concerns into sharper focus. As one of the 2006 symposium participants observed: "It's a war zone here. We're into triage in deciding what to sacrifice in the environment to achieve border security" (Cohn 2007, 96). Confirming these sentiments, it has been observed that in general the US-Mexico border "is an area characterized by environmental degradation, economic and political inequality, and conflicting norms and priorities" (Doughman 2002, 190). Overall, it strongly appears that the United States has "chosen to prioritize national security over the environment and acted unilaterally [in militarizing the border], forgoing negotiations with its neighbor" (Magee 2011), and taking advantage of the fact that Mexico is "economically and militarily inferior to the United States" (Dinar 2011, 179).

Still, perhaps with due regard to the inescapable fact that "the U.S.-Mexico border shares common air, rivers, and underground waters" (Bernstein 2002, 7), there have been examples of environmental cooperation predating construction of the border wall. In 1983, for instance, the two countries signed the La Paz Agreement to address issues of pollution, sewage, toxic substances, and wastes (Bernstein 2002, 9). The Integrated Border Environment Plan was issued in 1992, followed by the five-year US-Mexico Border XXI Program in 1996 that established binational working groups on issues including air, water, pollution, natural resources, and environmental health (Bernstein 2002, 9). In 2012, a gathering of environmental experts and government officials from both the United States and Mexico was held "to build binational consensus on conservation priority areas" along the Rio Grande/Río Bravo corridor; the project—organized by the Commission for Environmental Cooperation (CEC), and titled the Big Bend-Río Bravo Collaboration for Transboundary Landscape Conservation—focused on developing a binational cooperative conservation plan "for one of North America's most important cross-border ecosystems" (CEC 2012). Still in its early stages, this initiative aims to develop a model for transboundary conservation efforts that can inform similar projects in other cross-border locales.

Peacebuilding on the US-Mexico Border

Such efforts to transform border conflict are informed by environmental peacemaking tenets indicating that crises such as violence, militarism, and competition over resources can be utilized as moments to draw people together rather than accentuating rifts. In this light, it has been argued that "water cooperation efforts in the U.S.-Mexico border region have the potential to improve U.S.-Mexico relations in many respects [and] could help to move the border from a zone of uneasy transition and human insecurity to a zone of peace" (Doughman 2002, 191). Significantly, as noted at the beginning of this chapter, the agreement signed in 2012 concerning the quantity and quality of Colorado River waters reaching Mexico is an important, albeit tenuous, step in this direction; likewise, the conservation efforts of the CEC and other groups are also a positive sign. As detailed above, the problems plaguing the region are numerous, and include grave ecological concerns not only about water but about pollution and toxification, soil contamination, loss of habitat and biodiversity, and the environmental toll of mass human migration. At the same time, it is also perceived that efforts to turn this zone of sacrifice into one of sustainability and peace could provide "an opportunity to strengthen trust, reciprocity, long-term planning, interdependence, shared norms, and trans-societal linkages" (Doughman 2002, 199). Indeed, at the US-Mexico interface, "shared natural resource initiatives continue even in a time of increased attention to border security" (Sifford and Chester 2007, 212).

Despite the failure to date in establishing a transborder peace park or equivalent on the US-Mexico border, it remains the case that "the establishment of cross-border protected areas could actually help diminish current, seemingly irreconcilable, tensions while benefiting long-term cooperation in other arenas besides that of conservation" (Sifford and Chester 2007, 218). In order to accomplish this, cooperation and coordination between the United States and Mexico on transboundary environmental efforts is essential (cf. Bernstein 2002, 10), including "coordinated binational conservation" efforts and the "preservation of transborder connectivity" for habitats and species (Lasky, Jetz, and Keitt 2011, 7). In the dualistic spirit of transborder peace ecology, such environmental efforts could readily be coupled with mutually supportive initiatives to "deemphasize national sovereignty" and gradually dismantle "the legacy of defensive boundaries" (Scott 1989, 140), while at the same time working to "reinstate environmental regulation of border security efforts" (Lasky, Jetz, and Keitt 2011, 12). While these sorts of positive outcomes have yet to cohere in the case of the US-Mexico border, there is cause for hope that a confluence of issues and actors could unite around these tenets of peace ecology.

Interestingly, notwithstanding the presence of the world's first formally recognized peace park (Waterton-Glacier) on the US-Canada border, the potential for transborder peacebuilding initiatives has been less analyzed in a North American context than it has on most other continents around the world. [It is also worth considering why the United States has failed to "effect similar strategies along the US-Mexico border in the south" despite the success of Waterton-Glacier (Ramutsindela 2007a, 30).] This may be due to the unique role that the United States plays in global affairs, generally serving not only as a regional hegemon but a global one as well. In light of ostensible US military and economic dominance in recent decades, coupled with an increasing tendency toward obsessive national security at home and unilateral action abroad in the post–9/11 era, some may perceive the United States (especially on its own shores) as beyond cooperation when it comes to resources. Indeed, by reputation and actual practice alike, it might be surmised that neither "peace" nor "ecology" factor very strongly into US policymaking.

Putting this tenable cynicism aside, we have seen that there are actually a number of constructive transborder peace ecology efforts to be found along the US-Mexico border. These nascent steps suggest a strong nexus between landscapes and cultures, politics and people, and peacebuilding and the environment—thus meriting our attention in some detail. By themselves, none of these regional actors would likely be sufficient to establish a cross-border environmental peacemaking initiative such as a peace park. But viewed as a whole, we can begin to see the strands of a conjoined civil society effort to help mediate the social and ecological conflicts on the border. Such efforts have worked in other locales, once the key players are identified:

Commission for Environmental Cooperation (www.cec.org) (CEC) was established in 1994 by the North American Agreement on Environmental Cooperation to support transnational conservation efforts among the United States, Mexico, and Canada, and to address environmental issues of continental concern.

Frontera de Cristo (www.fronteradecristo.org) focuses on building relationships and understanding across borders, facilitating the crossing of borders of hundreds of persons per year to support brotherhood and sisterhood between people in the United States and Mexico.

International Sonoran Desert Alliance (www.isdanet.org) (ISDA) works with US, Mexican, and indigenous constituencies to promote conservation and educational projects in the bioregion, emphasizing both the cultural and ecological resources that are paramount for spurring action and achieving sustainable solutions.

Kino Border Initiative (www.kinoborderinitiative.org) is a binational organization—located in Nogales, Arizona, and Nogales, Sonora, Mexico—that seeks to foster humane, just, and workable migration between the United States and Mexico, and to promote US-Mexico border and immigration policies that affirm the dignity of the human person and a spirit of binational solidarity.

No More Deaths (www.nomoredeaths.org) is an organization whose mission is to end death and suffering on the US-Mexico border through civil initiative, in the belief that people of conscience must work openly and in community to uphold fundamental human rights.

Northern Jaguar Project (www.northernjaguarproject.org) has partnered with the Mexican conservation organization, Naturalia, creating the Northern Jaguar Reserve which encompasses 78 square miles of prime jaguar habitat just 125 miles south of the Arizona border.

Sierra Club Borderlands Project (www.sierraclub.org/borderlands) seeks to restore and protect the borderlands that have been damaged by failed border policies, and supports "rational and transparent border policies rather than adhering to symbolic mandates to construct walls."

Sonoran Institute (www.sonoraninstitute.org) works with local communities and government agencies on both sides of the US-Mexico border to protect and enhance the distinctive character of the Sonoran Desert and Gulf of California region—including the Colorado River Delta Legacy Program, which focuses on restoring environmental water flows to the Colorado River Delta.

Southeast Arizona Area Health Education Center (www.seahec.org) works on both sides of the international boundary, seeking to enhance the well-being of people living in Southeastern Arizona's US-Mexico border region by collaborating with communities on both sides for better prevention and care—premised on the view that "neither health nor disease has a border."

Trans-Border Institute (www.sandiego.edu/peacestudies/tbi), an initiative of the Joan B. Kroc School of Peace Studies at the University of San Diego, works to promote "understanding, dialogue, and cooperation" across the US-Mexico border by emphasizing sustainable development, cross-border collaborations, and educational exchange.

Tucson Samaritans (www.tucsonsamaritans.org) are people of faith who respond directly to the human crisis at the US-Mexico border; prompted by the mounting deaths among border crossers, they formed to provide emergency medical assistance, food, and water to people crossing the Sonoran Desert.

While an overarching transborder peace ecology initiative on the US-Mexico border has yet to coalesce, we can see here the seeds for a viable effort imbued with the core principles involved with successful projects in other locales. Many of the nongovernmental actors focusing on environmental issues are duly cognizant of human rights concerns at the same time; and likewise many of the more sociopolitical groups comprehend the deeply intertwined nature of ecological concerns with their efforts. The confluence of these perspectives is quintessential to peace ecology, and suggests that we broaden the definition of terms like *transnational* and *transborder*. One of the paradoxes of environmental peacemaking (and similar efforts) when applied in a transborder context is that there is an impetus to transcend the nation-state as the unit of analysis, while at the same time often relying upon those same nation-states as the primary actors in terms of negotiating agreements and establishing cross-border initiatives. A broader view, however, and one that is more consistent with the overall scope of peace ecology as a local *and* global phenomenon, would include not only states but also regional actors (e.g., grassroots organizations, NGOs, faith groups) as potential drivers of transborder collaborative efforts.

In the case of the US-Mexico border, it is apparent that many of the conditions for success established in the literature are in place: a history that includes examples of "cooperation and collaboration between Mexican and U.S. officials" (Bernstein 2002, 10); the presence of regional "pressure groups [that] attempt to convince national governments of the benefits of supporting cooperative schemes" (Scott 1989, 155); efforts toward "coordinated binational conservation" (Lasky, Jetz, and Keitt 2011, 7); an emphasis on "transboundary connectivity" and "landscape connectivity" in terms of habitats, animal populations, and human cultures alike (Flesch et al. 2009, 2); a combination of both "upstream" and "downstream" positions between the two nations as to air, water, waste, and the like that promotes a sense of interconnection and mutual reliance (cf. Dinar 2011, 179–180); and a condition of relative scarcity of essential resources such as water that can foster "substantial long-term incentives to develop outcomes that avoid conflict" (Turton, Patrick, and Julien 2006, 27). As a general matter, it becomes clear that balancing the nation-state and its interests with those of other regional actors yields the potential to "allow more room for local transborder initiative to meet local needs" (Scott 1989, 140).

Toward a Sustainable Peace

In the final analysis, this nexus of local/regional initiatives in the context of international relations is a critical element in transborder peace ecology. The upshot is that conservation efforts can serve to promote mutuality and social justice, and that cooperative and collaborative projects can likewise work to restore and maintain the environment. Environmental peacemaking, peace parks, shared river basins, and other forms of transborder collaboration indicate that "environmental cooperation can be an effective general catalyst for reducing tensions, broadening cooperation, fostering demilitarization, and promoting peace," and furthermore that there can be "positive side effects from such cooperation that can create positive synergies for peace, in the form of trust building [and] the identification of mutual gains" (Conca and Dabelko 2002, 9–11). While it would be an overstatement to say that environmental cooperation *causes* peace, it is clear that such efforts can "support peace by enabling communities in fragile states to increase their resilience [and] establish collaborative and cooperative relationships," in the recognition that "shared resource systems and ecological interdependence are part of a durable peace" (Leroy 2010, 339–340).

Even as much work yet remains to achieve this aim, the theories and examples cited in this chapter can help point the way toward a more just, sustainable, and peaceful world. In order to accomplish this transformation, however, we need to move beyond merely dividing up the raw materials toward a reconsideration of our overall relationship to the world around us. Some of the actors in the US-Mexico border region have sought to move the discussion of environmental issues beyond the commodity-based constructions that prevail among many governmental and business entities. The ISDA in particular, with its specific inclusion of indigenous perspectives, "constructs water in ecological terms, viewing the Colorado River [as being] among the richest biological treasures in the world" (García-Acevedo 2001, 84). As Pamela Doughman (2001, 204) has observed, some groups in the border region "see water as an integral part of the ecological and cultural identity of communities." A central aim of many of these activists and advocates who are working tirelessly on social and environmental issues in the region is "the creation of an international biosphere reserve that would protect both biota and indigenous people from the harmful side effects of border economic development" (García-Acevedo 2001, 84). Integrating grassroots perspectives with those of governmental (and often more pro-development) entities such as the CEC could yield positive results in terms of promoting environmental cooperation.

While the establishment of a transborder conservation zone, peace park, or other similar initiative can be a powerful step toward a sustainable peace, it is also the case that if we do not break out of the commodity mindset that sees the products of nature as mere "goods" for human utilization, then we are only likely to continue exacerbating the patterns of inequality and degradation that undergird conflicts at all levels. The transborder context provides a unique opportunity to simultaneously confront the material and ideological issues that often demarcate the realm of geopolitics, which must be surmounted for a sustainable peace to take hold. Integral to this task are perceptions and beliefs, which appear as equally fundamental to the "hardware" issues of resources, borders, territories, landscapes, and the like that we have been considering thus far. This essential emphasis on "software" will be the subject of the next chapter.

Chapter Eight
Collective Reenchantment

There may never have been a time when humans truly and completely existed in harmony with one another and in balance with the environment; our unique makeup, biologically and socially speaking, would seem to mitigate against the reality of some bygone idyllic Eden. Longing for such a quixotic condition—in the past, present, or future—thus appears to be an exercise in futility, even as it may serve to assuage despair and cultivate optimism in an era rife with grave challenges. As such, when we consider pressing matters of conflict, violence, degradation, or despoliation, we are talking more about questions of degree than absolutes; these are all foundational appurtenances to existence itself, susceptible to alleviation but never elimination. By necessity, we must take life in order to survive at all, as individuals and collectively. Yet the questions remain: Of what sort, at what scale, and will we do so malevolently or not? Indeed, nature itself (of which we are a part) is not always benign, with predator-prey relationships and life-death cycles casually manifested in its processes—but to term this "violence" would likely be an overstatement. Natural systems tend toward an overall balance, a big-picture quest for equilibrium that can also be a guidepost for how we humans conduct ourselves during our time here.

The critical point thus becomes whether we can achieve that elusive balance, putting back in as much as we take out of the systems that sustain us both socially and ecologically. This entails reducing levels of consumption quantitatively (how much) and qualitatively (in what manner), while simultaneously learning to "close the loop" as much as possible through the cultivation of restorative practices where waste is minimized, systems are regenerated, and creativity is abundant. In so doing, it is fundamentally important to maintain a positive vision in our minds, at the very least in order to set a high bar for our actions as we seek to move from what *is* to what *could be*. As Starhawk (2011) has observed, a constructive vision can be a "gift" and a strong motivator for collective action, inspiring "a deeper level of passion, commitment and creativity." Even small-scale examples of relative peace and ecological balance, especially those we directly experience in our lives, serve as reminders of how far we have come—and how far we yet have to go. Part of the task for peacemakers and environmentalists alike is to make it safe to suspend our disbelief and reclaim a sense of wonder about ourselves and the world around us. This need not invariably become a pursuit of mysticism, nor should it be reduced to mere self-preserving pragmatism. It is, more precisely, a way of rethinking our relationships at every level, including those that exist in both the material and ideological realms.

Pursuing this course, we come to realize that our crises and opportunities alike are composed of equal parts hardware and software. How we develop our systems of governance, economics, and resource allocations tells a large part of the story about whether we will surmount contemporary challenges and continue the experiment of human evolution. But equally telling is how we perceive the world in which we reside and of which we are a part. To a not-insignificant extent, modern humans have consistently abolished the sacred in favor of the profane, and in the process have externalized our collective relationship with the divine. Competition and conflict among ourselves mirror the overarching views held toward nature as inert, mechanical, consumable, exploitable, and disposable. The peace ecology framework developed in this volume does not merely ask us to reconsider how we divide up the wealth, but perhaps even more so calls upon us to redefine our moral, emotional, and spiritual relationships with the world that is simultaneously around, among, and within us. In the end, peace ecology is a *perspective* more than a specific goal, more about fostering a process than a particular result.

This burgeoning perspective is informed by many spheres of thought and practice, including ecofeminism, ecopsychology, nature spirituality, Gaia theory, deep ecology, social ecology, spiritual ecology, engaged Buddhism, and liberation theology (cf. Macy and Brown 1998, 22). While this chapter will not include a detailed discussion of these areas, its sensibility is imbued with lessons and insights drawn from them. The aim here will not be to survey all of the extant approaches to notions such as enchantment or the sacred, but rather to focus on the ways that alterations in ideology and perception can be powerful tools for building peace and justice, and likewise for promoting resiliency and sustainability (cf. Orr 2005, 61). Throughout much of this volume, we have looked at the hardware that implicates such processes, from war and resources to borders and rivers. We have also considered a range of software-oriented concepts such as cooperation, peacemaking, empathy, solidarity, and compassion—drawing upon these notions in the context of *interconnection* as it relates to peace and ecology alike. Here, we will take this further and explore these themes through the lens of *reenchantment*, which can be viewed in spiritual and/or secular terms depending upon one's predilection. Ultimately, the question becomes whether humankind can rekindle its love for life itself.

Falling Back in Love with the World

While humans may never have lived in a perfect state of harmony with nature, there does seem to have been a time when greater reverence was held for the world around us. We need to take care not to idealize or romanticize the pacific, ecoconscious tendencies of so-called primitive cultures or "indigenous peoples," and counterexamples can certainly be found in the anthropological record. Nevertheless, we can surmise that people living before the industrial era had a closer connection to the land and one another, with cornerstones such as food and water often taking on spiritual significance in rituals and ceremonies (cf. Shiva 2002; Garcia and Santistevan 2008). Creation mythologies around the world convey a sense of wonder and an attribution of sacredness to nature, interweaving the physical and psychological bases of life. It will not be fruitful, again, to reify these qualities as curiosities or museum pieces, and it is incumbent upon us to let people and cultures define themselves on their own terms, as Winona LaDuke asserts in her 2005 book *Recovering the Sacred*. From whatever culture we trace our personal origins, if we go far enough back we will discover at least some vestigial reverence for nature and its life-giving properties. In many ways, it is precisely our relative inability as modern-day humans to reconnect to this ethos that has pushed us to the collective brink.

As I write this, I am also following a discussion thread on an activist listserv about the dichotomization of love and hate as motivating factors in bringing about change. Some have argued for the primacy of love and compassion as moving forces, while others maintain that there is a place in our work for righteous indignation and even hatred of that which oppresses. Undoubtedly, humans are capable of both love and hate, even as some spiritual practices may counsel the abolition of hate altogether in favor of universal love. What I want to suggest here is neither the exclusive elevation of love nor the moralistic suppression of rage; rather, it seems to me that in our human-human and human-environment relationships there is already more than enough of the latter for those inclined to embrace its virtues. On some level, we can perceive that modern humans often display a form of collective self-loathing and a general disdain for other beings in our actions, if not our sentiments. Sometimes this is explicit, as with slurs and epithets used to describe enemies during time of war; at other times it is implicitd, as with the cruel treatment of animals for fast-food consumption that is widely known yet cognitively ignored.

There are myriad treatments of the "power of love" in music, art, literature, and even science. In the realms closely connected to peace ecology, we have eloquent figures such as David Suzuki (1999, viii, 159) characterizing love as a "mutual attraction [that is] built into the very structure of all matter in the universe," and further intoning that "as social and spiritual creatures, we need love and spirit if we are to lead rich, full lives." For Suzuki (1999, 6), the challenge before us devolves upon "the need to find a way to live rich, fulfilling lives without destroying the planet's biosphere"; in so doing, it becomes incumbent upon us to procure "the non-negotiable human needs" without making ourselves the enemy of each other and the world. In his influential work *The Reenchantment of the World*, Morris Berman (1984, 300) suggested that this goal is actually the means to its own attainment, in that the "preservation of this planet may be the best guideline for *all* our politics" and thus may be "the ultimate safety valve in the emergence of a new consciousness." In this sense, the notion of reclaiming our sense of wonder toward and love for the world is both a process for averting cataclysm and an end in itself, as renowned ecophilosopher Joanna Macy (in Tippett 2012) inferred: "The other face of our pain for the world is our love for the world, our absolutely inseparable connectedness with all life."

The Earth Charter (www.earthcharterinaction.org), a comprehensive document that links peace with sustainability, emphasizes the need to identify "ourselves with the whole Earth community" and to care for this community with "understanding, compassion, and love." Likewise, in 2011 a collective of writers and scholars came together as the Blue River Quorum, authoring a joint manifesto called "The Blue River Declaration." The sensibility contained in this brief document is noteworthy for its combination of humility and forthrightness, urging in no uncertain terms that humankind must "align its ethics with the ways of the Earth." The text reminds us that "humans are kin to one another and to all the other beings on the planet," and that in an interconnected system we all possess the capacity and responsibility to care for the whole. Urging an approach based on reciprocity, cooperation, and creativity, the statement acknowledges the beauty and grandeur of life, asserting the overarching proposition that "the world is worthy of reverence, awe, and care." The fact that we even need to be reminded of these principles is telling in its own right, and yet the basic tenets put forth in the Earth Charter and the Blue River Declaration are hardly controversial even as some will dismiss them. For those inclined to see the world through a prism of gratitude and kindredness, it is sometimes hard to understand the blunt materialism and rampant desacralization that pervades modern life.

Saving Sacred Spaces

"The presence of the sacred is like returning to a home that was always there and a truth that has always existed," writes Charles Eisenstein (2011, xvii).

Again, this need not be a strictly spiritual matter, for surely pragmatists and secularists alike can relate to the experience of being at "home." The intention here is not to mystify such concepts, but rather to demystify the workings of the global military-industrial economy—the system that replaces a nurturing *home* with a numbered house, if one is even fortunate enough to have one anymore. It is certainly easy (and understandable) to become disenchanted with such a stifling system that replaces meaning with money, tools with technology, and love with lust at nearly every turn. Corporate culture has a routinely sacrilegious quality to it, turning the mundane into the momentous and leaving no stone unturned in its quest for profit. Perhaps, in the end, it is not that we have become disenchanted, but that we are actually too enamored with ourselves to the exclusion of everything else. If "pride goeth before a fall" (also rendered as "pride goeth before destruction" in the Book of Proverbs), then our misplaced human hubris may indeed be the preamble to our self-inflicted demise.

If you think this sounds like too strong an assessment of our fate, you may be (and hopefully are) right—even as mounting evidence suggests that the "Doomsday Clock" (which actually exists!) is rapidly ticking. Ironically, it is the dominant culture that is most fatalistic about its own prospects, openly embracing a widespread creation myth that also predicts its ultimate doom for exactly the sorts of hubristic reasons we have been investigating here. One can deny the reality of being on a sinking ship, choose to avert one's gaze from the iceberg ahead, take a pill to ease the pain of anticipated demise, or even mock the spectacle by taking cell phone pictures of it and posting them online for friends to see—but that doesn't make it any less real. As Berman (1984, 1) contends, "Western life seems to be drifting toward increasing entropy, economic and technological chaos, ecological disaster, and ultimately, psychic dismemberment and disintegration." The list of intersecting crises in our midst is long; most of this volume has been an attempt to articulate an equally robust catalogue of viable alternatives. Yet sometimes we need to immerse ourselves in a problem in order to see potential solutions.

To take but one small example, the San Francisco Peaks in northern Arizona (mentioned in Chapter One) are considered sacred by over a dozen of the area's Native American tribes, but developers have nonetheless forged ahead with plans to expand ski runs and increase snowmaking with reclaimed sewage water. In recent years there have been dozens of arrests at the site, as demonstrators have engaged in nonviolent civil disobedience to protect the sacred peaks. Following years of rancorous public debate and coming on the heels of circuitous court proceedings, the developers of the site have expanded the slopes and laid a pipeline for the bringing of wastewater to make artificial snow, over the objections of indigenous communities and environmental activists alike. Shortsighted thinking, combined with unaddressed health risks and insufficient environmental impact assessments, threatens to turn the Peaks into yet another sacrifice zone for the sake of a buck, constituting "dirty money" in every sense of the phrase. Concomitantly, mining interests have raised the specter of extracting uranium from the Grand Canyon, which is adjacent to the Peaks, adding yet another unfortunate chapter to the story.

For the Hopi people in particular, the *kachinas* (spirit beings that represent manifestations of nature)—including the well-known fertility deity, Kokopelli—are said to live on the Peaks. Thirteen local tribes accord religious significance to the Peaks, including the Havasupai, Zuni, and Navajo, for whom the Peaks represent the sacred mountain of the west, called the Dook'o'oosłííd. The development of the Peaks has been a longstanding point of contention, dating to the earliest days of Forest Service–sanctioned recreational development in the 1930s. In the early 1980s, when outside investors sought to greatly expand the ski area on the Peaks, the tribes unsuccessfully sued to block the expansion as a violation of their religious freedom. In 2008, additional major expansions were announced by developers, including the use of reclaimed sewage effluent to make artificial snow. Another suit followed, in which native elders testified in federal court as to the Peaks' essential spiritual significance. The tribes initially won this lawsuit, but it was reversed on appeal, and the development has now proceeded despite numerous concerns about the cultural issues as well as the health effects of wastewater that includes untested levels of chemicals, pharmaceuticals, and potential endocrine disruptors.

The net effect of this regional conflict has been to squarely raise the issue of whether anything can be said to be sacred anymore. This is not a rhetorical question. The answer will decide whether our essential humanity has a future in a world increasingly dominated by technological abstractions and the relentless pursuit of profit over the interests of people and places.

As noted above, some may be uncomfortable with invocations of the sacred, preferring that arguments remain grounded in rational "facts." In the case of Snowbowl, however, the facts have been argued for years in city council proceedings, legal briefs, Forest Service public comment processes, and more. Still, the powerful interests have not listened, making it necessary to dig a bit deeper into ourselves (and our comfort zones) in order to keep the last remaining pristine places in our midst from being dug into any further. Similarly intact habitats everywhere possess special qualities including their biodiversity and life-giving properties. In this case, ecologists have found the Peaks to contain six distinct "life zones" (Sonoran desert, Pinyon-juniper woodland, Ponderosa pine forest, mixed conifer forest, spruce-fir forest, and alpine tundra) in an arid region where life in general is tenuous and often-times a struggle to sustain.

Whatever your views, it is incumbent upon us to find a basis for agreeing that some places simply ought to remain wild, if only as symbolic reminders of the natural wellspring from whence come the essentials of human exis-tence. Relegating any region's most iconic geographical features to the status of just another place for wanton development represents a narrow-minded, and ultimately self-defeating, enterprise. What would be the implication if nature had "In God We Trust" stamped on it, or if you had to raise your right hand and swear an oath before entering it? Perhaps then more people would be fine with icons like the Peaks being called *sacred*—a word that actually derives in part from the idea of being "set apart" or remaining "whole." Is it too much to ask that we maintain even a few places in our midst set apart from human conquest? Prioritizing the recreational desires of the leisure class over the spiritual and cultural needs of indigenous nations is a travesty with historical reverberations. But it isn't just native sensibilities that suffer in this process; the exploiters eventually render their own habitat unlivable and, in the process, sow the seeds of their own ultimate destruction.

The residents and activists protesting the further desecration of the Peaks are keenly aware of the magnitude of the stakes involved. When explicitly sacred areas are subject to the developer's merciless blade, it renders every-thing disposable. The anachronism of skiing in the desert likewise connotes an attitude of human superiority that turns the world—including the people in it—into little more than a commodity to be bought and sold according to the whims of an unsustainable market ideology. "The logical end point of this worldview is a feeling of total reification," as Berman (1984, 3) writes, where "everything is an object." Against this narrative of relentless commodification, activists have been working to tell another story. Among those arrested defending the sacred peaks have been Klee Benally, a Navajo filmmaker and community organizer. As he was chained to an excavator, Benally (2011)—who has been deeply committed to the cause, including making the award-winning film *The Snowbowl Effect*—spoke about his motivations: "This is not a game. This is not for show. This is not for the media. This is to stop this desecration from happening." Also arrested for attempting to halt the destruction was noted author (of *Going Through Ghosts*, among other books) Mary Sojourner (2011), who addressed the crowd that had gathered in support as she was being handcuffed and led away: "I took action not just for the Mountain, but ... so that older women and men would see that one doesn't have to be young to stand up for a place and community that you love."

These sentiments unite the work for peace and justice with the preservation of the environment, asking us to take heed—and action—lest the remaining natural landmarks in our midst be sacrificed on the altar of greed. The conjoined quality of being motivated by love for one's community and respecting the sacredness of nature is not mere happenstance; indeed, it is foundational to the pursuit of peace and nonviolence, as Thomas Merton (2007, 17) observed: "Hence the cornerstone of all Gandhi's life, action, and thought was the respect for the sacredness of life and the conviction that 'love is the law of our being'." Oftentimes it is precisely those concerned with the "fundamental issues ... of *meaning*" (Berman 1984, 2) that are most inclined to take a stance. Vandana Shiva (2002, 138–139), another strong voice for peace and the environment, has observed that "sacred sites ... have very high value but no price," and can serve to "carry us beyond the marketplace" and into a world where we all bear the right and responsibility to participate in "shaping the creation story of the future." Protecting sacred spaces, planting trees and gardens, resisting militarism and commodification of the environment, cultivating nature experiences, and arousing consciousness are all potent acts of "intergenerational optimism" (cf. Nixon 2011). In the end, we come to learn that "nature is to be cherished and valued, not simply for what it *is* but for what it *foreshadows*" (McGrath 2002, 185), and that our ability to persist into the future is bound up with how we treat it in the present.

Healing the Whole

An exercise I have used in my courses and workshops—one that I was introduced to by the aforementioned Sojourner—is to have people share an experience in which they felt most at "home" or at "peace" in their lives. Overwhelmingly, people select a nature-oriented experience, often grouping along lines of water (e.g., lakefronts, beaches) or earth (e.g., mountains, farms). Many of these stories encapsulate a sense of belonging, integration, acceptance, or wholeness. As with the longing for being in community with others, there is often an equivalent longing for communion with something larger than ourselves. Just as we can see the effects on people denied nurturing relationships or supportive communities, we can also see—at the micro and macro levels—what becomes of people who are disconnected from their environment. The relatively recent loss of this original connection, in which humans were enchanted with the world *and* construed as a part of it, "has destroyed the continuity of the human experience and the integrity of the human psyche. It has very nearly wrecked the planet as well" (Berman 1984, 10). Macy (in Tippett 2012) further laments that "we have been treating the earth as if it were a supply house and a sewer," and David Orr (2005, 133) thus concludes that we "cannot do such things for long without bringing about economic ruin, endless wars, more terror, political turmoil, isolation, and finally, ecological collapse." To behave "in such a massive way with so little regard for our own future is a kind of collective insanity that is suicidal" (Suzuki 1999, 151).

Rather than deepen the well of despair (and thus foment wider disengagement), these insights are intended to serve as a wakeup call so that we might reconnect to the world around us in a spirit of "active hope" (Macy and Johnstone 2012). Reflecting on economically distressed Detroit, Rebecca Solnit (2007, 73) discerned in it "the hope that we can reclaim what we paved over and poisoned, that nature will not punish us, that it will welcome us home." As Alan Weisman (2008, xv) opined in the introduction to Thich

Nhat Hanh's book *The World We Have: A Buddhist Approach to Peace and Ecology*, things are indeed this simple, and urgent: "The environment unites every human, of every nation and creed. If we fail to save it, we all perish. If we rise to meet the need, we and all to which ecology binds us—other humans, other species, other everything—survive together. And that will be peace." Hanh (2008, 2, 37) himself calls for a "collective awakening" in which we can "begin the work of healing" the individual, society, and the environment, and Suzuki (1999, 12) reminds us that "human beings hold enormous responsibility" to do this work. Instructively, Orr (2005, 134) thus divines a palpable "common ground around an agenda of peace, nonviolence, fairness, protection of communities, restoration of degraded places, ecological sustainability, an extended view of human rights as well as the rights of species and nature, and least, the rights of our children and those yet to live on Earth."

For Orr (2005, 135), it is apparent that "we are called to higher things," and are on the cusp of "a new enlightenment." Shiva (2003, 45) adduces a "new way of thinking and being on this planet," and invites us to embrace "a new worldview in which compassion not greed is globalized"—where we can be "connected to each other and the world in the common fabric of life." Suzuki (1999, 198) likewise observes "the beginning of a new way of thinking about the world—as sets of relationships rather than separated objects." As such, the same moment of crisis, and even potential extinction, is also a profound opportunity to usher in a paradigm shift that takes us to the core of our relationships with each other and the world. This is precisely what Macy (2013) urges with her concept of "the great turning," which she describes as "the essential adventure of our time: the shift from the Industrial Growth Society to a life-sustaining civilization." This effort entails taking direct action to slow the rate of destruction, developing creative and collaborative alternatives, and cultivating "a profound shift in our perception of reality"—ultimately coming to recognize that "our world is a sacred whole, worthy of adoration and service" (Macy 2013). As Berman (1984, 301) concludes, "If we are lucky, by 2200 A.D. the old paradigm may well be a curiosity, a relic of a civilization that seems millennia away."

However, we will not get there through luck alone; the path ahead will require fortitude and perseverance, coupled with nothing short of a revolution in our thoughts and deeds alike. One of the most poignant voices calling for this revolution of consciousness and conduct has been Chellis Glendinning. Her landmark 1994 book (re-released in 2007), *My Name Is Chellis and I'm in Recovery from Western Civilization*, remains a classic in the field of ecopsychology, highlighting the alienation and suffering that come with our increasing disconnection from the earth. The problem is not merely one of individual choices, but more so about the kind of society in which we are participating: mechanical, hyper-technological, dehumanizing, objectifying, monocultural, murderous, and toxic. For Hanh (2008, 88), it remains the case that "when we are in harmony with each other, we are also in harmony with the land"—and vice versa. Extending this logic, the opposite would equally be true, namely that disharmony also begets disharmony. This is part of the import of Glendinning's (1990) teachings, namely that we cannot attain human well-being, either individually or collectively, unless and until we come to grips with the myriad ways in which our societies "are out of control and desecrating the fragile fabric of life on Earth." We remain, unfortunately, subservient to and conditioned by remote technologies and oppressive ideologies alike, comprising a "psycho-socioeconomic system" based on principles of "standardization, efficiency, linearity, and fragmentation" (Glendinning 1995, 45).

It is little wonder that we frequently go mad, individually and collectively. How could it be otherwise, when the baseline of our technologically constructed lives contrasts so blatantly with the natural rhythms that lay at the core of our genetic memories and long-forgotten cultural narratives? We are addicted to a system we can neither control nor easily resist, as Glendinning discerns, and like an addict we must take responsibility for our actions (and inactions) before genuine healing can begin. It is not *them* who wage war, perpetrate violence, despoil the earth, and decimate sacred spaces, but rather *us* who suborn it, pay for it, buy it, watch it, consume it, wear it, eat it, drive it, and let it stand uninterrupted without rising up to throw the proverbial "moneychangers out of the temple." Even so, many of us do struggle against the hardware and software of injustice, working in our communities to reclaim and reconnect with "the same qualities and conditions in which our species lived for more than 99.997 percent of its existence" (Glendinning 1995, 52). But the work has been slow, and the time to change grows short.

Fortunately, we have a number of viable templates for what we are after as conscientious practitioners of peace ecology. Our needs are relatively few, and are time-tested in their wide applicability: "physical nourishment, vital community, fresh food, continuity between work and meaning, unhindered participation in life experiences, personal choices, community decisions, and spiritual connection with the natural world" (Glendinning 1995, 53). Our demand is not for a return to a pristine past, real or imagined, or for a perfected utopia here and now. As Glendinning (1990) has advanced, akin to the elements of Macy's Great Turning, we seek the dismantling of unhealthy, oppressive, destructive technologies (both of the mechanical and sociopolitical varieties), in favor of new technologies that foster autonomy and exist at the appropriate scale, including community-based, renewable energy sources; organic technologies in food, medicine, and transportation; conflict resolution practices based on cooperation and restoring relationships; and decentralized sociopolitical systems that empower people, foster participation, and promote responsibility at all levels. In the end, consistent with the vision of peace ecology brought forth in this volume, we seek a world premised on the mutuality of "human dignity and nature's wholeness" (Glendinning 1990), recognizing that we cannot attain one without the other.

Continuing the Story

The truly remarkable aspect of this nascent vision is that we already possess all of the tools we need to manifest it. Nothing referenced here is reliant upon some future technological breakthrough or miraculous discovery. We can make the transition to a more peaceful, just, balanced, and sustainable world with far less effort and commitment of resources than it takes to maintain the current one—the one that is consuming everything (including us) on the way to its predestined demise. We know what needs to be done, and we have the resources to do it; all that we require at this juncture is the political will and personal wherewithal to make it so. The concept of reenchantment can serve as a touchstone for deepening our engagement with these issues and rekindling our passion for the world and that which we will leave to our children. Are we really content to go about our business, purposefully ignorant of our impacts, and be the generation of humans forever remembered (assuming anyone is here to remember) as the one that crashed the system through its profligacy and waste? We can and must do better than this.

Advocating for peace ecology almost comes down to arguing for patently self-evident items such as clean air and water, healthy food, meaningful work, cooperation, political voice, an end to the futility and devastation of war, and a better future for our children. It is hard to fathom that there could be an opposing view on these issues; more often than not, it takes the form of a "realist" stance arguing that such notions may be good ideas in theory but they are idealistic at best and dangerously naïve at worst. We are told that humans simply cannot get along, that there is "evil" in the world that must be combated at every turn, that the current system is imperfect but is the best one we have ever had, that science and progress will yield technological solutions to the problems that plague us, that predictions of impending doom are alarmist, and that only by staying the course can we achieve relative stability in a dangerous and uncertain world. This is a seductive tale that seems plausible to many, since it relieves them of the responsibility to directly engage the issues before us, but it is beginning to erode in many places as the paternalistic figures propagating it reveal their lack of regard for people and nature alike in ways that are increasingly difficult to ignore even for the well-fed and financially solvent among us. In the end, "it is business as usual that is the utopian fantasy" (Speth 2010, 22), not peace ecology.

Casting a light directly on these issues, the nexus between peace and the environment that has been steadily growing in recent years provides a basis for drawing out the foundational components of a new ethic to replace the dominant one of complicit capitulation. For instance, Christos Kyrou (2006, 10) has argued that peace studies and environmental studies share many affinities, including a belief in diversity, interdependence, and nonviolence, concluding that peace ecology is reliant upon two key and mutually inclusive principles: the "capacity to maintain ecological integrity with humans residing responsibly in and as part of nature," and an "effectiveness in managing conflicts constructively while eliminating the various forms of violence." Kent Shifferd (2011, 109, 172) envisions an integrated "peace system" that is global, comprehensive, and reflective of "a radical vision of the whole."

For Shifferd (2011, 173, 201), such a system includes the peaceful resolution of conflicts, an economy in which everyone's basic needs are met, and sustainable human-environment relations based on "the interdependence of all beings who together make up a web of life, the biosphere." Echoing these themes, David Barash and Charles Webel offer a comprehensive peace ecology perspective:

> A world at peace must be one in which all living things are "at home." . . . The health, well-being, and security of every individual become inseparable from the health, well-being, and security of the Earth itself. . . . We cannot fully make "peace" until we make peace with our planetary environment. . . . Peace may ultimately require a much broader view of the human community, in which people are responsible not only for their own actions, the actions of other people, and their effects on other people but also for their effects on all other life forms. . . . All things, quite literally, are linked to all others. Accordingly, any striving for peace must take account of this connectedness. (2009, 397–419)

Academics and mystics alike recognize the power and utility of such synergies. Perhaps at the end of the day, what we are really seeking is a new narrative, another story that binds us together and to the world around us. Often invoking images of the sacred, creation stories can "help us to reconcile conflicts and contradictions and describe a coherent reality" (Suzuki 1999, 185). For those disinclined to embrace anything as quaint as a creation myth, especially one grounded in arcana like sacredness or enchantment, consider that we are already living out our lives largely beholden to such stories, whether or not we recognize them as such. The pervasive idea that humans are inherently uncooperative and untrustworthy is one such myth, as is its corollary proposition that rational entities seek to maximize their own self-interest. We are thoroughly beholden to narratives that define progress as inevitable and growth as good, that dichotomize the relationship between humans and nature, that render non-human life as inferior and subordinate, and that likewise create such untenable divisions within our human societies as well. None of this is immutable—it is merely what we tell ourselves along the way.

The old story of an inert, lifeless earth put here for our wanton consumption and for us to exercise power over is reaching its inevitable conclusion and belongs in history's dustbin. We need a new story—or an even older one, as the case may be—that recognizes the living systems all around us and that strives for a sense of power *with* rather than over one another and the world. This new story can be spiritual for those so inclined, but it need not be rendered as such. Indeed, it is eminently pragmatic to survive, after all. Beyond that, we have the capacity to promote resiliency, responsibility, regeneration, and renewal from the personal to the global levels. We can help restabilize the systems that support us, turning the current vicious cycle of degradation-conflict into one of sustainability-peace. We can still have complex, modern lives as new challenges and opportunities emerge, without the pervasive pathologies and self-destructive behaviors that dominate today. This does not mean that we suddenly wake up and act well or that our intrinsic nature changes overnight—but more so that we find our way home again, as Albert Einstein opined in terms that remain relevant (if linguistically dated) today:

> A human being is part of the whole, called by us the universe. A part limited in time and space. He experiences himself, his thoughts and feelings, as something separate from the rest, a kind of optical delusion of his consciousness. This delusion is a kind of prison for us, restricting us to our personal desires and to affection for a few persons nearest to us. Our task must be to free ourselves from this prison by widening our circle of compassion to embrace all living creatures. (in Suzuki 1999, 26)

If anyone wants to argue with Einstein, please be my guest! The rest of us will be forging ahead with the essential work of reinvigorating our societies and restabilizing our place in the world.

CONCLUSION
RESTABILIZING THE HABITAT, AND OURSELVES

The central thesis advanced in this book is complex in its full implications, yet relatively straightforward in its basic rendering. The core problems confronting humankind can be grouped into two primary spheres: on the one hand, there is *sociopolitical violence* in all of its various manifestations (e.g., warfare, oppression, disempowerment, competition, privatization, control), and on the other there is *environmental degradation* and its associated processes (e.g., climate change, loss of biodiversity, diminution of essential resources, toxicity, pollution, waste). What I have posited here is that violence and degradation are inherently interrelated, potentially existing in a feedback loop in which one reinforces the other as, for example, with the increasing co-optation of the global food supply by ecologically unfriendly corporations, or with the militaristic race to extract and control the last planetary reserves of minerals and energy sources. With the nexus of violence and degradation thus coming into sharper relief, there is also the concomitant potential to tap into these same relational patterns for more positive and productive purposes. In presenting such arguments and exemplars—often circumscribed by their spatial reach in given localities and regions, with the question of their scalability to the *global* remaining open—the essence of this volume has been to articulate a framework linking peace and nonviolence with ecology and sustainability, in the belief that this union is the crux of the matter.

Peace ecology contends that there needs to be a paradigmatic shift in how we view our relationship to the biosphere. Specifically, we cannot think merely about temperatures or technologies, but rather in terms of the overall *destabilization* of the planet's capacity to support human habitation—since, at root, life "depends on a kind of fundamental, underlying stability" (Barash and Webel 2009, 399). Such a move requires us to assume responsibility for the continuation of the conditions of our own existence. The premise is simply that we can and must take dramatic action—not in some abstract "Save the Earth" sense, but more so to save ourselves. Indeed, the accumulated footprint of civilization in just a few centuries of industrialism has contributed to an escalating erosion of precisely the conditions required for us to survive. This is the paradox of the human enterprise, namely that too much of the very things that enable us to flourish can sow the seeds of our destruction. Addressing the interlinked crises leading to this pervasive sense of destabilization requires a reorientation of our mindset away from conflict and consumption and toward collaboration and conservation. As Albert Einstein once said, "We can't solve problems by using the same kind of thinking we used when we created them." The road ahead will be arduous—"There's no easy way out of the trouble we're in," as Bill McKibben (2010) has asserted—but every great journey starts with small steps.

From Crises to Opportunities

Let us then be clear about the implications of embarking on this course of action. The challenges of perpetual war, climate change, resource depletion, and escalating societal violence are not going to magically vanish overnight. Moving from a paradigm rife with crises to one defined by opportunities will take more than a rhetorical gesture, and hard choices will have to be made even as many people around the world continue to suffer from the acute effects of business as usual. The elite interests that manage the military-industrial complex are unlikely to suddenly abdicate their positions of power and privilege in the name of sustainability and social justice, even when confronted by incontrovertible evidence and/or large-scale demonstrations of protest. However, there is no aspect of this global system that is not contingent upon our assent and participation on some level. The more we learn to leverage that requisite consent, the more we can exercise control over our collective course of action, and the more we can envision scenarios in which small-scale actions yield widespread impacts; indeed, this is the basic teaching of Gandhian nonviolence, namely that we have a moral duty to refuse to cooperate with injustice while at the same time advancing the pursuit of just outcomes both socially and ecologically.

This push-pull strategy has been deployed in manifold settings, and often-times works (as Gandhi's challenge to the British Empire did) to help those opposing change see the error of their ways; Gandhian nonviolence is "an active engagement in compassion" (Shiva 2005, 116). We can surmise that even those thoroughly invested in the dominant paradigm are interested in leaving a better (or even habitable) world for their children and their children's children. Their ostensible "rationality" might even be appealed to as the evidence of looming cataclysm steadily mounts. With empirical observations and the grim predictions of most credible scientists firmly in hand (e.g., Rockström et al. 2009), it seems more irrational *not* to accept that the paradigm in which we have been living is rapidly approaching its prophesied closure point. Part of the peacemaker's task is to bring this realization to those either not yet aware or actively opposed to its implications. A peace ecology revolution would strive to uplift everyone, not merely supplant one ruling force with another, and it would equally place environmental issues on a par with sociopolitical ones in terms of building a wide movement to confront the crises of the day.

Eschatological notions of "collapse" and the like can be disempowering on some level, with the apocalyptic sensibility at times breeding apathy and cynicism, as well as courting even further displays of fascism and militarism in the process (cf. Lilley et al. 2012). Peace ecology is expressly framed in the affirmative, in the belief that people are more likely to be motivated by working *for* something positive rather than merely struggling *against* negativities. It reminds us of our obligation to get up every day and keep trying to promote the values of peace and justice in our lives, communities, bioregions, and the larger world. Whatever the ineluctable combination of fate and free will has in store for us, it remains incumbent upon us to roll up our sleeves and work to avert the self-inflicted cataclysm we have been relentlessly courting in recent years. Establishing a predominant ethos of "engaged restabilization" in our outlooks and actions strikes close to the heart of the matter and could be the ticket for righting the ship in the nick of time. As Aldo Leopold's "land ethic" famously asserts, "A thing is right when it tends to preserve the integrity, stability, and beauty of the biotic community" (in Barash, ed. 2010, 155). We need to reclaim our place in this community and seek to promote its continuity. "Our brash exuberance over our incredible inventiveness and productivity," writes David Suzuki (1999, 207), "has made us forget where we belong." Chief among these forgotten attributes are the "ancient virtues" of humility, respect, love, faith in ourselves, and harmonious relations.

Consider the proposition that we have lived in relative harmony with each other and the world around us for more of our time here than we have been egocentric, militaristic dominators. The post-industrial arc that is pushing to the limit the planet's capacity to continue supporting us is but a mere blip in the cosmic spectrum of existence, even in the time span of our brief human experiment. But let us not sugarcoat the magnitude of our task. Simply being kind and appreciating the wonder of nature will not apply the brakes to our collective immolation overnight. We also need to immediately take the harder steps of weaning ourselves off the consumer addictions that have turned most of us into the agents of our own destruction, and we likewise need to promptly abandon both the hardware and software of devastation with which we have laced the emerging global culture. Most of us, especially in the industrial societies, have been caught in a vicious cycle whereby our lives are conditioned upon the unsustainable extraction of resources—often secured under the auspices of a rapacious war machine—by a globalized economic system that pries open nations and strip-mines the depths of the earth. This system, however, merely serves to exacerbate the twin problems of depletion and degradation.

Fortunately, the same processes that create feedback loops in our economic and political arrangements can also be made to yield mutually supporting positive results as well. Greater appreciation for the environment lessens our rampant consumption, and transcending our imposed identities as consumers opens up the prospect of becoming co-creators instead. Being purveyors of peace creates fewer conflicts around us, and fewer global "hot spots" in turn promotes greater feelings of peaceableness. Relationships based on trust and mutual aid can cultivate instincts toward greater trustworthiness and adduce behavior further motivated beyond the narrow confines of egocentrism and unbridled self-interest. In this sense, a potential "self-fulfilling apocalypse" can just as likely become a self-fulfilling utopia. We need not wait for crises to deepen in order to change course; rather, our task is "to develop alternatives to existing policies, to keep them alive and available until the politically impossible becomes politically inevitable" (Speth 2010, 22). In essence, we are charged with keeping the present from precluding the future—and thus staving off the ravages of escalating crises a bit longer.

Again, this will not be easy, requiring a reinvigorated spirit of sacrifice and collective responsibility; it will also demand of us an eternal vigilance in order to keep the positive feedback loop, well, "positive." Whatever the challenges involved in this transition, they will likely pale before the ones that are already beginning to manifest in our midst. In the end, we can either choose to alter course and turn crisis into opportunity, or have the same (for all intents and purposes) imposed upon us by the inescapable laws of nature; peace ecology asserts an unequivocal preference for the former. "The question, then," writes David Orr (2005, 57), "is not whether we will change, but whether the transition will be done with more or less grace and whether the destination will be desirable or not." Rather than pass the responsibility on to remote lawmakers or future generations, peace ecology counsels that we can and must account for our own personal contributions to the overall social and ecological systems in which we participate, and further that we should utilize this insight to break out of a mindset of self-loathing and/or powerlessness in favor of one that gives us a key role to play in the planet's future.

There are two specific changes we must make in order to accomplish this. First, as noted above, there needs to be a paradigmatic shift in how we view our relationship to the balance of life on the planet. Specifically, we cannot focus merely on climate change or resource depletion, but rather should think in terms of the planet's overall capacity to support human habitation. This sharpens the focus specifically to the human-induced changes in evidence as they impact human life, and further calls upon us to take responsibility for the continuation of the conditions of our own existence. Second, we need to reintegrate humankind as part of nature. This doesn't mean that every technological intervention we will make is somehow to be deemed "natural" or that we can otherwise ignore the impacts of our collective actions. "Complexity is our glory, but also our vulnerability," writes McKibben (2010), and "we're moving quickly from a world where we push nature around to a world where nature pushes back." Unlike most other species, humankind possesses the unique capacity to critically reflect upon our conduct and gauge its level of integration with the balance of the biosphere. This quality accords us a special role in engaging environmental issues—one that must be exercised with diligence and a sense of the whole in order to be viable.

Peace ecology posits that this shift (from degradation to destabilization, and from separation to integration) can serve as a means for addressing not only vital ecological issues, but for harmonizing our diverse sociopolitical perspectives as well. The basic notion is to move from generic concepts like "climate change" to the more focused notion of considering the "destabilization of the planet's capacity to support human habitation" as a rubric that could cut across ideological orientations. Whatever differences we possess, we might at least converge on the desirability of continued human existence. The premise is simply that we can and must take serious action now in order to preserve the habitability of the biosphere; this is the piece of the puzzle that we can rightly be said to own, both ethically and politically. Saving the entire planet retains too much of the hubris that got us into this mess to be truly useful; indeed, the planet will quite likely do just fine in our absence, should that come to pass. It is, in the end, our human-driven impacts that are the ones most responsible for imperiling our own existence. Like it or not, we are not masters of this world but are simply part of a community. It is time to act like it.

"Why are we as a species destroying the very basis of our survival and existence?" asks Vandana Shiva (2005, 111). Our patterns of wanton consumption, the disposability of commodities, the false externalization of wastes, and the extraction of vast resources for pleasure rather than purpose have pushed us to the limit of the planet's carrying capacities. The results are evident everywhere we look. Toxification, pollution, drought, maldistribution of food and other essentials, energy-intensive production methods, perpetual resource wars, increasing rates of industrial-age diseases, species extinctions, loss of biodiversity, and degradation of arable soils are all measurable phenomena. We have seen a rapid increase in overall planetary temperature and concomitant alterations in climate patterns. The polar ice caps are receding at an alarming rate, releasing methane and other gases that can trigger a runaway greenhouse effect. The oceans are rising, acidifying, and losing their capacity to support life. Resource wars are explicitly touted as a means to secure material necessities in a world where supplies are diminishing, even as warfare is extremely resource-intensive and contributes greatly to further toxification and degradation in the process. Corporate agriculture requires massive energy and water inputs, and winds up displacing and decimating more people than it is capable of feeding. Nuclear power leads to disastrous effects at every level, from the mining of uranium to uncontainable disasters. Geoengineers want to "seed" the atmosphere and manipulate more of the earth's processes as a solution to the already-devastating effects of human manipulation of the environment.

We can list the negative effects of these downward-spiral processes ad nauseum, but that will not bring us any closer to a solution. Mere knowledge of impending disaster seems to be a less-than-robust motivator for altering destructive behavior, since many seem convinced that the worst effects can be deferred to the future—perhaps when we have found high-tech "solutions" to the challenges before us. Others deflect the mounting crises by placing faith in the realm of either "divine origins" or some other "natural cycle" that explains and excuses our own contributions. This, however, represents another form of abdication. Simply put, we have to own up to the responsibility of what we have wreaked on the world around us in the name of progress, and likewise what we have visited upon ourselves in the process. The moving principle of continued human existence, whatever we ascribe to our origination, remains firmly in our own hands at this point. We can choose to exercise that power wisely, or perish in its misapplication. Peace ecology asserts that there is strong evidence to suggest that we retain an inherent capacity to realize the former condition of wisdom, and that we can do so while there is still time. As Suzuki (1999, 154) has appropriately urged, "We must rein in our destructive ways and then provide conditions to encourage the return and regrowth of life." We have the capacity to do this.

Yes We Can—but Will We?

Moving toward closure on an optimistic note, it is useful to focus on viable alternatives and strategies for change that we can employ in our everyday lives and local communities. Let us be clear, of course, that the genuine solution to the problems of endemic warfare, escalating societal violence, widening economic inequality, environmental degradation, climate change, and the despoliation of the habitat involves no less than completely remaking and restabilizing the nature of our relationships with one another and our collective engagement with the balance of life on the planet. Yet this often appears as an aspirational aim, one that strains our capacity for implementation, and can thus serve to perpetuate greater disengagement. Even in the era of globalization, it is barely conceivable for most of us how we might act globally. Instead, we can focus our efforts around specific areas where our individual and collective choices still matter:

> Localization: Our patterns of consumption have brought us to the brink of survivability. The embedded costs of energy and transportation in our food alone would disable most of us from eating at all if they were reflected in the actual price. Rescaling our lives to support local economies is a crucial step toward restoring balance and realizing a sustainable society. We will still be socially and ecologically linked with others, regionally and even globally, but the baseline of our lives must be rooted in our locales and bioregions. Humans have lived this way for a long time, and we can do so as well. "The social unit that will have the greatest stability and resilience into the future is the local community" (Suzuki 1999, 213).
>
> Basics: Not only the scale but the scope of our lives can be reframed to reduce our impact on the world. The necessary elements to sustain human life are relatively basic, and all the rest is excess and waste that threatens our very survival. We don't have to return to caves or give up all creature comforts, but working to bring our lives closer to the level of *need* than *want* is crucial. Food, water, energy, and shelter have long defined the parameters of human existence, and

with good reason. We can reclaim the capacity to produce these essentials in a just manner. "Only by meeting all [people's basic] needs can society … achieve true sustainability" (Suzuki 1999, 213).

Energy: The question of how to generate power is central to promoting a sustainable future. The coal-petroleum-nuclear economy has done apparent wonders for productivity and expansion, but the returns on investment are actually false profits when the real costs are included. If the subsidies given to fossil and atomic fuels were dedicated to green energy sources and their development, the world could change rapidly. We can help usher this change in by minimizing our energy consumption and opting for greener and localized sources right now. Connect your own energy use to consumption and lifestyle choices, "work to get your home as ecologically benign as possible [and] make 'disposable' an obscene word" (Suzuki 1999, 215).

Education: The greatest driver of human behavior remains education. Beyond schools there are also the more informal modes of cultivating societal norms, including most prominently the media. If these sources were recalibrated to include a few basic lessons, the ripple effects would be palpable. Indeed, we can use the channels of discourse—including texts such as this one—to foster cooperation as much as competition, and interdependence as a complement to individualism. Teaching people to teach others multiplies the effect and helps build a sense of solidarity and the ethos of a shared human future. "The thousands of positive news stories to report from all over the world," observes Suzuki (1999, 219), provide a "basis for real hope."

Of course, hope alone cannot remake the map of the world overnight. Nor would it be prudent to suggest that relatively localized, small-scale actions will turn the paradigm in short order. But a critical mass has to start somewhere—and in light of modern science suggesting that the "tipping point" for a new idea to spread through a population takes merely 10 percent of the people holding it (Science Daily 2011), perhaps we might not be as far away as it often appears. It is entirely conceivable that social movements will continue arising in response to escalating crises and that they will find greater salience, thus resulting in a sea change as to popular views on fundamental issues. Whether this will occur in time to avert the sort of cataclysmic sea change anticipated as a result of climate destabilization remains unclear; one of the rationales for this book is to add my voice to the growing chorus of those working to see that it in fact does.

In order to achieve such a critical mass in time, there are a number of related factors that could be explored in subsequent treatments and interventions. Deeper case studies on, and broader empirical support for, the processes of environmental peacemaking and peacebuilding are warranted, in particular as to how these principles apply at local, regional, and global scales alike. Academic and scientific explorations of the pertinent issues should include greater participatory bases and action-oriented emphases, inviting readers not only to deepen their knowledge but to turn it into tangible results as well. Likewise, the agglomeration of "best practices" arising from the peace ecology vision can be brought to bear more straightforwardly in policy discussions, thus potentially scaling up their impact. The solutions proposed ought to be appropriately complex to match the challenges at hand, avoiding quick fixes and invocations of right/wrong or winners/losers, and meeting the needs of multiple constituencies in terms of their applicability, durability, and capacity to be continued into the future. It is also incumbent upon us to develop evaluative tools for measuring the success of our initiatives, rather than simply taking them on faith or falling into a feel-good mindset while objective conditions worsen. I have tried to sketch the terms under which some of this might occur, with due regard to the limitations of space and time. This work is intended as a starting point—a floor, perhaps, rather than a ceiling.

And in the End . . .

Some readers may recall the Beatles' lyrical intonation that "the love you take is equal to the love you make." In its poetic sensibility, this encapsulates the basic notion that any healthy relationship is based on a balance between the parties. Ecologically speaking, we must recognize that "we cannot take more away from the land than we—or nature—put back," and moreover that "it is ethically unacceptable, and ultimately impractical as well, to purchase short-term gratification and growth while robbing future generations" (Barash and Webel 2009, 407). In this sense, there is both a spatial and a temporal element to the process of *restabilization*, as we confront not only our relationship with the earth but also with its future inhabitants. This is the essence of *sustainability*, in its best sense, embodying the creation of "long-term economic, political, and moral arrangements that secure the well-being of present and future generations" (Orr 2005, 57). This term has been used throughout this volume notwithstanding its diverse associations, ranging from relatively shallow aspects such as recycling and "green" consumerism, to deeper incursions based on subsistence and structural change. "I have long been impatient with 'sustainability', as if it were an end in itself. Isn't it more important to think about what we want to sustain, and therefore what we want to create?" (Eisenstein 2011, 249). The central idea is not to merely continue present structures and patterns, but to invent new ones.

We certainly do not lack for cogent suggestions and viable alternatives, many of which have been mentioned in the preceding pages: community gardening, organic farming, collaborative water management, reinvigorating the commons, demonetizing our relationships, decommodifying the stuff of nature, preserving the environment for its own sake and as a potential pathway to peacebuilding, navigating crises through mutual aid, forestalling crises through sustainable practices, resisting militarism on all levels, practicing compassion and radical generosity, moving toward green energy sources, relocalizing the foundation of our lives, respecting diversity both sociopolitically and ecologically, and working across borders of all types. Above all, we should realize that (a) there is still time to act although it is rapidly dwindling, and (b) we have the power and ability to redefine our baseline relationships with each other and the earth. In both cases, there is no place for abdication—it is incumbent upon us to act well, and right now. Again, this will surely be difficult, yet what is the alternative? Checking out, self-medicating, resigning ourselves to inevitability, giving up altogether—none of these make for an especially peaceful or sustainable life. We will need to leverage our innate creativity and engage our imaginations to point the way forward, and we might just save a world in the process.

Perhaps this is what we were destined for all along. Being the ones upon whom the choice has squarely fallen—will it be conflagration or continuation?—confers upon us something of a unique status. On the one hand, we might feel compelled "to preserve what remains and dedicate ourselves to restoring what we have lost" (Hawken 2008, 172); at the same time, we are not "trying to *save* the world," but rather are "trying to *remake* the world" (Hawken 2008, 177, emphases in original). It is not easy to be old-school and cutting-edge at the same time, all while working to stave off the ravages of the present. Yet this is what has befallen us. Rather than thinking in terms of specific goals and outcomes, there is a penchant in the sociopolitical and ecological spheres alike to emphasize *process* instead. In this view, the "solution" to warfare and violence is often seen more as a combination of preventive actions coupled with healing and reconciliation in the aftermath. For their part, environmentalists increasingly favor the notion of *resilience*, which is sometimes seen as "a more useful concept than that of sustainability" (Hopkins 2009) due to its dynamic, process-oriented qualities.

In essence, resilience is the capacity to absorb and adapt to disturbances and changes, while maintaining stability and cohesion—a quality that is "as true for social systems as it is for environmental ones" (Hawken 2008, 172). It is not a blueprint, but rather an array of patterns and processes that serve to restore our capacity to be restorative, to help us rekindle our love for loving relationships at all levels, to heal our tattered ability to be healers. Resilience devolves upon "a strong local community with deep connections," one that helps "each of us to inspire others by first inspiring ourselves" (Martenson 2010, 2). It is about how we procure life's essentials—food, water, energy, shelter—with our local communities at the core of the effort. It is about creating social and political systems patterned on ecological concepts such as redundancy, interdependence, diversity, self-reliance, and feedback loops (cf. Hopkins 2009). We have seen in this volume a number of working visions that embrace this ethos, with the common thread being the cultivation of our capacity to turn crises into opportunities, since the former are never in short supply and may well be the most abundant present-day resource of all.

And in this, we come full circle—or, more appropriately—full cycle. Peace ecology is eminently cyclical, fostering interconnections and generating dynamic exchange, illuminating the synergies between self, society, and nature, and seeking to connect the past, present, and future. An attempt has been made here to highlight the positive aspects of this paradigm, even as we have considered the challenges of militarism, injustice, degradation, and destabilization. We have posited that a working version of "structural peace" could serve as a constructive counterpoint to "structural violence," that the commons might be reclaimed in the face of privatization, that borders can unite rather than divide people and landscapes, and that a vision of interconnectedness may be the antidote to apathy, isolation, and despair. None of this has been asserted lightly, as if a magical ascendance somehow follows our commitment to peace and environmentalism; likewise, there are counterfactuals and opposing arguments to consider, some of which may be of service to help refine whatever nascent "truths" we hold to be self-evident in the halcyon days ahead. There will always be conflicts in our communities and societies, and we will always have to be vigilant about the consequences of our human impacts—which is as it should be.

In the end, I am reminded of a conversation I had with my six-year-old son on one of our many adventurous hikes in the high desert. We had been talking about how trees, and people as well, sometimes get diseases that are caused by tiny life forms. "But Dad," he asserted, "Mother Nature must have had a good reason for making those little creatures, too, right?" To which I replied: "Of course, even if we don't always know what it is." "Maybe it's because if we get sick sometimes, we appreciate it even more when we're healthy," he said. And I nodded, smiling.

References

Acharya, Sourya, and Samarth Shukla. 2012. "Mirror Neurons: Enigma of the Metaphysical Modular Brain." *Journal of Natural Science, Biology and Medicine* 3 (2): 118–124.

Adley, Jessica, and Andrea Grant. 2003. "The Environmental Consequences of War." *Sierra Club of Canada.* http://www.sierraclub.ca/national/postings/war-and -environment.html.

Agyeman, Julian, Robert D. Bullard, and Bob Evans. 2003a. "Joined-Up Thinking: Bringing Together Sustainability, Environmental Justice and Equity." In *Just Sustainabilities: Development in an Unequal World*, edited by Julian Agyeman, Robert D. Bullard, and Bob Evans, 1–16. Cambridge, MA: The MIT Press.

———. 2003b. "Towards Just Sustainabilities: Perspectives and Possibilities." In *Just Sustainabilities: Development in an Unequal World*, edited by Julian Agyeman, Robert D. Bullard, and Bob Evans, 323–335. Cambridge, MA: The MIT Press.

Ali, Saleem H. 2007. "Introduction: A Natural Connection Between Ecology and Peace?" In *Peace Parks: Conservation and Conflict Resolution*, edited by Saleem H. Ali, 1–17. Cambridge, MA: The MIT Press.

Ali, Saleem H., ed. 2007. *Peace Parks: Conservation and Conflict Resolution.* Cambridge, MA: The MIT Press.

Allouche, Jeremy. 2011. "The Sustainability and Resilience of Global Water and Food Systems: Political Analysis of the Interplay Between Security, Resource Scarcity, Political Systems and Global Trade." *Food Policy* 36: 53–58.

Amster, Randall, and Michael Nagler. 2010. "War and Planet Earth: Toward a Sustainable Peace." *Waging Nonviolence* (December 21). http://wagingnonviolence.org /feature/war-and-planet-earth-toward-a-sustainable-peace/.

Anderson, Terry L., and P. J. Hill. 1977. "From Free Grass to Fences: Transforming the Commons of the American West." In *Managing the Commons*, edited by Garrett Hardin and John Baden, 200–216. San Francisco, CA: W. H. Freeman and Co.

Austin, Jay E., and Carl E. Bruch, eds. 2007. *The Environmental Consequences of War: Legal, Economic, and Scientific Perspectives.* Cambridge, UK: Cambridge University Press.

Axelrod, Robert. 1984. *The Evolution of Cooperation*. New York: Basic Books.

Babatunde, Abosede. 2010. "Environmental Conflict and the Politics of Oil in the Oil-Bearing Areas of Nigeria's Niger Delta." *Peace and Conflict Review* 5 (1). http://www.review.upeace.org/index.cfm?opcion=0&ejemplar=20&entrada=107.

Bajaj, Monisha, and Belinda Chiu. 2009. "Education for Sustainable Development as Peace Education." *Peace & Change* 34 (4): 441–455.

Barash, David P., ed. 2010. *Approaches to Peace: A Reader in Peace Studies* (2nd edition). New York: Oxford University Press.

Barash, David P., and Charles P. Webel. 2009. *Peace and Conflict Studies* (2nd edition). Thousand Oaks, CA: SAGE.

Barlow, Maude. 2009. *Blue Covenant: The Global Water Crisis and the Coming Battle for the Right of Water*. New York: The New Press.

———. 2010. "Water for All." In *All That We Share: A Field Guide to the Commons*, edited by Jay Walljasper, 160–166. New York: The New Press.

Barnett, Jon. 2003. "Security and Climate Change." *Global Environmental Change* 13: 7–17.

———. 2007. "Environmental Security and Peace." *Journal of Human Security* 3 (1): 4–16.

Barnett, Jon, and W. Neil Adger. 2007. "Climate Change, Human Security and Violent Conflict." *Political Geography* 26: 639–655.

Basolo, Victoria. 2009. "Environmental Change, Disasters, and Vulnerability: The Case of Hurricane Katrina and New Orleans." In *Global Environmental Change and Human Security*, edited by Richard A. Matthew, Jon Barnett, Bryan McDonald, et al., 97–116. Cambridge, MA: The MIT Press.

Benally, Klee. 2011. "Arresting Developments." *New Clear Vision* (August 19). http://www.newclearvision.com/2011/08/19/arresting-developments/.

Berman, Morris. 1984. *The Reenchantment of the World*. New York: Bantam.

Bernstein, Tobie. 2002. *Strengthening U.S.-Mexico Transboundary Environmental Enforcement*. Washington, DC: The Environmental Law Institute.

Berry, Wendell. 2001. *In the Presence of Fear: Three Essays for a Changed World*. Great Barrington, MA: The Orion Society.

Bhavnani, Ravi. 2009. "Scarcity, Abundance, and Conflict: A Complex New World." *The Whitehead Journal of Diplomacy and International Relations* 10 (2): 65–80.

Blatter, Joachim, Helen Ingram, and Pamela M. Doughman. 2001. "Emerging Approaches to Comprehend Changing Global Contexts." In *Reflections on Water: New Approaches to Transboundary Conflicts and Cooperation*, edited by Joachim Blatter and Helen Ingram, 3–29. Cambridge, MA: The MIT Press.

Blatter, Joachim, Helen Ingram, and Suzanne Lorton Levesque. 2001. "Expanding Perspectives on Transboundary Water." In *Reflections on Water: New Approaches to Transboundary Conflicts and Cooperation*, edited by Joachim Blatter and Helen Ingram, 31–53. Cambridge, MA: The MIT Press.

Blue River Quorum. 2011. "The Blue River Declaration: An Ethic of the Earth." *New Clear Vision* (November 4). http://www.newclearvision.com/2011/11/04/the-blue-river-declaration/.

Boaz, Peter, and Matthew O. Berger. 2010. "Rising Energy Demand Hits Water Scarcity 'Choke Point'." *Inter Press Service* (September 22). http://www.ipsnews.net/2010/09/rising-energy-demand-hits-water-scarcity-choke-point/.

Bonfiglio, Olga. 2008. "Growing Green in Detroit." *Christian Science Monitor* (August 21). http://www.csmonitor.com/The-Culture/Gardening/2008/0821 /growing-green-in-detroit.

Boulding, Elise. 1987. "Building Utopias in History." In *Towards a Just World Peace: Perspectives from Social Movements*, edited by Saul H. Mendlovitz and R. B. J. Walker, 213–233. London: Butterworths.

Boulding, Kenneth E. 1977. "Commons and Community: The Idea of a Public." In *Managing the Commons*, edited by Garrett Hardin and John Baden, 280–294. San Francisco, CA: W. H. Freeman and Co.

Boyle, Mark. 2013. "Beyond Money: Living Without the Illusion of Independence." *Positive News* (April 1). http://positivenews.org.uk/2013/economics_innovation/11748 /money-living-illusion-independence.

Bratman, Steven (with David Knight). 2001. *Health Food Junkies: Orthorexia Nervosa: Overcoming the Obsession with Healthful Eating.* New York: Broadway.

Broughey, Michael V. 2013. "Soldiers Deploy to MBTA Subway Stations Following the Boston Marathon Bombing." *Army.mil* (April 24). http://www.army.mil/article /102044/Soldiers_deploy_to_MBTA_subway_stations_following_the_Boston _Marathon_bombing/.

Brown, Lester R. 2012. *Full Planet, Empty Plates: The New Geopolitics of Food Security.* New York: W. W. Norton & Co.

Brunnschweiler, Christa N., and Erwin H. Bulte. 2009. "Natural Resources and Violent Conflict: Resource Abundances, Dependence and the Onset of Civil Wars." Oxcarre Research Paper, Oxford Centre for the Analysis of Resource Rich Economies, No. 2009-18.

Buckles, Daniel, and Gerett Rusnak. 2000. "Conflict and Collaboration in Natural Resource Management." In *Cultivating Peace: Conflict and Collaboration in Natural Resource Management*, edited by Daniel Buckles, 1–10. Ottawa, Canada: IDRC Books.

Burger, Joanna, et al. 2001. "Introduction: Common-Pool Resources and Commons Institutions." In *Protecting the Commons: A Framework for Resource Management in the Americas*, edited by Joanna Burger, Elinor Ostrom, Richard B. Norgaard, David Policansky, and Bernard D. Goldstein, 1–15. Washington, DC: Island Press.

Butler, Smedley. 1935. *War Is a Racket.* http://www.ratical.org/ratville/CAH/warisaracket .html.

Button, Gregory. 2010. *Disaster Culture: Knowledge and Uncertainty in the Wake of Human and Environmental Catastrophe.* Walnut Creek, CA: Left Coast Press.

Caplan, James A. 2010a. *The Theory and Principles of Environmental Dispute Resolution.* San Bernardino, CA: edrusa.com.

———. 2010b. *The Practice of Environmental Dispute Resolution.* San Bernardino, CA: edrusa.com.

Carius, Alexander. 2006. "Environmental Cooperation as an Instrument of Crisis Prevention and Peacebuilding: Conditions for Success and Constraints." Report commissioned by the German Federal Ministry for Economic Cooperation and Development. http://userpage.fu-berlin.de/ffu/akumwelt/bc2006/papers/Carius_Peacemaking .pdf.

———. 2007. "Special Report: Environmental Peacebuilding: Conditions for Success." *United Nations Environment Programme.* http://www.unep.org.

Castro, A. Peter. 2010. "Communities and Natural Resource Conflicts in Africa: Reflections on Conflict Management Options for Peace-Building in Darfur." In *Environment and Conflict in Africa: Reflections on Darfur*, edited by Marcel Leroy, 341–354. Addis Ababa, Ethiopia: University for Peace.

CEC. 2012. "Conservation Experts from Both Sides of U.S.-Mexico Border Pinpoint Priority Conservation Actions in Big Bend/Río Bravo Region." *Commission for Environmental Cooperation* (September 10). http://www.cec.org/Page.asp?PageID=122&ContentID=25281&SiteNodeID=655.

Chaitin, Julia, Fida Obeidi, Sami Adwan, and Dan Bar-On. 2002. "Environmental Work and Peace Work: The Palestinian-Israeli Case." *Peace and Conflict Studies* 9 (2): 64–94.

Clancy, Tim. 2004. "The War on Bosnia." *World Watch* 17 (2): 12–23.

Clayton, Mark. 2004. "Environmental Peacemaking." *The Christian Science Monitor* (March 4).

Clonan, Tom. 2008. "U.S. Generals Planning for Resource Wars." *Irish Times* (September 22).

Cloud, John. 2010. "Why Your DNA Isn't Your Destiny." *TIME* (June 6). http://content.time.com/time/magazine/article/0,9171,1952313,00.html.

Cohn, Jeffrey P. 2007. "The Environmental Impacts of a Border Fence." *BioScience* 57 (1): 96.

Conca, Ken, and Geoffrey D. Dabelko, eds. 2002. *Environmental Peacemaking*. Baltimore, MD: Johns Hopkins University Press.

Cool, Lisa Collier. 2011. "New Eating Disorders: Are They for Real?" *Yahoo! Health* (April 7). http://health.yahoo.net/experts/dayinhealth/new-eating-disorders-are-they-real.

Crawford, Stanley. 1989. *Mayordomo: Chronicle of an Acequia in Northern New Mexico*. New York: Anchor Books.

Cruz, Diego. 2011. "US-Mexico Border Disturbs Ecology." *The Daily Texan* (July 14). http://www.dailytexanonline.com/news/2011/07/14/us-mexico-border-disturbs-ecology.

Dangl, Benjamin. 2010. "Profiting from Haiti's Crisis." *Toward Freedom* (January 18). http://towardfreedom.com/home/content/view/1827/1/.

de Carbonnel, Alissa. 2010. "Putin Says Arctic Must Remain 'Zone of Peace'." *AFP/Google News* (September 23). http://www.google.com/hostednews/afp/article/ALeqM5j3kfjZrYnSA5ckzjblraADmRKL1w.

de Soysa, Indra. 2002. "Ecoviolence: Shrinking Pie, or Honey Pot?" *Global Environmental Politics* 2 (4): 1–34.

Dear, John. 2012. "Making Peace in Inner-City Oakland, One Block at a Time." *National Catholic Reporter* (February 21). http://ncronline.org/blogs/road-peace/making-peace-inner-city-oakland-one-block-time.

Democracy Now! 2007. "*Unbowed*: Nobel Peace Laureate Wangari Maathai on Climate Change, Wars for Resources, the Greenbelt Movement and More." *Democracy Now!* (October 1). http://www.democracynow.org /2007/10/1/unbowed_nobel_peace_laureate_wangari_maathai.

———. 2010. "US Accused of Militarizing Relief Effort in Haiti." *Democracy Now!* (January 19). http://www.democracynow.org/2010/1/19/us_accused_of_militarizing_relief_effort.

Di John, Jonathan. 2007. "Oil Abundance and Violent Political Conflict: A Critical Assessment." *Journal of Development Studies* 43 (6): 961–986.

Dinar, Shlomi. 2009. "Scarcity and Cooperation Along International Rivers." *Global Environmental Politics* 9 (1): 109–135.

————. 2011. "Conflict and Cooperation Along International Rivers: Scarcity, Bargaining Strategies, and Negotiation." In *Beyond Resource Wars: Scarcity, Environmental Degradation, and International Cooperation*, edited by Shlomi Dinar, 165–199. Cambridge, MA: The MIT Press.

Dinar, Shlomi, ed. 2011. *Beyond Resource Wars: Scarcity, Environmental Degradation, and International Cooperation*. Cambridge, MA: The MIT Press.

Dinar, Shlomi, Ariel Dinar, and Pradeep Kurukulasuriya. 2011. "Scarcity and Cooperation Along International Rivers: An Empirical Assessment of Bilateral Treaties." *International Studies Quarterly* 55: 809–833.

Dolšak, Nives, and Elinor Ostrom. 2003. "The Challenges of the Commons." In *The Commons in the New Millennium: Challenges and Adaptations*, edited by Nives Dolšak and Elinor Ostrom. 3–34. Cambridge, MA: The MIT Press.

Dolšak, Nives, et al. 2003. "Adaptation to Challenges." In *The Commons in the New Millennium: Challenges and Adaptations*, edited by Nives Dolšak and Elinor Ostrom, 337–359. Cambridge, MA: The MIT Press.

Doughman, Pamela M. 2001. "Discourses and Water in the U.S.-Mexico Border Region." In *Reflections on Water: New Approaches to Transboundary Conflicts and Cooperation*, edited by Joachim Blatter and Helen Ingram, 189–211. Cambridge, MA: The MIT Press.

————. 2002. "Water Cooperation in the U.S.-Mexico Border Region." In *Environmental Peacemaking*, edited by Ken Conca and Geoffrey D. Dabelko, 190–219. Washington, DC: Woodrow Wilson Center Press.

Dyer, Gwynne. 2010. *Climate Wars: The Fight for Survival as the World Overheats*. New York: Oneworld Publications.

Editorial. 2009. "The Climate and National Security." *New York Times* (August 17).

Ehrenfeld, David. 2005. "The Environmental Limits to Globalization." *Conservation Biology* 19 (2): 318–326.

Eisenstein, Charles. 2011. *Sacred Economics: Money, Gift & Society in the Age of Transition*. Berkeley, CA: Evolver Editions.

EPA. n.d. "Future Climate Change." *Environmental Protection Agency* (ca. May 2013). http://www.epa.gov/climatechange/science/future.html.

Escamilla, Heriberto. 2005. "You Are My Other Self." *La Prensa San Diego* (April 15). http://laprensa-sandiego.org/archieve/april15-05/self.htm.

Evans, Tina Lynn. 2012. *Occupy Education: Living and Learning Sustainability*. New York: Peter Lang Publishing.

Fettweis, Christopher J. 2011. "Is Oil Worth Fighting For? Evidence from Three Cases." In *Beyond Resource Wars: Scarcity, Environmental Degradation, and International Cooperation*, edited by Shlomi Dinar, 201–233. Cambridge, MA: The MIT Press.

Flesch, Aaron D., Clinton W. Epps, James W. Cain, et al. 2009. "Potential Effects of the United States–Mexico Border Fence on Wildlife." *Conservation Biology* 24 (1): 171–181.

Flores, Jose. 2010. "Detroiters Find 'Way!' Out of No Way." *Urban Habitat: Weaving the Threads* 17 (2). http://urbanhabitat.org/17-2/flores.

Foster, John Bellamy, Brett Clark, and Richard York. 2010. *The Ecological Rift: Capitalism's War on the Earth*. New York: Monthly Review Press.

Gallegos, Joseph C. 1998. "Acequia Tales: Stories from a Chicano Centennial Farm." In

Chicano Culture, Ecology, Politics: Subversive Kin, edited by Devon G. Peña, 235–248. Tucson, AZ: The University of Arizona Press.

Galtung, Johan. 1996. *Peace by Peaceful Means: Peace and Conflict, Development and Civilization*. Thousand Oaks, CA: SAGE.

Garcia, Paula. 2000. "Community and Culture vs. Commodification: The Survival of Acequias and Traditional Communities in New Mexico." *Voices from the Earth* 1 (2).

Garcia, Paula, and Miguel Santistevan. 2008. "Acequias: A Model for Local Governance of Water." In *Water Consciousness: How We All Have to Change to Protect Our Most Critical Resource*, edited by Tara Lohan, 110–119. San Francisco, CA: AlterNet Books.

García-Acevedo, María Rosa. 2001. "The Confluence of Water, Patterns of Settlement, and Constructions of the Border in the Imperial and Mexicali Valleys (1900–1999)." In *Reflections on Water: New Approaches to Transboundary Conflicts and Cooperation*, edited by Joachim Blatter and Helen Ingram, 57–88. Cambridge, MA: The MIT Press.

Gartzke, Erik. 2012. "Could Climate Change Precipitate Peace?" *Journal of Peace Research* 49 (1): 177–192.

Gelobter, Michel. 2001. "Integrating Scale and Social Justice in the Commons." In *Protecting the Commons: A Framework for Resource Management in the Americas*, edited by Joanna Burger, Elinor Ostrom, Richard B. Norgaard, David Policansky, and Bernard D. Goldstein, 293–326. Washington, DC: Island Press.

Giordano, Mark F., Meredith A. Giordano, and Aaron T. Wolf. 2005. "International Resource Conflict and Mitigation." *Journal of Peace Research* 42 (1): 47–65.

Gleditsch, Nils Petter. 2012. "Whither the Weather? Climate Change and Conflict." *Journal of Peace Research* 49 (1): 3–9.

Gleditsch, Nils Petter, Kathryn Furlong, Håvard Hegre, Bethany Lacina, and Taylor Owen. 2006. "Conflicts over Shared Rivers: Resource Scarcity or Fuzzy Boundaries?" *Political Geography* 25: 361–382.

Gleick, Peter H. 2010. "Has the U.S. Passed the Point of Peak Water?" *Huffington Post* (October 12). http://www.huffingtonpost.com/peter-h-gleick/has-the-us-passed -the-poi_b_758698.html.

Glendinning, Chellis. 1990. "Notes Toward a Neo-Luddite Manifesto." *Utne Reader* (March/April).

———. 1995. "Technology, Trauma, and the Wild." In *Ecopsychology: Restoring the Earth, Healing the Mind*, edited by Theodore Roszak, 41–54. San Francisco, CA: Sierra Club Books.

———. 2007. *My Name Is Chellis and I'm in Recovery from Western Civilization*. Gabriola Island, BC: New Catalyst Books.

Goldman, Rafi. 2007. "Palestine and Israel: A Co-operative Approach to Conflict Resolution." In *Co-operatives and the Pursuit of Peace*, edited by Joy Emmanuel and Ian MacPherson, 335–340. Victoria, BC: New Rochdale Press.

Goldsmith, Edward. 1974. "The Ecology of War." *The Ecologist* (May).

Gottlieb, Robert, and Anupama Joshi. 2010. *Food Justice*. Cambridge, MA: The MIT Press.

Gunderson, Lance. 2010. "Ecological and Human Community Resilience in Response to Natural Disasters." *Ecology & Society* 15 (2): 18–28.

Hanh, Thich Nhat. 2008. *The World We Have: A Buddhist Approach to Peace and Ecology*. Berkeley, CA: Parallax Press.

Hanjra, Munir A., and M. Ejaz Qureshi. 2010. "Global Water Crisis and Future Food Security in an Era of Climate Change." *Food Policy* 35: 365–377.

Hardin, Garrett. 1968. "The Tragedy of the Commons." *Science* 162: 1243–1248.

———. 1977a. "Denial and Disguise." In *Managing the Commons*, edited by Garrett Hardin and John Baden, 45–52. San Francisco, CA: W. H. Freeman and Co.

———. 1977b. "Living on a Lifeboat." In *Managing the Commons*, edited by Garrett Hardin and John Baden, 261–279. San Francisco, CA: W. H. Freeman and Co.

Harnden, Toby. 2005. "Threatened with Eviction at Gunpoint, the Big Easy Holdouts Are Now Hailed as Heroes." *The Telegraph* (September 18). http://www.telegraph .co.uk/news/worldnews/northamerica/usa/1498677/Threatened-with-eviction-at -gunpoint-the-Big-Easy-holdouts-are-now-hailed-as-heroes.html.

Hastings, Tom H. 2000. *Ecology of War and Peace*. Lanham, MD: University Press of America.

Hauter, Wenonah. 2008. "Agriculture's Big Thirst: How to Change the Way We Grow Our Food." In *Water Consciousness: How We All Have to Change to Protect Our Most Critical Resource*, edited by Tara Lohan, 72–81. San Francisco, CA: AlterNet Books.

———. 2012. *Foodopoly: The Battle Over the Future of Food and Farming in America*. New York: The New Press.

Hawken, Paul. 2008. *Blessed Unrest: How the Largest Social Movement in History Is Restoring Grace, Justice, and Beauty to the World*. New York: Penguin Books.

Heinberg, Richard. 2010. "Beyond the Limits to Growth." In *The Post Carbon Reader: Managing the 21st Century's Sustainability Crisis*, edited by Richard Heinberg and Daniel Lerch. Healdsburg, CA: Watershed Media.

Hinton, Christopher. 2011. "Iraq War Ends with a $4 Trillion IOU." *MarketWatch (Wall Street Journal)* (December 15). http://articles.marketwatch.com/2011 -12-15/general/30778140_1_iraq-war-iraq-and-afghanistan-veterans-budgetary -assessments.

Hiscock, Geoff. 2012. *Earth Wars: The Battle for Global Resources*. Hoboken, NJ: Wiley.

Hobbes, Thomas. 1974 [1651]. *Leviathan*. New York: Collier Books.

Hoerner, J. Andrew, and Nia Robinson. 2008. "A Climate of Change: African Americans, Global Warming, and a Just Climate Policy in the U.S." *Environmental Justice and Climate Change Initiative*. http://www.rprogress.org/publications/2008 /climateofchange.pdf.

Homer-Dixon, Thomas F. 1999. *Environment, Scarcity, and Violence*. Princeton, NJ: Princeton University Press.

Hopkins, Rob. 2009. "Resilience Thinking." *Resurgence Magazine* 257 (November/ December).

Hou, Jeffrey, Julie M. Johnson, and Laura J. Lawson. 2009. *Greening Cities, Growing Communities: Learning from Seattle's Urban Community Gardens*. Seattle, WA: University of Washington Press.

Kahn, Si, and Elizabeth Minnich. 2005. *The Fox in the Henhouse: How Privatization Threatens Democracy*. San Francisco, CA: Berrett-Koehler Publishers.

Kane, Thomas M. 2007. "Hot Planet, Cold Wars: Climate Change and Ideological Conflict." *Energy & Environment* 18 (5): 533–547.

Kaplan, Robert D. 1994. "The Coming Anarchy." *The Atlantic* (February).

Kaye, Jennifer. 2011. "Nipun Mehta: An Economy to Feed Your Soul." *YES! Magazine*

(December 13). http://www.yesmagazine.org/issues/the-yes-breakthrough-15/nipun-mehta-an-economy-to-feed-your-soul.

Kayyem, Juliette. 2012. "After Sandy, Environmentalists, Military Find Common Cause." *Boston Globe* (November 5).

Kemkar, Neal A. 2006. "Environmental Peacemaking: Ending Conflict Between India and Pakistan on the Siachen Glacier Through the Creation of a Transboundary Peace Park." *Stanford Environmental Law Journal* 25 (1): 1–56.

Kim, Ke Chung. 2007. "Preserving Korea's Demilitarized Corridor for Conservation: A Green Approach to Conflict Resolution." In *Peace Parks: Conservation and Conflict Resolution*, edited by Saleem H. Ali, 239–259. Cambridge, MA: The MIT Press.

King, Martin Luther, Jr. 1963. "Letter from a Birmingham Jail" (April 16). http://mlk-kpp01.stanford.edu/index.php/resources/article/annotated_letter_from_birmingham/.

———. 1967. "Beyond Vietnam" (April 4). http://mlk-kpp01.stanford.edu/index.php/encyclopedia/documentsentry/doc_beyond_vietnam/.

Klare, Michael T. 2002. *Resource Wars: The New Landscape of Global Conflict.* New York: Owl Books.

———. 2009. *Rising Powers, Shrinking Planet: The New Geopolitics of Energy.* New York: Holt Paperbacks.

———. 2012a. *The Race for What's Left: The Global Scramble for the World's Last Resources.* New York: Metropolitan Books.

———. 2012b. "Oil Wars on the Horizon." *TomDispatch* (May 10). http://www.tomdispatch.com/blog//175540/.

Klein, Naomi. 2007. *The Shock Doctrine: The Rise of Disaster Capitalism.* New York: Picador.

———. 2013. "How Science Is Telling Us All to Revolt." *New Statesman* (October 29). http://www.newstatesman.com/2013/10/science-says-revolt.

Kramer, Mattea, and Miriam Pemberton. 2013. "Beating Swords into Solar Panels: Re-Purposing America's War Machine." *Common Dreams* (September 19). http://www.commondreams.org/view/2013/09/19-5.

Kyrou, Christos N. 2006. "Peace Ecology: An Emerging Paradigm in Peace Studies." Paper presented at the annual meeting for the International Studies Association, March 22–25, in San Diego, CA.

LaDuke, Winona. 2005. *Recovering the Sacred: The Power of Naming and Claiming.* Cambridge, MA: South End Press.

———. 2009. "Uranium Mining, Native Resistance, and the Greener Path." *Orion Magazine* (January/February).

Lanier-Graham, Susan D. 1993. *The Ecology of War: Environmental Impacts of Weaponry and Warfare.* New York: Walker & Co.

Lappé, Frances Moore. 2009. "The City That Ended Hunger." *YES! Magazine* (February 13). http://www.yesmagazine.org/issues/food-for-everyone/the-city-that-ended-hunger.

Lasky, Jesse R., Walter Jetz, and Timothy H. Keitt. 2011. "Conservation Biogeography of the US-Mexico Border: A Transcontinental Risk Assessment of Barriers to Animal Dispersal." *Diversity and Distributions: A Journal of Conservation Biogeography* 17 (4): 1–15.

Le Billon, Philippe. 2001. "The Political Ecology of War: Natural Resources and Armed Conflicts." *Political Geography* 20: 561–584.

———. 2005. *Fuelling War: Natural Resources and Armed Conflict*. New York: Routledge.

Lecoutere, Els, Ben D'Exelle, and Bjorn Van Campenhout. 2010. "Who Engages in Water Scarcity Conflicts? A Field Experiment with Irrigators in Semi-arid Africa." MICROCON (A Micro Level Analysis of Violent Conflict), Working Paper 31. Brighton, UK: University of Sussex.

Lee, James R. 2009. *Climate Change and Armed Conflict: Hot and Cold Wars*. New York: Routledge.

Leroy, Marcel, ed. 2009. *Environment and Conflict in Africa: Reflections on Darfur*. Addis Ababa, Ethiopia: University for Peace.

Letman, Jon. 2010a. "In Search of Real Security, Part One: A Closer Look at Our Basic Needs in a Time of Crisis." *Truthout* (August 26). http://archive.truthout.org/in -search-real-security-part-one-a-closer-look-our-basic-needs-a-time-crisis62823.

———. 2010b. "In Search of Real Security, Part Two: Societies, Like All Living Things, Need Air and Light to Live." *Truthout* (August 30). http://archive.truthout.org/in -search-real-security-part-two-societies-like-all-living-things-need-air-and-light -live62869.

Lewis, Michael. 2008. "New Orleans: The Day After." *New York Times (The Lede Blog)* (September 2). http://thelede.blogs.nytimes.com/2008/09/02/new-orleans -the-day-after/.

Lilley, Sasha. 2012a. "The Apocalyptic Politics of Collapse and Rebirth." In *Catastrophism: The Apocalyptic Politics of Collapse and Rebirth*, 1–14. Oakland, CA: PM Press.

———. 2012b. "Great Chaos Under Heaven: Catastrophism and the Left." In *Catastrophism: The Apocalyptic Politics of Collapse and Rebirth*, 44–76. Oakland, CA: PM Press.

Lilley, Sasha, David McNally, Eddie Yuen, and James Davis. 2012. *Catastrophism: The Apocalyptic Politics of Collapse and Rebirth*. Oakland, CA: PM Press.

Linn, Karl. 2005. "Reclaiming the Sacred Commons." *New Village Journal* 1: 42–49.

Living on Earth. 2012. "Working Woods for Carbon and Cash." http://www.loe.org /shows/shows.html?programID=13-P13-00003.

Lohan, Tara. 2009. "Blue Gold: Have the Next Resource Wars Begun?" *The Nation* (March 31).

López, Alexander. 2009. "Environmental Transborder Cooperation in Latin America: Challenges to the Westpahalia Order." In *Global Environmental Change and Human Security*, edited by Richard A. Matthew, Jon Barnett, Bryan McDonald, et al., 291–304. Cambridge, MA: The MIT Press.

Lovett, Ian. 2012. "U.S. and Mexico Sign a Deal on Sharing the Colorado River." *New York Times* (November 20).

Machlis, Gary E., and Thor Hanson. 2008. "Warfare Ecology." *BioScience* 58 (8): 729–736.

Macy, Joanna. 2013. "The Great Turning." *Center for Ecoliteracy*. http://www.ecoliteracy .org/essays/great-turning.

Macy, Joanna, and Molly Young Brown. 1998. *Coming Back to Life: Practices to Reconnect Our Lives, Our World*. Gabriola Island, BC: New Society Publishers.

Macy, Joanna, and Chris Johnstone. 2012. *Active Hope: How to Face the Mess We're in Without Going Crazy*. Novato, CA: New World Library.

Magdoff, Fred, and Brian Tokar. 2010. "Agriculture and Food in Crisis: An Overview." In *Agriculture and Food in Crisis: Conflict, Resistance, and Renewal*, edited by Fred Magdoff and Brian Tokar, 10–30. New York: Monthly Review Press.

Magee, Megan. 2011. "The U.S.-Mexico Border Wall: An Environmental and Human Rights Disaster." *Prospect: Journal of International Affairs at UCSD* (May 18). http://prospectjournal.org/2011/05/18/the-u-s-mexico-border -wall-an-environmental-and-human-rights-disaster/.

Marom, Yotam. 2012. "The Best Response to Disaster: Go on the Offensive." *Waging Nonviolence* (December 3). http://wagingnonviolence.org/feature/the-best -response-to-disaster-go-on-the-offensive/.

Martenson, Chris. 2010. "Personal Preparation." In *The Post Carbon Reader: Managing the 21st Century's Sustainability Crisis*, edited by Richard Heinberg and Daniel Lerch. Healdsburg, CA: Watershed Media.

Martin, Michelle. 2011. "The Possibility Alliance: Ethan Hughes' Educational Homestead." *Mother Earth News* (April 25). http://www.motherearthnews.com/nature-and -environment/possibility-alliance-ze0z11zmar.aspx#axzz2TYf7LK94.

Matthew, Richard A. 2010. "Climate Change and Peace." In *Voices for a Culture of Peace*, SGI-USA Distinguished Speakers Series, 34–53. Santa Monica, CA: Culture of Peace Press.

Matthew, Richard A., and Ted Gaulin. 2001. "Conflict or Cooperation? The Social and Political Impacts of Resource Scarcity on Small Island States." *Global Environmental Politics* 1 (2): 48–70.

———. 2002. "The Ecology of Peace." *Peace Review* 14 (1): 33–39.

Matthew, Richard A., Michael Brklacich, and Bryan McDonald. 2004. "Analyzing Environment, Conflict, and Cooperation." In *Understanding Environment, Conflict, and Cooperation*, produced by United Nations Environment Programme, 5–15. Nairobi, Kenya: UNEP.

Mauss, Marcel. 1925 [2000]. *The Gift: The Form and Reason for Exchange in Archaic Societies* (trans. W. W. Norton). New York: W. W. Norton & Co.

McGrath, Alister. 2002. *The Reenchantment of Nature: The Denial of Religion and the Ecological Crisis*. New York: Doubleday.

McHenry, Keith. 2012. *Hungry for Peace: How You Can Help End Poverty and War with Food Not Bombs*. Tucson, AZ: See Sharp Press.

McIntosh, Alistair. 2004. *Soil and Soul: People versus Corporate Power*. London: Aurum Press.

McKibben, Bill. 2010. "Breaking the Growth Habit." *Scientific American* (March 18).

Mehta, Nipun. 2012. "Would Gandhi Use Social Media?" *Daily Good* (February 21). http:// www.dailygood.org/story/182/would-gandhi-use-social-media-nipun-mehta/.

———. 2013. "Do Nothing Generosity." *ServiceSpace Blog* (May 8). http://www .servicespace.org/blog/view.php?id=12848.

Merton, Thomas, ed. 2007 [1965]. *Gandhi on Non-Violence*. New York: New Directions.

Mische, Patricia, and Ian Harris. 2008. "Environmental Peacemaking, Peacekeeping, and Peacebuilding." *Encyclopedia of Peace Education*. New York: Columbia University Teachers College. http://www.tc.edu/epe.

Moore, Hilary, and Joshua Kahn Russell. 2011. *Organizing Cools the Planet: Tools and Reflections to Navigate the Climate Crisis*. Oakland, CA: PM Press.

Morales, Aurora Levins. 1998. *Medicine Stories: History, Culture and the Politics of Integrity*. Cambridge, MA: South End Press.

Murcott, Anne. 1999. "Scarcity in Abundance: Food and Non-Food." *Social Research* 66 (1): 305–339.

Mychalejko, Cyril. 2013. "Turtles and Tomahawk Missiles, Together at Last? War Is Not the Answer to Climate Change." *Truthout* (January 15). http://truth-out.org/news/item /13917-turtles-and-tomahawk-missiles-together-at-last-war-is-not-the-answer-to -climate-change.

Nel, Philip, and Marjolein Righarts. 2008. "Natural Disasters and the Risk of Violent Civil Conflict." *International Studies Quarterly* 52: 159–185.

Nixon, Rob. 2011. "Planting the Seeds of Peace." *Counterpunch* (September 27). http:// www.counterpunch.org/2011/09/27/planting-the-seeds-of-peace/.

No Border Wall. n.d. "Environmental Impacts." http://www.no-border-wall.com /environmental-impacts.php.

Ordonez, Franco. 2012. "Scientists Work to Bridge Political Gap Between Cuba, U.S." *McClatchy Newspapers* (May 21). http://www.mcclatchydc.com/2012/05 /21/149603/scientists-work-to-bridge-political.html.

Orr, David W. 2005. *The Last Refuge: Patriotism, Politics, and the Environment in an Age of Terror.* Washington, DC: Island Press.

Ostrom, Elinor. 1990. *Governing the Commons: The Evolution of Institutions for Collective Action.* Cambridge, UK: Cambridge University Press.

———. 2001. "Reformulating the Commons." In *Protecting the Commons: A Framework for Resource Management in the Americas*, edited by Joanna Burger, Elinor Ostrom, Richard B. Norgaard, David Policansky, and Bernard D. Goldstein, 17–41. Washington, DC: Island Press.

Parenti, Christian. 2011. *Tropic of Chaos: Climate Change and the New Geography of Violence.* New York: Nation Books.

Parker, Meaghan, Moira Feil, and Annika Kramer. 2004. "Environment, Development and Sustainable Peace: Finding Paths to Environmental Peacemaking." Report based on Wilton Park Conference 758, in cooperation with Adelphi Research (Berlin) and the Woodrow Wilson International Center for Scholars (Washington, DC).

Patel, Raj. 2012. *Stuffed and Starved: The Hidden Battle for the World Food System* (2nd edition). Brooklyn, NY: Melville House.

Paz, Yehuda. 2007. "Working for Peace: The Role of Co-operatives in Conflict Resolution." In *Co-operatives and the Pursuit of Peace*, edited by Joy Emmanuel and Ian MacPherson, 327–333. Victoria, BC: New Rochdale Press.

Peña, Devon G. 1998. "A Gold Mine, an Orchard, and an Eleventh Commandment." In *Chicano Culture, Ecology, Politics: Subversive Kin*, edited by Devon G. Peña, 249–277. Tucson, AZ: The University of Arizona Press.

———. 2005. *Mexican Americans and the Environment: Tierra y Vida.* Tucson, AZ: The University of Arizona Press.

Pfeiffer, E. W. 1990. "Degreening Vietnam." *Natural History* 99 (11): 37–41.

Phillips, Macon. 2010. "The Clinton Bush Haiti Fund." *Whitehouse.gov* (January 16). http://www.whitehouse.gov/blog/2010/01/16/clinton-bush-haiti-fund.

Philpott, Daniel, and Gerard F. Powers, eds. 2010. *Strategies of Peace: Transforming Conflict in a Violent World.* New York: Oxford University Press.

Pimentel, David. 2010. "Reducing Energy Inputs in the Agricultural Production System." In *Agriculture and Food in Crisis: Conflict, Resistance, and Renewal*, edited by Fred Magdoff and Brian Tokar, 241–266. New York: Monthly Review Press.

Postel, Sandra. 2010. "Water: Adapting to a New Normal." In *The Post Carbon Reader: Managing the 21st Century's Sustainability Crisis*, edited by Richard Heinberg and Daniel Lerch. Healdsburg, CA: Watershed Media.

Ramutsindela, Maano. 2007a. *Transfrontier Conservation in Africa: At the Confluence of Capital, Politics and Nature*. Oxfordshire, UK: CABI Publishing.

———. 2007b. "Scaling Peace and Peacemakers in Transboundary Parks: Understanding Glocalization." In *Peace Parks: Conservation and Conflict Resolution*, edited by Saleem H. Ali, 69–81. Cambridge, MA: The MIT Press.

Reardon, Betty. 1994. "Learning Our Way to a Human Future." In *Learning Peace: The Promise of Ecological and Cooperative Education*, edited by Betty Reardon and Eva Norland. Albany, NY: SUNY Press.

Rees, William E., and Laura Westra. 2003. "When Consumption Does Violence: Can There Be Sustainability and Environmental Justice in a Resource-Limited World?" In *Just Sustainabilities: Development in an Unequal World*, edited by Julian Agyeman, Robert D. Bullard, and Bob Evans, 99–124. Cambridge, MA: The MIT Press.

Regan, Margaret. 2013. "Nonviolence and the Drug War." *Sojourners* 42 (2): 34–37.

Renner, Michael, and Zoë Chafe. 2007. *Beyond Disasters: Creating Opportunities for Peace*. Washington, DC: Worldwatch Institute.

Ride, Anouk, and Diane Bretherton, eds. 2011. *Community Resilience in Natural Disasters*. New York: Palgrave Macmillan.

Risen, James. 2010. "U.S. Identifies Vast Mineral Riches in Afghanistan." *New York Times* (June 13).

Rivera, José A. 1998. *Acequia Culture: Water, Land, and Community in the Southwest*. Albuquerque, NM: University of New Mexico Press.

Rockström, Johan, et al. 2009. "Planetary Boundaries: Exploring the Safe Operating Space for Humanity." *Ecology and Society* 14 (2): 32–65.

Rodríguez, Sylvia. 2006. *Acequia: Water Sharing, Sanctity, and Place*. Sante Fe, NM: SAR Press.

Rowland, Marty. 2005. "A Framework for Resolving the Transboundary Water Allocation Conflict Conundrum." *Ground Water* 43 (5): 700–705.

Sanders, Barry. 2009. *The Green Zone: The Environmental Costs of Militarism*. Oakland, CA: AK Press.

Salehyan, Idean. 2008. "From Climate Change to Conflict? No Consensus Yet." *Journal of Peace Research* 45 (3): 315–326.

Schlager, Edella, and William Blomquist. 2001. "Water Resources: The Southwestern United States." In *Protecting the Commons: A Framework for Resource Management in the Americas*, edited by Joanna Burger, Elinor Ostrom, Richard B. Norgaard, David Policansky, and Bernard D. Goldstein, 133–159. Washington, DC: Island Press.

Schumacher, E. F. 1975. *Small Is Beautiful: Economics as if People Mattered*. New York: Harper.

Science Daily. 2011. "Minority Rules: Scientists Discover Tipping Point for the Spread of Ideas." *Science Daily* (July 26). http://www.sciencedaily.com/releases/2011/07/110725190044.htm.

Scott, James Wesley. 1989. "Transborder Cooperation, Regional Initiatives, and Sovereignty Conflicts in Western Europe: The Case of the Upper Rhine Valley." *Publius: The Journal of Federalism* 19 (1): 139–156.

Shifferd, Kent D. 2011. *From War to Peace: A Guide to the Next Hundred Years.* Jefferson, NC: McFarland.

Shiva, Vandana. 2000. *Stolen Harvest: The Hijacking of the Global Food Supply.* Cambridge, MA: South End Press.

———. 2002. *Water Wars: Privatization, Pollution, and Profit.* Cambridge, MA: South End Press.

———. 2003. "Earth Democracy." *Tikkun* 18 (1): 43–45.

———. 2005. *Earth Democracy: Justice, Sustainability, and Peace.* Cambridge, MA: South End Press.

———. 2010. "Time to End the War Against the Earth." *The Age* (November 4). http://www.theage.com.au/opinion/society-and-culture/time-to-end-war-against-the-earth-20101103-17dxt.html.

Sierra Club. n.d. "Sierra Club Borderlands Campaign: Overview." http://www.sierraclub.org/borderlands/overview.aspx.

Sifford, Belinda, and Charles Chester. 2007. "Bridging Conservation Across *La Frontera*: An Unfinished Agenda for Peace Parks Along the US-Mexico Divide." In *Peace Parks: Conservation and Conflict Resolution*, edited by Saleem H. Ali, 205–225. Cambridge, MA: The MIT Press.

Sirimarco, Elizabeth. 1993. *War and the Environment.* Milwaukee, WI: Gareth Stevens Publishing.

Slack, Gordy. 2007. "I Feel Your Pain." *Salon.com* (November 5). http://www.salon.com/2007/11/05/mirror_neurons/.

Smith, Brendan. 2010. "Fighting Doom: The New Politics of Climate Change." *Common Dreams* (November 23). http://www.commondreams.org/view/2010/11/23-1.

Smith, Jackie, and Ernesto Verdeja, eds. 2013. *Globalization, Social Movements, and Peacebuilding.* Syracuse, NY: Syracuse University Press.

Smith, Jeremy N. 2010. *Growing a Garden City.* New York: Skyhorse Publishing.

Sojourner, Mary. 2011. "From Sacrilege to Sacredness," *New Clear Vision* (August 19). http://www.newclearvision.com/2011/08/19/from-sacrilege-to-sacredness/.

Solnit, Rebecca. 2007. "Detroit Arcadia: Exploring the Post-American Landscape." *Harper's Magazine* (July) 315: 65–73.

———. 2009. *A Paradise Built in Hell: The Extraordinary Communities That Arise in Disaster.* New York: Penguin Books.

———. 2012. "Revolutionary Plots: Urban Agriculture Is Producing a Lot More than Food." *Orion Magazine* (July/August).

Speth, James Gustave. 2010. *A New American Environmentalism and the New Economy.* Tenth Annual John H. Chafee Memorial Lecture on Science and the Environment. Washington, DC: National Council for Science and the Environment.

Starhawk. 2011. *The Empowerment Manual: A Guide for Collaborative Groups.* Gabriola Island, BC: New Society Publishers.

Stevens, Michelle L. 2007. "Iraq and Iran in Ecological Perspective: The Mesopotamian Marshes and the Hawizeh-Azim Peace Park." In *Peace Parks: Conservation and Conflict Resolution*, edited by Saleem H. Ali, 313–331. Cambridge, MA: The MIT Press.

Strand, Erik. 2004. "Orthorexia: Too Healthy?" *Psychology Today* (September 1). http://www.psychologytoday.com/articles/200412/orthorexia-too-healthy.

Suzuki, David (with Amanda McConnell). 1999. *The Sacred Balance: Rediscovering Our Place in Nature.* Toronto, ON: Greystone Books.

Swain, Ashok. 2002. "Environmental Cooperation in South Asia." In *Environmental Peacemaking*, edited by Ken Conca and Geoffrey D. Dabelko, 61–85. Washington, DC: Woodrow Wilson Center Press.

Tang, Shui Yan. 1992. *Institutions and Collective Action: Self-Governance in Irrigation*. San Francisco, CA: ICS Press.

Tanner, Randy, Wayne Freimund, Brace Hayden, and Bill Dolan. 2007. "The Waterton-Glacier International Peace Park: Conservation Amid Border Security." In *Peace Parks: Conservation and Conflict Resolution*, edited by Saleem H. Ali, 183–199. Cambridge, MA: The MIT Press.

Tippett, Krista. 2012. "A Wild Love for the World with Joanna Macy." *On Being* (November 1). http://www.onbeing.org/program/wild-love-world/transcript/4905#main_content.

Tokar, Brian. 2010. *Toward Climate Justice: Perspectives on the Climate Crisis and Social Change*. Porsgrunn, Norway: Communalism Press.

Trotz, Alissa. 2010. "We Must Stand with Haiti: Solidarity, Not Help." *Stabroek News* (January 18). http://www.stabroeknews.com/2010/features/01/18/we-must-stand-with-haiti-solidarity-not-help/.

Tully, John 1993. "Vietnam: War and the Environment." *Green Left Weekly* 106 (July 14).

Turton, Anthony R., Marian J. Patrick, and Frédéric Julien. 2006. "Transboundary Water Resources in Southern Africa: Conflict or Cooperation?" *Development* 49 (3): 22–31.

UNDESA. n.d. "International Decade for Action: 'Water for Life' 2005–2015." *United Nations Department of Economic and Social Affairs* (ca. April 2013). http://www.un.org/waterforlifedecade/water_cooperation.shtml.

UNEP. 2009. "From Conflict to Peacebuilding: The Role of Natural Resources and the Environment." *United Nations Environment Programme*. http://www.unep.org.

Urdal, Henrik. 2005. "People vs. Malthus: Population Pressure, Environmental Degradation, and Armed Conflict Revisited." *Journal of Peace Research* 42 (4): 417–434.

Van Schoik, Rick. 2004. "Biodiversity on the U.S.-Mexican Border." *World Watch Magazine* 17 (6) (November/December). http://www.worldwatch.org/node/567.

Vidal, John. 2010. "A Planet at War with Itself." *The Guardian* (September 14). http://www.guardian.co.uk/global-development/2010/sep/14/mdg7-afghanistan-health-environment.

Vintila, Peter. 2007. "Climate Change War or Climate Change Peace." *PostKyoto Journal* (Spring). http://www.postkyoto.org/journal.pdf.

VornDick, Wilson. 2012. "Thanks Climate Change: Sea-Level Rise Could End South China Sea Spat." *The Diplomat* (November 8). http://thediplomat.com/2012/11/08/can-climate-change-wash-away-south-china-sea-dispute/.

Wagner, Cynthia G. 2003. "War Crimes Against Nature." *The Futurist* 37 (3).

Walljasper, Jay. 2010. *All That We Share: A Field Guide to the Commons*. New York: The New Press.

Ward, Diane Raines. 2003. *Water Wars: Drought, Flood, Folly, and the Politics of Thirst*. New York: Riverhead Books.

Ward, Katherine. 2013. "A Fistful of Lindens." *New York Magazine* (April 7).

Washington Post Staff. 2013. "Transcript: Obama's U.N. General Assembly Speech." *Washington Post* (September 24). http://articles.washingtonpost.com/2013-09-24/politics/42340329_1_challenges-war-u-n-general-assembly.

Watts, Michael. 2004. "Violent Environments: Petroleum Conflict and the Political Ecology of Rule in the Niger Delta, Nigeria." In *Liberation Ecologies: Environment, Development, Social Movements* (2nd edition), edited by Richard Peet and Michael Watts, 273–298. New York: Routledge.

Weinthal, E., A Vengosh, A. Marei, A, Gutierrez, and W. Kloppmann. 2005. "The Water Crisis in the Gaza Strip: Prospects for Resolution." *Ground Water* 43 (5): 653–660.

Weisman, Alan. 2008. "Introduction." In *The World We Have: A Buddhist Approach to Peace and Ecology*, by Thich Nhat Hanh, viii–xv. Berkeley, CA: Parallax Press.

Weitzner, Viviane, and Marvin Fonseca Borrás. 2000. "Cahuita, Limón, Costa Rica: From Conflict to Collaboration." In *Cultivating Peace: Conflict and Collaboration in Natural Resource Management*, edited by Daniel Buckles, 129–150. Ottawa, Canada: IDRC Books.

Weller, Philip and Peter Rickwood. 1999. "Kosovo: War on the Environment." *The Ploughshares Monitor* 20 (3).

Welzer, Harald. 2012. *Climate Wars: Why People Will be Killed in the 21st Century*. Malden, MA: Polity Press.

Wenden, Anita L., ed. 2004. *Educating for a Culture of Social and Ecological Peace*. Albany, NY: SUNY Press.

Westing, Arthur H., Warwick Fox, and Michael Renner. 2001. "Environmental Degradation as Both Consequence and Cause of Armed Conflict." Working Paper prepared for Nobel Peace Laureate Forum (PREPCOM subcommittee on Environmental Degradation), June.

Williams, Matt. 2013. "US Troops Sent to Niger to Bolster Military Presence in West Africa." *The Guardian* (February 22). http://www.guardian.co.uk/world/2013/feb/22/us-troops-niger-west-africa.

Wittman, Hannah. 2007. "Planting Peace: MST Co-operatives and Agrarian Justice in Brazil." In *Co-operatives and the Pursuit of Peace*, edited by Joy Emmanuel and Ian MacPherson, 121–146. Victoria, BC: New Rochdale Press.

World Wildlife Fund. 2012. "Google Helps WWF Stop Wildlife Crime." http://worldwildlife.org/stories/google-helps-wwf-stop-wildlife-crime.

Yuen, Eddie. 2012. "The Politics of Failure Have Failed: The Environmental Movement and Catastrophism." In *Catastrophism: The Apocalyptic Politics of Collapse and Rebirth*, 15–43. Oakland, CA: PM Press.

Zohar, Asaf, Stuart Schoenfeld, and Ilan Alleson. 2010. "Environmental Peacebuilding Strategies in the Middle East: The Case of the Arava Institute for Environmental Studies." *Peace and Conflict Review* 5 (1): 1–20.

Index

＊

ABOUT THE AUTHOR

Randall Amster, J.D., Ph.D., is Director of the Program on Justice and Peace Studies at Georgetown University and serves as Executive Director of the Peace and Justice Studies Association. His articles have appeared in journals including *Peace Review*, *Contemporary Justice Review*, and the *Journal of Sustainability Education*, and he has been a regular contributor to online publications including *Common Dreams*, *Huffington Post*, and *Truthout*. Among his works in the field of peace studies are the co-edited volumes *Building Cultures of Peace: Transdisciplinary Voices of Hope and Action* (2009) and *Exploring the Power of Nonviolence: Peace, Politics, and Practice* (2013).